12
American
Women

12
American

Women

Elizabeth Anticaglia

Nelson-Hall Co.   nh   Chicago

Library of Congress Cataloging in Publication Data

Anticaglia, Elizabeth, 1939–
    12 American women.

    Bibliography: p.
    CONTENTS: Anne Hutchinson.—Mercy Otis Warren.—Emma
Hart Willard.—Margaret Fuller.—Susan B. Anthony. [etc.]
    1. Women—United States—Biography. I. Title.
HQ1412.A57   920.72   74–23229
ISBN 0–88229–102–5

ISBN 0–88229–102–5

Manufactured in the United States of America.

Dedicated to
Joe—
With love and affection

Contents

Preface

Where are the women in American history? A familiar question, implying that there aren't any women in American history—at least, not outside the log cabin or off the plantation. Women, it is assumed, were involved only with childbearing, child raising, soap and candle making, spinning, weaving, and in general, struggling to convert the raw environment to a civilized place for their children. It is accepted that American women were too absorbed in domesticity to step out into the world of business, academia, or science.

Although the opening question is not unfair, the underlying assumption of universal female passivity is false. American women *are* in history; they are absent only from history books. When a child grows up in the traditional male-oriented, male-directed educational system, where female elementary school teachers are really middle people between students and the educational hierarchy, it is not surprising that the impression gained from history texts is that the male sex alone was responsible for the growth of American civilization.

Reading about the early settlers, students learn the names of John Winthrop and John Rolfe; in the Revolutionary period, they learn about John Hancock, the two male Adamses, Benjamin Franklin, and George Washington; in the Civil War era are Lincoln, Grant, and Lee. Heroes abound— "Buffalo Bill" Cody, "Wild Bill" Hickok, Teddy Roosevelt, the Minutemen—all male.

Men stand for achievement in every area—politics, social reform, literature, education, science, religion. Except for weddings and births, women are inconsequential. Those female names sprinkled here and there in the pages of a history text are there to provide human interest. They are romantic figures, like Pocahontas and Priscilla Alden, or nurturing, like Clara Barton, or they provide comic relief, like Calamity Jane.

Occasionally, we come across a paragraph or two in a history text on the suffragist and the temperance movements (often confused or combined), fifty years encapsulated in fifty words. Rarely do the women of these movements emerge as other than frustrated, neurotic, and overly moralistic. They are certainly "unfeminine." As a result, male students gain little respect for women's achievements, endeavors, or capabilities aside from the domestic ones, and even worse, female students lack historical models or heroines.

Yet, there were exciting and important women in our history. So many, in fact, that my most difficult job was deciding which women to include. How do I justify omitting Clara Barton, Mary Baker Eddy, and Charlotte Perkins Gilman? Why choose Anne Hutchinson over Ann Lee or Jemima Wilkinson? Who best represents the Revolutionary period, Abigail Adams or Mercy Otis Warren? Which educator? Which crusader?

It was obvious that the criteria would have to be rather severe. First, the woman must have made a concrete contribution to American civilization. Without Dorothea Dix's efforts, for example, improvements in mental health care might well have been retarded another fifty years. The progress in birth control rests squarely on the work of one person, Margaret Sanger.

This collection has more than a "first person to" approach. The effects of the efforts of those chosen had to be long lasting. For this reason, I omitted Prudence Crandall, who made a courageous contribution to racial equality in the early 1800s by integrating her school. But that contribution, though inspired, had short-lived results. By this criterion, I had to leave out the colorful pioneer women of the West and the Underground Railroad workers of the East. Their contributions were certainly noteworthy, but did not produce the sociological changes I wished to chronicle.

Next, I wanted women who lived in different periods. Because the middle of the nineteenth century had several reform movements, many remarkable women had to be omitted, for example, Clara Barton, Mary Bickerdyke, Mary Walker. It is the story of Dorothea Dix which best fits the criterion of durable contribution.

Another aim was to deal with a variety of life styles— married, single, unconventional, traditional. I did not include those whose life styles were their contribution, as valid as this might be. I looked for enduring, universal ideals: Victorian-age Jane Addams was a drop-out from middle-class affluence, and we can easily picture Mercy Otis Warren as a presentday newspaper columnist venting her indignation with imagination and intelligence as she observed the political chicanery of the 1970s.

The final criterion was subjective. Certain women became my own heroines and others took on new dimensions. Observing how some women are capable of overcoming the most oppressive burdens was inspiring, but at the same time, noting that many of the oppressions of a hundred years ago are still at work was discouraging. Before the suffrage amendment was passed, women were warned of the breakup of the family if they exercised their right to vote. In 1974, the Equal Rights Amendment was being opposed with the same dire prediction. Margaret Sanger was accused of advocating racial suicide when she distributed contraception information, and today, proponents of woman's right to abortion are called murderers.

Although I tried to avoid drawing similarities between the women in this book, there emerged similarities that proved interesting. Several of the women, for instance, had liberal religious views. Many were influenced to achieve by their mothers, fathers, or grandparents. A few women—Susan B. Anthony and Margaret Sanger—were influenced by the life of drudgery their mothers led.

Still, parental influence was only part of the story. These women all succeeded in spite of the psychological deterrents to female brain power and achievement, especially of the earlier eras of American history.

In her memoirs, Eleanor Roosevelt wrote, "A real picture of any human being is interesting in itself, and it is especially interesting when we can follow the play of other personalities upon that human being and perhaps get a picture of a group of people and of the influence on them of the period in which they lived."

America is still the New World, and its women are an inspiration for any society and any era. Those included here each took a firm hold of their world, shook it up, and sent it off in an entirely new direction. They deserve recognition and our sincere thanks.

Many people and agencies helped to make this book a reality. I wish to thank especially the Emma Willard School, the late Alma Lutz for her help and her excellent volumes, the Bryn Mawr College Library staff, and especially the staff of the Radnor Memorial Library in Wayne, Pennsylvania.

Acknowledgments

The author wishes to express her thanks to the following for granting permission to reprint material:

Beacon Press for material from *Emma Willard: Pioneer Educator of American Women* by Alma Lutz, Beacon Press, 1964. The Belknap Press of Harvard University Press for material from *The Adams Papers, Adams Family Correspondence* edited by L. H. Butterfield, Cambridge, Mass.: Harvard University Press, Belknap Press, 1963, and *Diary and Autobiography of John Adams* edited by L. H. Butterfield, Harvard University Press, The Belknap Press, 1961. Dodd, Mead and Company for material from *Miss Ruth* by Walter Terry. Doubleday and Company, Inc., for material from *One Thousand and One Night Stands* by Ted Shawn with Gray Poole, Copyright © 1960 by Ted Shawn, and for material from *Susan B. Anthony* by Katherine Anthony, Copyright © 1954 by Katherine Anthony.

Harper and Row, Publishers, Inc., for material from *The Sense of Wonder* by Rachel Carson, and from *The Autobiography of Eleanor Roosevelt* by Eleanor Roosevelt. Harvard College Library for material from a manuscript of dramatic writings of Mercy Otis Warren. Houghton Mifflin Company for material from *Silent Spring* by Rachel Carson, and from *Since Silent Spring* by Frank Graham. The Institute of Early American History for material from *Saints and Sectaries* by Emery Battis, University of North Carolina Press, 1962. Lawrence Lader for material from *The Margaret Sanger Story and the Fight for Birth Control,* Doubleday and Company, Inc., 1955.

Macmillan Publishing Company, Inc., for material from *Twenty Years at Hull House* by Jane Addams, Copyright 1910 by The Macmillan Company, renewed 1938 by James W. Linn, and from *Jane Addams: A Centennial Reader* edited by Emily Cooper Johnson, Copyright © The Macmillan Company, 1960. McIntosh and Otis, Inc., for material from *Margaret Sanger: Pioneer of the Future* by Emily Taft Douglas, Holt, Rinehart and Winston, Copyright © 1970 by Emily Taft Douglas. William Morrow and Company, Inc., for material from *Blackberry Winter* by Margaret Mead, Copyright © 1972 by Margaret Mead.

W. W. Norton and Company, Inc., for material from *Eleanor and Franklin* by Joseph Lash, Copyright © 1971 by Joseph Lash, from *Eleanor: The Years Alone* by Joseph Lash, Copyright © 1972 by Joseph Lash, and from *The Feminine Mystique* by Betty Friedan. Quadrangle Books for material from *Everyone Was Brave: The Rise and Fall of Feminism in America* by William L. O'Neill, Quadrangle Books, 1969.

Redbook for material from "Women: A Time for Change" by Dr. Margaret Mead, reprinted from *Redbook Magazine,* March 1970, Copyright © 1970 by The McCall Publishing Company. *Time* for material from "Margaret Mead Today: Mother to the World," reprinted by permission from *Time,* The Weekly Newsmagazine, Copyright Time Inc.

The Bettmann Archive

Anne Hutchinson

"To be a religious rebel was wicked," wrote historian Andrew Sinclair, "but to be a woman rebel was devilish."

To the Puritan establishment in America, Anne Hutchinson was surely a "devil." She challenged the religious base of the Puritan government and rattled the political framework it supported. By demonstrating her own rejection of the silent female role, Hutchinson threatened the entire Massachusetts Bay Colony.

Anne Hutchinson was punished with excommunication and banishment to the New England wilderness, not only for her religious challenge but also for her intolerable gender "insubordination." The Bay Colony indicted her because she was an inspiration to other women to become more of a "husband than a wife," more assertive than submissive. This the seventeenth-century Puritan New World could not digest.

Anne Hutchinson was a magnetic personality, as introspective as she was gregarious. Displaying a brilliant mind and eloquent speech, she was intolerant of lesser talents. Headstrong, independent, and "fierce" was how her Puritan foe Governor John Winthrop saw her. He admitted,

however, that Hutchinson was a "woman of ready wit and
bold spirit"—a bold spirit that had no place in the Puritan
grand experiment of trying to form a community out of a
religious principle.

   While her "bold spirit" may have been threatening, Ms.
Hutchinson's generous nature was certainly beneficial to the
young settlement. Just as her intellect was respected, her
kindness was loved. She was nurse and healer to many in the
colony, often mixing her own herbal cures. She was married
to a successful merchant and community leader and bore
fifteen children; she labored all day for her family, typical of
the colonial woman, and added to her duties by visiting the
sick and delivering babies. She comforted and she cured, and
then she spent half the night poring through the Bible,
searching for verification of a "truth" she refused to deny.

   This truth grew out of Hutchinson's own nature. In the
Old World, Puritan sects had evolved with the goal of
"purifying" the Church of England, which was wavering
between Roman Catholicism and Protestantism. One arm of
the discontented body, the Pilgrims, had sailed to America in
1619. They were the first to officially break away from the
English church. The second group of Puritans, led by John
Winthrop, sailed ten years later. This branch held a unique
charter which allowed the members to govern the colony
themselves. The charter itself was brought to the New World;
it was not kept in Mother England. Therefore, the
Massachusetts Bay Colony was relatively independent of
Europe.

   John Winthrop's Puritans were spiritual descendants of
John Calvin, believing that salvation was possible only
through prayer, church attendance, and charity. They
believed that reason and self-control must rule passion. This
ideal was called the Covenant of Works. Winthrop's plan was
to marry the Covenant of Works to community government,
thereby forming a new world based on the Puritan ethic.
When he led the first of his followers to America in 1630, he
sought to inspire them with these words:

"We shall be as a City upon a Hill, the eyes of all people are upon us; so that if we shall deal falsely with our God in this work we have undertaken, and so cause him to withdraw his present help from us, we shall be made story and a by-word through the world."

To keep God's "help," the Puritans became nearly as intolerant of alien ideas as were their oppressors in Europe. They were not interested in honing truth to its essence; they wanted to form an America out of the "truth" which they had already accepted. Daniel Boorstin describes the Puritans as "self-selected conformists." No speculation was allowed. Punishment for religious or civil dissenters was carried out on the marketplace pillory or whipping post—a public warning to all. Judgments were founded on the intuition of the leaders and on the Bible. Other religions, mores, and ideas were not welcome; in short, American Puritanism was almost the complete opposite of the vigorous, variable Puritanism of England.

Anne Hutchinson, who arrived in the New World four years after Winthrop, could appreciate the necessity for all this. She believed that in order for the Puritan experiment to work, it must have God's favor; she realized that God's favor depended upon total obedience from all men and women, with no questions asked.

Anne Hutchinson understood this, but she could not accept it. Such a way of living was intolerable to her; she needed a faith which allowed her restless temperament and quick mind to communicate directly and personally with God. To Hutchinson, the Holy Spirit, or Grace, was the only force that could guide a person to salvation—no amount of "good works" alone could propel one into the Kingdom of God. This Covenant of Grace led her to experience revelations from God, and these visions were her only ruling light. Obviously, the magistrates of Massachusetts could not allow this, especially in a woman.

Winthrop once explained that if he let a woman defy the established religion, men would try to do the same in business and law, and then the entire experiment would crumble. Besides, the place of woman in the settlement was a vital one, written down long before: "Woman in her greatest perfection was made to serve and obey man, not to rule and command him."

Colonial America was just over a quarter of a century old when Anne Hutchinson arrived. Women of that era were allowed little education and few rights. In church, a woman listened in silence. At home she was a breeder and a manufacturer of necessary goods. Her house was virtually a factory to which men brought wool, grain, and meat for her to spin, wash, prepare, and preserve. She made the candles and soap, brewed the ale, cured the meat, and watched over the children and servants while her husband watched over her. Usually, she married young and bore children until she died, often up to twenty of them. A woman's greatest hope for liberty lay in marriage to an old man, for when he passed on, she would be left a widow, sought after but independent, not only of her husband, but of her father and brothers as well.

Ms. Hutchinson didn't reject these traditional duties; she accepted and expanded on them. She did all she was supposed to do and more. It was straining against the bonds that limited the activities and interests of women, that put Anne Hutchinson into the role of rebel.

She was born July 1591, the second of thirteen children, into a spiritual but nonconformist household north of London. Her father, Francis Marbury, was a minister who battled the English church until he was removed from his pulpit. Anne soon fell under the magnetic, spiritual spell of her father. Throughout her life, she lived by his rules. He told her that England's ministers were unfit because they had not studied the Scriptures enough, so Ms. Hutchinson was to closely examine the Bible in her quest for the truth. The Marburys never relied on regular religious leaders for guidance, so Hutchinson later rejected rulers too. Her father demanded a great deal from her—so Anne demanded much from herself and, eventually, from others. Francis Marbury was obstinate, independent, moral and contemptuous of the Establishment, and his daughter emulated him. Critics indicted them with some of the same observations. Francis was called "an overthwart, proud Puritan knave," and his daughter "a woman of haughty and fierce carriage . . . and a very voluble tongue."

The Marbury family focused on personal meditation with God, which led Anne Hutchinson to strive all her life for inner security and personal identity. In his later years, Francis Marbury once more received a pulpit from which to preach. The family moved to London, where young Anne reveled in the luxury of a literary, civilized city. Then her father died. One year later, Anne Marbury, now at the advanced age of twenty-one, married.

Her groom, William Hutchinson, was nothing like the late Reverend Marbury. Rather than being intellectually active, he was a placid tradesman. While Francis had been an outcast in his profession, Will was a success in his. What Will had in common with Marbury was a great love for Anne. His main concern from the wedding day on was providing his wife and children with comfort and security. He denied her nothing and admitted that he was more tied to his wife than to his church. In later years, John Winthrop affirmed this, calling Will "a man of very mild temper and weak parts and wholly guided by his wife."

But during those pampered years, Ms. Hutchinson was directionless. Without her father's spiritual guidance, she was left with only herself to supply truth, and she was neither mature nor experienced enough to find it. She was not a beautiful woman, but she was proud, straight, and exceptionally strong; she bore fifteen children and, remarkably, they all survived infancy.

Though floundering intellectually, Hutchinson loved her family and was devoted to it. The Hutchinsons lived in Lincolnshire for twenty-two years. And then the second intellectual influence entered her life.

John Cotton was a Calvinist minister in a nearby town. A

mild, self-effacing man, he believed in the inevitability of
God's love and tender mercy. So humble was Cotton, in fact,
that he often seemed indecisive. Nevertheless, once Anne
Hutchinson heard him preach his theory of dependency upon
God alone, she joined the numerous worshippers who traveled
miles every week to be assured that once a person accepted
Grace, God would not extinguish it, no matter how frail that
person might be.

Cotton was gentle enough not to stifle or compete with
Hutchinson's aggressiveness; he was intellectual enough to
stimulate her mind. In the years to come, she was to interpret
his theories, to begin speaking to groups, and eventually to
lead others. But this confidence and sense of calling followed
fifteen years of concentrated study, meditation, and self-
searching.

Europe, meanwhile, was falling into religious turmoil.
The Counter Reformation threatened German Protestants;
Richelieu, in France, harangued the Huguenots; and in
England, Charles Stuart took a Catholic bride, shaking the
security of the Puritans in the House of Commons. In 1629,
King Charles dismissed Parliament and the Puritans decided
that their survival depended upon establishing the City of
God in the New World. John Cotton followed John Winthrop
and the first wave of theological intellectuals to the
Massachusetts Bay Colony.

After Cotton left, Anne Hutchinson was desolate.
England was in the midst of a general depression. Harvests
were poor; wool sat unused on the docks. Then, to add to
Anne's despair, the Hutchinsons' oldest daughter Susanna,
died at age fourteen, and one month later, eight-year-old
Elizabeth also died—probably from the plague. Anne
Hutchinson plunged into mourning, crying out against God's
cruel inflictions. She withdrew from the world. During this
period of intense meditation, Hutchinson reported a sudden
spiritual revitalization. A message had come to her: "Every
spirit that confesseth not that Jesus Christ is come in the
flesh is the spirit of Antichrist." What did it mean?

The next winter, a second message came to her: "He that
denies the testament denies the testator." Suddenly
everything became clear: The Antichrist lived in those who
refused the Covenant of Grace. For her, the idea of the
Puritan religion of good works, which was held by the leading
Puritans of England, including Winthrop, was spiritually
dead.

Whether or not Anne Hutchinson actually had these
revelations is, of course, debatable. She had always craved
moral and intellectual direction, and when her mortal leader
left her, God took his place. Then the deaths of her children
led her to seek even more intense comfort. Whatever the case,
Hutchinson gained tremendous self-definition and power
through these visions, and this power eventually led her to
become one of America's first rebels.

Anne Hutchinson now decided to follow John Cotton to
America, hoping she could freely pursue her individualistic
religious principles which were so like Cotton's. Cotton had
become a leading preacher in the New World, well known and
well respected. It was in the summer of 1634 that the
Hutchinson family, including a newborn infant, settled itself
aboard the small ship *Griffin* and began the long sail across
the ocean.

The voyage was tiring and hot, with cattle lowing in the
hold and the sun glaring above. But Ms. Hutchinson was
vibrant and curious. She questioned the clergy so incessantly
that when they landed they reported her to the authorities as
being potentially dangerous.

Once in Boston, Will Hutchinson was immediately
invited to join the church, which meant he could become a
community participant. But Governor Winthrop and the
magistrates held up Anne's application for several months
because of her behavior during the voyage and her insistence
that Grace was more important than good works. She was
finally allowed to enter the church, however. Her sex
probably helped her to be accepted. The church leaders were
certain that females were by nature indecisive and emotional.

Once Ms. Hutchinson settled down to family life again, she
would adjust.

And they were right. The Hutchinsons were assigned a
half-acre lot opposite the governor's own home, among the
"best" townspeople. William built an ample two-story wooden
house, complete with cellar, centered around a huge brick
chimney with fireplaces opening into the larger rooms. Anne
planted an herb garden and an orchard behind the house, and
further back were the stable and sheds for horses, cows, and
pigs.

Anne Hutchinson became a model citizen, resuming
medicine making and nursing, delivering babies, and
rescuing the townsfolk from the superstitions of old Mrs.
Hawkins, the former "nurse." She was as energetic and
generous as she had been in England. Will quickly
established himself as an important merchant and
community leader. Despite the difficult New England
winters, the Puritan prohibition against any recreation,
festivals, or games, the rocky land, and constant threat of
attack by Indians, life was not unbearable for Anne
Hutchinson. However, she could not deny her growing
spiritual strength.

Hutchinson was contemptuous of Winthrop's creed that
"man must prepare himself for God's election." She felt that
man could in no way "prepare" himself for salvation; God
bestows Grace through direct revelation. Yet, ironically,
Anne Hutchinson was a living example of the "good works"
principle donating her time and energy to the community.
But, she adhered to the Covenant of Grace, and eventually
her belief led to direct action.

First, she interrupted those sermons she felt were false.
Next, she began inviting neighboring housewives to her home
on Sunday nights, when she would repeat John Cotton's
sermons of that day. The women were eager to listen. In
church they were segregated from their husbands and had to
sit in silence. But here was a woman who was intelligent and
far from silent. They found they could talk to her, and later

they grew to depend upon her for spiritual guidance.

The women-only sessions were soon expanded to include men. Hutchinson added a second weekly meeting and began drawing all the individualistic, tolerant, imaginative elements of Bay society. One of her admirers said of her, "I'll bring you a woman that preaches better Gospel than any of your black-coats that have been at the Ninniversity, a woman of another kind of spirit, who hath many revelations of things to come. . . . I had rather hear such a one that speaks from the mere motion of the spirit, without any study at all, than any of your learned Scholars, although they may be fuller of Scripture."

Hutchinson was soon addressing gatherings of up to eighty people in her spacious parlor. She was no longer simply repeating Cotton's sermons; she was also criticizing orthodox preachers. It wasn't long before the preachers learned of Anne's activities and quickly labeled her an Antinomian. This was a serious charge; they were accusing Ms. Hutchinson of freeing herself not only from the laws of the Puritan church but also from the generally accepted standards of morality of the community.

It was not the most opportune time for Anne Hutchinson to be critical of the church. Winthrop was very concerned about the condition of his experiment. Only six years old, the Bay Colony was overcrowded, with dirty winding streets. Inflation raged, food was expensive, and fuel scarce. A smallpox epidemic had broken out the year before, and the community was busy mopping up the vestiges of the disease. Ms. Hutchinson had borne another baby even as her oldest son was preparing to return to England for his bride. And to top all this, the prestigious colony cofounder and conventional minister, John Wilson, had returned to Boston after a sojourn in England, and he immediately set about fervently preaching the Covenant of Works.

Yet, Anne Hutchinson was not to be silenced. In fact, she now traveled to neighboring communities, drawing to her the spiritually insecure and intellectually curious. Then one day

a dashing young man named Sir Henry Vane sailed into
Boston Harbor. Drawn by Anne's magnetism, he joined the
Hutchinson forces. He soon charmed the Bostonians and was
elected governor in 1636.

It became obvious to the ruling powers of the colony that
Anne Hutchinson must be stopped. Earlier it had seemed
unnecessary to worry about a woman's ramblings, for how
much could one person—a female at that—accomplish? But
Hutchinson was demonstrating that she could accomplish
quite a bit by stirring up minds and imaginations, especially
Henry Vane's, and so John Wilson was sent to intervene.

Rather than going straight to Anne Hutchinson herself,
Wilson headed for her friend, John Cotton, probably believing
that her old mentor could persuade her to halt her activities.
But Cotton was too indecisive to take a firm stand. He
believed in Hutchinson, but not enough to oppose the
traditionalists. Cotton went only as far as telling her that a
rumor that she was a dangerous heretic was circulating.
Hutchinson denied being a heretic. However, the middle
ground of the controversy was never presented to the
Bostonians—they heard Hutchinson's side and Winthrop's—
and, consequently, the city was divided into two camps.

A third party entered the picture when John
Wheelwright sailed into the harbor. A British minister
planting his feet firmly on the side of Ms. Hutchinson,
Wheelwright had recently married into the Hutchinson clan
and upheld the validity of the idea that people were
dependent solely upon God's free Grace. Anne welcomed him
with open arms, insisting that he be given John Wilson's
pulpit and that Wilson be ousted. Winthrop refused to let
Wheelwright near a pulpit, but when the new minister began
preaching anyway, Winthrop knew he had another foe to
combat and action had to be taken.

The Puritan leaders were prepared to fight hard to
survive. They had escaped the religious persecution in
England and they were not going to tolerate any threat on
these shores. To them, Anne was a political, social, and

religious rebel; Winthrop insisted she be squelched because
"if [women] be allowed in one thing, [they] must be admitted
a rule in all things; for they being above reason and
Scripture, they are not subject to control." To him, her
revelations were "bottomless." In Winthrop's spiritual
aristocracy, each "saint" was responsible for defending not
only himself against heretics, but also his fellows—especially
against vocal, female heretics. If Anne Hutchinson would not
be reformed, then she must be exiled from the rest of the
community, which meant, in the early settlement days,
probable death in the wilderness.

Winthrop's first step was to address the populace,
declaring that if Hutchinson's position of the Holy Ghost's
presence in every person was correct, then each person must
be an individual God-Man. This was not only absurd, he
insisted, but heretical.

A series of swift actions followed. William Hutchinson
was ousted from his post as a magistrate. In the next election,
the remaining Hutchinson supporters were swept away, and
Winthrop was reelected governor. Shortly thereafter,
Wheelwright went into exile for his "seditious" lectures, and
the Court of Elections passed a law excluding from the colony
anyone who did not meet the approval of the ruling members.
Sir Henry Vane, disillusioned and angry, sailed back to
England. The pro-Hutchinson Bostonians reacted to all of this
by refusing to join the military expeditions against the
Indians.

It was in this raging climate that Winthrop called a
synod of all the churches in the Bay Colony; once and for all,
the "breeder and nourisher of all these distempers, one
Mistress Hutchinson," would be silenced.

August 1637 was steamy. Despite the suffocating heat
spell, the synod convened in a meeting house packed with
curious spectators, anxious to see what would happen next.
But the synod, too, was uncomfortable in the steamy
atmosphere and dispersed without taking a stand.

Ms. Hutchinson should have been relieved, but she was

not. She had a strange foreboding. She had just celebrated her forty-sixth birthday. She was pregnant and suffering from headaches, dizziness, hot flashes, and cold spells. She had not eased up on her midwife duties nor on mixing her herbal cures, nor had she lessened her endless housekeeping chores.

She fell into an acute depression for a time, searching for the inner spirit which held the "truth." The climactic moment came when her close friend and disciple, Mary Dyer, needed Anne's help in delivering her baby. It was November and an icy fist held Boston as Hutchinson made her way to the Dyer home. When she arrived, she realized that the fetus was in a breech position and had to be manually turned. This she did, and after an interminable labor, Mary Dyer gave birth to a dead, deformed child. Hutchinson was sure it was an evil omen. She fled to John Cotton for comfort and advice. Why had such a horrible thing happen to one of her followers?

Cotton soothed her. He told her to bury the child inconspicuously and to say nothing more about it. Cotton was well aware of how Hutchinson's enemies could distort such an event. They would use it against her, claiming it was evidence of God's wrath. She did as he advised.

The court reconvened. It had decided to meet outside Boston and thus evade the anger of Hutchinson's supporters. One by one, Hutchinson watched her friends condemned. She, herself, was allowed no jury trial. Winthrop acted as prosecutor and judge. When she was finally called before the court, Anne Hutchinson was visibly shaken but stood defiant, with her head held high.

"Mrs. Hutchinson," droned John Winthrop, "you are called here as one of those that have troubled the peace of the commonwealth and the churches here. You are known to be a woman that hath a great share in the promoting and divulging of those opinions that are causes of this trouble." Looking up, he offered her a chance to redeem herself with an apology and in this way become "a profitable member here among us." If she refused, the court warned, it "may take such course that you may trouble us no further."

Hutchinson replied clearly, "I am called here to answer before you but I hear no things laid to my charge."

Winthrop told Hutchinson that she was believed to be guilty of joining a seditious faction, of holding conspiracies in her house, of seducing honest people from their work and families. But worst of all she had broken the Fifth Commandment—honor thy father and thy mother.

Hutchinson exclaimed that Winthrop was neither her father nor her mother. Winthrop replied that "father and mother" meant anyone in authority.

"Parents who do not honor the Lord as wisely as their children might be disobeyed with impunity," replied Hutchinson.

After hours of debate, the court was adjourned and Hutchinson went home to pore over the transcripts and the Bible. When she returned the next day, she accepted the fact that no one, not even John Cotton, could be depended upon to defend her. Frustrated, she launched a tirade against the entire commonwealth, telling them God's curse would be upon them because of the course they were taking.

Weakly, she listened to her sentence: "Mrs. Hutchinson, the court you hear is that you are banished from out of our jurisdiction as being a woman not fit for our society, and are to be imprisoned till the court shall send you away."

"I desire to know wherefore I am banished," said Ms. Hutchinson. "Say no more, " replied Winthrop. "The court knows wherefore and is satisfied."

Before sending her away, however, the court wanted to make clear its claim of her heresy. Hutchinson was placed in the custody of an orthodox minister until spring, with visiting rights granted only to family and clergy. For the four months of her confinement, Hutchinson meditated with the Scriptures open before her. Her story blazed through the Bay Colony, and an explosive point came when a group of her sympathizers announced that they were leaving Massachusetts of their own accord.

Winthrop responded with an order of martial law. Homes

were searched and guns, pistols, powder, shot, match, and swords were confiscated. All ammunition was collected and stored outside Boston. The citizens were in a turmoil—some criticized Hutchinson's unfair trial, others were intimidated by Winthrop's strong stand and crept forward to confess their "errors."

In March 1638, Anne Hutchinson, pale, uneasy, and heavy with pregnancy, faced the reassembled court to hear sentence of heresy and excommunication. This time she saw her old supporter, John Cotton, rise before the magistrates and falteringly state that Anne Hutchinson had indeed endangered the spiritual welfare of the community and had led many weak souls astray. Bewildered, she heard Cotton predict that her attack upon the clergy was only a forerunner of her decline from morality, possibly leading to infidelity to her husband. Questions she asked during her imprisonment were now distorted and presented to the court in the form of heretical statements.

It was clear to Hutchinson that all her contributions, her work, her laboring for the community were erased. Discouraged, she hesitated over her answers. Her decisiveness cracked. In a blur, she heard the final sentence of excommunication.

"Foreasmuch as you, Mrs. Hutchinson, have highly transgressed and offended ... and troubled the Church with your Errors and have drawn away many a poor soule, and have upheld your revelations; and foreasmuch as you have made a Lie ... Therefore in the name of our Lord Jesus Christ ... I doe cast you out and ... deliver you up to Satan ... and account you from this time forth to be a Heathen and a Publican ... I command you in the name of Christ Jesus and of this Church as a Leper to withdraw yourself out of the Congregation."

She was stunned. Turning heavily, she stumbled down the aisle, the silent, frightened eyes of the congregation upon her. Suddenly, she felt a gentle touch on her arm. Looking up,

Hutchinson saw it was Mary Dyer, who smiled and continued walking beside her. She gathered enough strength to direct one last warning back to the magistrates; "Better to be cast out of the church than to deny Christ." A few days later, she was on her way to Rhode Island.

Despite Hutchinson's exile, Winthrop was still uneasy. He learned that she was hard at work reforming the Rhode Island government by insisting that true authority lies with the people. William Hutchinson had been selected chief magistrate in their new colony, and laws were passed to guarantee jury trial, an end to class discrimination, universal suffrage, and religious tolerance. And the settlement was prospering. Winthrop decided to stop such liberalism by annexing Rhode Island to the Bay Colony.

To undermine Hutchinson's influence, Winthrop instigated a witch hunt. He searched for evidence to use against her, and a choice piece happened his way: he learned of Mary Dyer's deformed stillborn child. Immediately, Winthrop ordered the body exhumed. All this information he meticulously entered in his diary and in his reports to England.

In addition, Winthrop seized upon Hutchinson's own misfortune. There was the fact of her last pregnancy, which aborted as a hydatidiform mole soon after her exile.

"God's will had manifested itself," decided Winthrop.

William Hutchinson died in 1642, and his widow now felt completely vulnerable to Winthrop's relentless threats against her. She took her six youngest children and a handful of settlers and moved southward to the Dutch territory on Pelham Bay. Here she survived for just a few months before she and five children were attacked and massacred by a band of revengeful Indians, angered at being cheated by the Dutch.

"God's hand is . . . seen herein," gloated Winthrop.

Anne Hutchinson's behavior has been attributed to many causes, ranging from mysticism to the menopause. But whatever the causes of her actions were, she must be judged a dynamic pioneer in a new land. She pioneered religious tolerance and laid the groundwork for acceptance of such liberal religions as Quakerism, Unitarianism, and Universalism. She lifted her mind and her voice above the level of female submersion of the time and earned respect for having done so. In an age of rigid religious and social conformity, Anne Hutchinson began the tradition of challenging repressive rulings that is still helping to keep the American experiment alive.

2

Mercy Otis Warren

It was in a growing Massachusetts town called Plymouth during those ten tumultuous years preceding the final outbreak of the American Revolution that a group of men—educated, illustrious , passionate—met to plan the overthrow of their government. Their hostess, often more passionate and articulate than her guests, was the handsome, dark-eyed wife of one of the Revolutionaries. Her name was Mercy Otis Warren.

"In the influence she exercised," it has been said, "she was perhaps the most remarkable woman who lived during the Revolutionary period." Ms. Warren herself admitted that "by the Plymouth fireside were many political plans originated, discussed, and digested." These political plans included opposition to such British atrocities as the Stamp Act and the navigation acts. The small group succeeded in fanning colonial hostility to the point of repealing the Stamp Act and installing the nonimportation agreements which kept British products out of the colonies. Quite possibly, Mercy Warren's "famed hospitality," as her close friend Abigail Adams put it, encouraged such radical actions as the

destruction of Thomas Hutchinson's house after he pushed
through the Stamp Act and even instigated the Boston Tea
Party itself.

Mercy Warren's action in the Revolution was not typical
for an eighteenth-century lady, but neither was Mercy
Warren typical of colonial femininity. Her pen was pungent,
her language at times bawdy, and her character observations
uncanny. Mercy Warren was thrown into the midst of the
colonial intrigue because of two happenstances: first, she
grew up with her brother, superpatriot James Otis, and
second, she was the wife of Revolutionary strategist James
Warren. Although she corresponded with several women,
including Abigail Adams, wife of John Adams, and historian
Catherine Macaulay, Mercy Warren's friendships and
intellectual stimulation resulted from her intimacy with
these two men. Because of them she spent a lifetime
exchanging ideas with people like John and Samuel Adams,
Elbridge Gerry, Thomas Jefferson, and Henry Knox. It was
Knox who wrote to Ms. Warren after receiving her letter
outlining postwar problems: "I should be happy, Madam, to
receive your communications from time to time, particularly
on the subject enlarged on in this letter." Notes like this were
saved and savored, to be finally used as the basis for her great
project, *The History of the Revolution.*

Mercy Otis Warren was born into the lively and
respectable Otis family, who had settled on a large farm in
rural Cape Cod Barnstable. The house was surrounded by
meadows and farmland, ample enough room for a couple with
thirteen children and a crew of servants. Colonel James Otis,
Mercy's father, was a judge, though he preferred to use his
military title. He had married a hearty Connecticut girl,
Mary Allyne, and together the portly pair ruled over an
active, stimulating household. Of the original thirteen
children, seven survived childhood, including James, the
oldest, and Mercy, the third child, born September 14, 1728.
(Another daughter, Mary, married into a wealthy Boston

Tory family. Two other sons, Joseph and Samuel, also became political activists.)

Young James and Mercy became the intellectual stars of the family. The colonel, who was largely self-taught, worshipped learning and had high hopes for his children. He deposited Mercy and her brothers with his brother-in-law, the Reverend Jonathan Russell, for schooling. Russell pointed the way in literature and history, which later became Mercy Warren's chief interests. She read voraciously, from Pope and Milton to Raleigh's *History of the World*. She absorbed the Reverend Russell's Sunday sermons, which were literary rather than sentimental, and she patterned her later poetry and drama on his style. In addition to the Reverend Russell's literary interests, James and Mercy were exposed to the constant political arguments of the Otis household. There were a barrage of pamphlets and periodicals to be studied and the philosophy of patriotism, rather than pro-British loyalism, to be absorbed.

Mercy and James were particularly close. Young Otis, a brilliant student, took it upon himself to help tutor his bright younger sister, and when he was admitted, at fourteen, to Harvard College, Mercy was desolate. However, as a young colonial lady, Ms. Otis had her domestic education to undertake. In fact, she seems to have been quite capable as a seamstress; two pieces of her handwork have been passed down through her descendants. One is a card table cover with a cross-stitch design of field and garden flowers; the other is her "second-day" wedding dress, an elaborately embroidered satin gown. It was accomplishments like these which were lauded far more than any intellectual feats in a Cape Cod lady. But it was Ms. Otis's drive for mind improvement which gave her a place in history as one of the leading influences in the fight for liberty, a proclivity which lasted until her death at eighty-six.

While James studied at Harvard, Mercy followed his achievements from her Barnstable quarters. He wrote to her

about his discovery of John Locke and recommended she delve
into Locke's works at home. James was a tense, intellectual
boy, gregarious but given to bouts of wild emotion. In spite of
this, he managed to establish himself as one of the student
leaders at Harvard. It was his graduation which finally ended
his sister's temporary seclusion. In 1743, Mercy Otis made
her first foray to Cambridge.

When Mercy was fifteen, an age when her comtem-
poraries were thinking of marriage, she was enthralled
by a visit to Harvard for James's graduation—listening
to the sermon, watching the degrees being offered, picnicking
on elaborate baked goods and meats, and meeting and talking
with her brother's friends. Quite a heady experience for an
intellectual younger sister from calm Cape Cod.

One of James's friends, a year behind James at school,
was a witty, handsome lad from Plymouth named James
Warren. Mercy Otis was impressed by young Warren on this
graduation day. She later wrote that James Warren was "the
star which attracts my attention." (Warren probably
impressed her parents as well, since his family was descended
from the early Pilgrims.)

James Otis headed home to Barnstable after graduation
to study for a master's degree. Periodically, he would break
away for a wild revelry and then go back to his studies. His
next move was to Boston to study law for two years with one
of the leading attorneys; only then could James Otis finally
open his own law office in Plymouth. Here he renewed his old
friendship with one of the town's new merchants, James
Warren.

Mercy was drawn into this friendship by her brother, and
James Warren and Mercy Otis wove romance into their
ideological union. This was to be their style throughout their
lives. James Warren seemed impressed with his friend's
outspoken younger sister. Like another friend, John Adams,
he preferred a mate "well stocked with learning." And it was
obvious that this bright, literary girl was very much in love
with James. On an autumn day in 1754, when Mercy was

quite into spinsterhood at age twenty-six, the two were
married and moved to the Warren farm, "Clifford," on the Eel
River outside Plymouth.

Mercy Otis Warren was never an efficient farmwife.
Perhaps her interests in government and literature were too
strong, or perhaps she was just not physically sturdy enough
for the heavy labor demanded on a farm. Nevertheless, she did
love "Clifford"; her poetic nature responded to the view of the
river winding through the lush Warren land, and her house
was snug with its sloping roof to resist the Cape Cod squalls.

The Warrens had much the same life as the Otis family
had had—they were literary minded and very political. Mercy
Warren was like her brother. She was passionate and driving
in her quest for knowledge, while her husband was didactic,
deliberate, and calm. Yet, their marriage must have inspired
James Otis, for just after Mercy married, her brother began
his more ill-fated marriage.

Otis was thirty when, in 1755, he married the daughter
of one of Boston's outstanding merchants. Along with a place
in the most elite circles and an ample dowry, this budding
patriot acquired a decidedly Loyalist family. When Otis
entered politics several years later, the division in political
thinking was to split his marriage apart.

Mercy Warren, at the same time, continued to be
influenced by her brother's development as a revolutionary.
In 1760, the post of chief justice of the province, which had
been promised to old Colonel Otis, was handed instead to
Lieutenant Governor Thomas Hutchinson (a descendant of
Anne Hutchinson). James Otis was livid. Following this
affront, the government passed writs of assistance which
allowed customs officers to enter any home or shop as they
wished. This action was bitterly attacked by many merchants,
and young Otis, who had been prosecuting attorney for the
province, resigned his post to fight against those government
writs.

He argued before the Supreme Court judges, headed by
Hutchinson, on February 24, 1761. His oration lasted over

four hours and covered many of the principles he would later expand on in pamphlets, articles, and speeches during his political life. From this first speech came the rallying cry of the American Revolution: "Taxation without representation is tyranny." As John Adams later commented, "Then and there, the child Independence was born."

Stunned, Hutchinson and the other judges never responded. Nor were the writs of assistance ever enforced, so Otis apparently won his point. More important, he had set out on a campaign to win independence from Britain, and an illustrious line of patriots were following him. His wife, however, was not among them. A schism developed between them that would never heal but only widen through the years. For all practical purposes, they separated and went their own ways—Otis, the Patriot, and his wife, the Loyalist —and their paths would never again cross.

Several months later, Otis, now thirty-five, was elected to the House of Representatives. With this, he left his spasmodic merrymaking forever. He kept a tight rein on his periods of rebellion; he would not let his temper erupt. One goal obsessed him—liberty. His days were consumed by meetings, plans, caucuses, and writing such things as *The Vindication of the House of Representatives,* which John Adams later cited as the basis for the 1774 Declaration of Rights and Wrongs, the 1775 Declaration of Independence, the French Constitution, and Thomas Paine's *Common Sense, Crisis,* and *Rights of Man.*

In the meantime, three years after they married, Mercy and James bought a new house, the stately town dwelling of General John Winslow. The elder Warren had recently died, bequeathing James the job of sheriff, and since Mercy was expecting her first child, the couple decided an urban residence would be more convenient. She lived in this Plymouth house (the "breeding place" of the American Revolution) for much of the rest of her life. It was a large roomy house, and she particularly liked the northeast corner room. There she wrote and mused on the stormy changes in

her country and in the lives of her friends and her family.
("Clifford" was the Warren home in the summer, and Ms.
Warren did much writing there as well.)

Five sons were born to the Warrens: James in 1757,
followed by Winslow, Charles, Henry, and finally George in
1766. All this took place while her brother James, in Boston,
was shaping the ideas of the Revolution. The two corresponded occasionally, but her brother explained that he could
not visit as often as he'd like because of the political situation,
which was snowballing in intensity each year.

The year before George was born, the British climaxed
their colonial taxation and trade restrictions with the Stamp
Act. This act required that a tax stamp be put on all papers of
commerce, on communications, and on every legal document.
Otis and Warren, probably in the solitude of the Plymouth
house, planned a series of activities to denounce the tax.
These included hanging the stamp officer in effigy and
smashing the windows of his home, and wrecking the
mansion of Hutchinson (Otis's old enemy). The law was
rescinded.

Encouraged by this victory, Otis began protesting the old
navigation acts which prevented American manufacturers
from selling or buying goods and materials from any but the
British. The Patriots urged the people to purchase only
American made items. If the citizens couldn't make it
themselves, they were to do without.

In 1766, Otis was joined in the legislature by other
Patriots—Samuel Adams, John Hancock, and James Warren.
Young John Adams joined the cause, but by now, Otis's
behavior was becoming erratic, probably from the tension of
the times and the rift in his home. Sometimes he talked
brilliantly; other times he rambled on like an old man,
though he was just past forty. The Patriots demanded
everything of him in the way of ideals and advice. The climax
came when, in 1769, he strolled recklessly into the British
Tavern. There he was attacked and bludgeoned by a customs
officer, and left with a gaping scalp wound and a devastated

career. Though he recovered to some degree, Otis was to spend his last decade with his aging father in Barnstable, leaving the Revolution to his followers.

His sister Mercy was shattered. She shared the Otis temper, though she usually expressed herself on paper, as she did in this anguished letter: "I wish to know every circumstance of this guilty affair: is it possible that we have men among us under the guise of officers of the Crown, who have become open assassins? Have they with a band of ruffians at their heels attacked a gentleman alone and unarmed with a design to take away his life? Thus it is reported and are those the conservators of peace?"

Mercy Warren dedicated herself anew to carrying out her brother's work. She was solicitous about Otis's mental condition and always concerned about him. It was reported that only Mercy, in those last years, had the power to calm him "in his wildest moods of that insanity."

Of course, her sons were growing up with the Revolution, and Mercy Warren consigned a sizable part of her energies to them. With her husband in the legislature, she was left with the task of raising the boys, including educating them. In a letter to Abigail Adams, she bemoaned this task, calling it "a duty of the highest consequence to society—though this is for a number of years left almost wholly to our uninstructed sex." She deplored the lack of concern for female education. She once stated, "While we own the appointed subordination (perhaps for the sake of order in families) let us by no means acknowledge such an inferiority as would check the ardour of our endeavors to equal in all mental accomplishments the most masculine heights that when those temporary distinctions subside, we may be equally qualified to taste the full draughts of knowledge and happiness prepared for the upright of every nation and sex."

Mercy Warren was a permissive mother and was especially devoted to Winslow, her second son, whom Abigail Adams depicted as "soft, tender and pathetick." (In contrast, she characterized James, Jr., as showing "fire, spirit, and

vivacity" and Charles as "firm and intrepid.") Obviously, Ms.
Adams had grown to know her good friend's children quite
well. The boys were all devoted to their mother, and it turned
out later that only one, Henry, ever married. For the others,
no woman, it seemed, could compare to Mercy.

As the boys grew older, Mercy Warren turned her
strength once again to the Revolutionary movement. The
movement had wavered a bit after Otis's hand left the helm,
but in 1772, the Warrens' Plymouth house was once again
filled with activity. James Warren presented his idea that
committees of correspondence be set up in each of the
colonies. These would create and disseminate plans for
rebellion against the British government. Sam Adams,
excited and capable despite the nervous tremor in his hands,
returned to Boston and called a meeting to discuss putting the
Warren plan into effect. James Warren established his
committee in Plymouth and young Elbridge Gerry set up
another in Marblehead. Virginia and the other colonies joined
in, and the chain of correspondence was soon functioning
throughout the seaboard. These committees were to become
governing centers of each colony once the Revolution erupted.

Historians agree that Mercy Warren most probably had a
strong hand in helping James evolve his idea. Women, like
children in those times, were to be seen and not heard, but
Mercy was too immersed in events and too articulate to sit
silent. She was, however, enough a product of her time to
remain anonymous, not only in the movement but in her
writing as well. About this time, Ms. Warren's enthusiasm for
the Patriot cause was firing up her literary talents. She wrote
countless poems of inspiration, distributing them to her
friends and publishing them in the newspapers. Often she
used a pen name; she was "Philomena" (and Abigail Adams
was "Portia"). Like her pen name, Mercy Warren's poetry was
greatly influenced by the ornate literary fashion of the day,
and she modeled her style on Pope and Dryden almost to the
point of imitation.

Warren's poetry at this time reflected her love of nature,

her friendships, her devout Puritanism, as well as her pursuit
of democracy. Later, she turned to satire, focusing on her
enemies, the British government and American Loyalists.
Her friends enjoyed and encouraged these jabs. In fact, John
Adams once suggested to James Warren, "I wish to see a late
glorious event [the Boston Tea Party] celebrated by a certain
poetical pen, which has no equal that I know of in this
country."

This "poetical pen" was, of course, that of James's wife.
Mercy modestly replied to Abigail that John Adams himself
could well fulfill this request. Nevertheless, she did turn out a
flowery poem to "celebrate" the Boston Tea Party. It was
called *The Squabble of the Sea Nymphs*, and with it, Mercy
Warren became, at forty-six, the literary queen of her world.
In the poem, she describes sea deities receiving the tea which
was dumped by the Boston Patriots:

> Pour'd a profusion of delicious teas
> Which, wafted by a soft favonian breeze,
> Supply'd the watry deities, in spite
> Of all the rage of Jealous Amphytrite.

Ms. Warren turned next to Molière's style for her new
interest, writing plays. Although theater performances were
prohibited in Massachusetts, Warren felt the stage was the
most effective medium for expressing her ideas on morality.
These plays were not stageable, however, for they lacked
dramatic plot and abounded in crowd and parade scenes. Her
first play, published in 1772, was called *The Adulateur: A
Tragedy; As it is Now Acted In Upper Servia.* (Though the
play was published anonymously, historians accredit it to
Mercy Otis Warren.) It was the first of several aimed at her
father's and brother's foe, Thomas Hutchinson, who was now
royal governor of Massachusetts, and who used nepotism to
control public offices.

Less than a year later, Warren hit at Hutchinson again
with *The Defeat*, now bringing in a character, a turncoat, who

shifts from one side to the other. In a matter of months,
Hutchinson's career plummeted from royal governor to
unemployed, so he sailed back to England. Ms. Warren
characterized this sad figure harshly:

> He strikes a bargain with his country's foes,
> And joins to wrap America in flames.
> Yet with feigned pity, and satanic grin,
> As if more deep to fix the keen insult,
> Or make his life a farce still more complete,
> He sends a groan across the broad Atlantic,
> And with a phiz of crocodilian stamp,
> Can weep, and wreathe, still hoping to deceive;

In 1774, General Thomas Gage was sent from Britain to
replace Hutchinson and take over the rule of Boston. Mercy
Warren scribbled seething notes to her husband, who was still
in the legislature, which had now exiled itself to Concord. In
the spring of 1775, in her popular satire *The Group*, she
predicted General Gage's imminent attack on Concord, where
the rebels' supplies were held. James Warren forwarded *The
Group* to Adams in Philadelphia where it was printed,
spreading his wife's work outside her home ground. Adams,
ever encouraging, told her that "instead of being at fault to
use [your God-given talents for satire] it would be criminal to
neglect them."

It tore Ms. Warren apart to see the British occupying
Boston. When John Hancock and Dorothy Quincy wed, just
after the battle of Lexington and Concord, she wrote a mutual
friend, "Tell her [Dorothy] I hope yet to see her in her own
delightful habitation at Boston, notwithstanding the locusts
now crawling around it." Mercy Warren minced no words.

As far as she was concerned, the Revolutionary War
began right after the battle of Bunker Hill in June 1775. Her
husband became president of the Provincial Congress, and
then George Washington selected him for the post of
paymaster general in Cambridge. Ms. Warren, though upset

by the sight of the bedraggled Continental Army, made
several trips to Cambridge to be with James in the army
camp. There she met Martha Washington, who, it's reported,
was rather fearful of meeting Mercy Warren. Apparently the
meeting went well, for Ms. Warren wrote later to Abigail
Adams that, "I was received with that politeness and Respect
shown in a first interview among the well-bred and with the
Ease and Cordiallity of Friendship of a much Earlier date."

Mercy Warren had already become acquainted with the
leading generals and had her usual candid observations to
make. Washington, she commented, was "one of the most
amiable and accomplished gentlemen, both in person, mind,
and manners, that I have met with." Of Lee she said, "I think
plain in his person to a degree of ugliness, careless even to
unpoliteness—his garb ordinary, his voice rough, his manners
rather morose." Warren was sensitive enough to recognize
Lee's other qualities. She felt he was "learned, judicious, and
penetrating: a considerable traveller, agreeable in his
narrations, and a zealous indefatigable friend to the
American cause." She described Gates as being "a brave
soldier, a high republican, a sensible companion, an honest
man, of unaffected manners and easy deportment."

Later, of Lafayette, she had this to say: "Penetrating,
active, sensitive, and judicious, he acquits himself with the
highest applause in the public eye, while the politeness of his
manners, and the sociability of his temper, insure his
welcome at every hospitable board."

The two brightest women of the Revolution—Mercy
Warren and Abigail Adams—met often during this time.
They mended clothes and talked of children, comforting and
supporting each other. But while Adams kept her farm going
when her husband went to Philadelphia and later France,
Warren spent her time writing in the Plymouth house, and
the Eel River farm began to decay.

Then, good news. In March 1776, Gage's troops were
routed from Boston by General Washington, and a gleeful
Mercy Warren traveled to the Boston hills to watch the

retreat. But this victory introduced another problem. Since
Washington's army was to move south, her husband might
have to follow. Mercy was too open and emotional to keep her
fears from James, and she wrote him distraught letters
voicing her fear for his safety and for that of her oldest son,
who was about to enlist, and even for Winslow, uncertain
about his aims. Her prayers were partly answered when
James Warren was left behind by the advancing army to
promote the formation of an American navy. He was to
organize privateers to harass the British ships and would run
the navy board from its Boston headquarters.

It was surely a relief for Mercy Warren to have him so
close to her and so far away from the fighting, but he didn't
visit Plymouth very often, and the farm continued to fare
badly. And then Boston was invaded by a new enemy—
smallpox.

Mercy and James were inoculated in Boston. At the time,
Abigail Adams wrote, "Mrs. Warren is now struggling with it,
to one of her constitution it operates in faintings and
langour." At one point, Abigail Adams felt her friend would
not survive the effects of the vaccine, but she did and
returned to Plymouth to have her sons undergo the same
ordeal. She placed them in separate rooms and watched with
compassion ("my pen trembles") as they suffered the lesser
illness. In the midst of this domestic drama, Mercy Warren
heard that the Declaration of Independence had been signed.

Mercy Otis Warren, at home at bucolic "Clifford" or the
more urban Plymouth house, followed by letter the progress
of the war, the defeats in Long Island, the desolate retreat
through New Jersey, the Trenton and Princeton victories, and
the despair at freezing Valley Forge while British General
Howe was safe and warm in Philadelphia. This woman, vital
in her middle age, sat in a vortex while tragedy and struggle
swirled about her, and was somehow able to influence events
and to record them for history.

Closer to home, enemy General John Burgoyne was
brought back to Boston a prisoner. The local Loyalists came

out of hiding to entertain their British hero in elegant, elaborate style, and to provide an extremely pleasant imprisonment for Gentleman Johnny and his fellow officers. Burgoyne, delighted, penned for his hosts a droll satire ridiculing the ragtag rebel soldiers. This, of course, infuriated Mercy Warren, and she retaliated with *The Blockheads: or the Affrighted Officers, A Farce 1776*. The plot involved General Gage's soldiers being contained in Boston during the winter of 1775 by George Washington and how they fled like rats when spring came. She spared no chance to be as vindictive as possible, with the British saying such things as, "I would rather _____ my breeches than go without those forts to ease myself." Of course the Americans howled; Mercy Warren was moving her pen to move the war, and her side loved every word she wrote.

As the war moved southward, Boston entered a period of prosperity. Mercy Warren watched indignantly as citizens spent their money on frivolities while soldiers were dying for liberty. Her reaction resulted in her writing *The Motley Assemblage*. This time, instead of blasting the British, she hit out at Americans—the *nouveau riche* Patriot and the snobbish Loyalist. (Incidentally, this was the first play written in America with all American characters.)

At the same time, in the late 1770s, Ms. Warren was drifting into a period of depression. Winslow had moved to Boston, vaguely counting on his striking looks and winning charm to make him rich. Charles was studying at Harvard and James, Jr., had joined the new navy. Mercy, now over fifty, was suffering from fainting spells and "vapours," and her eyesight was failing. James, though sympathetic, could not visit her as often as he would have liked, but he did refuse the post of delegate to the Continental Congress so as not to move too far from his "little angel," whom he still adored.

Mercy Warren left play writing to concentrate on her growing collection of letters, especially to rereading the Adams correspondence. She wrote to Catherine Macaulay, historian *célèbre* of England, an admirer of James Otis. Just

as Mercy Warren could be a stubborn foe of men like
Hutchinson, she was a faithful friend once she chose to be.
When Ms. Macaulay married a man twenty-six years younger
than she, the literary world was aghast, but Warren defended
her, saying, "That lady's independency of spirit led her to
suppose she might associate for the remainder of her life with
an inoffensive, obliging youth with the same impunity a
gentleman of threescore and ten might marry a damsel of
fifteen."

Just before the war ended, Warren's beloved Winslow
sailed for Europe, a dangerous undertaking when many ships
were being threatened by the British navy. Winslow was
seized and promptly imprisoned in Newfoundland and then
London, but without inconvenience as far as he was
concerned. He was, in fact, allowed to move on to Holland
when anti-American feelings flamed up in London.

Meanwhile, Mercy and James decided to buy the old
estate of Thomas Hutchinson in Milton. It was close to the
Adams place, and since the navy was being abolished, James
thought he'd develop a fine farm to leave his heirs, while
Mercy hoped the elegant home would lure Winslow back.
Instead, Winslow petitioned his father to use some influence
in getting him a consulate job in Europe after the war. James,
however, could do nothing, for his influence was on the
decline.

During the move to Milton, tragedy struck the Warrens.
James, Jr., serving on *The Alliance*, was wounded, and
subsequently his leg was amputated. Distraught, the young
man suffered a mental breakdown and was moved to a
cousin's home to be nursed back to health. In later years, this
oldest son became his mother's mainstay. After his recovery
he taught school and served a stint as postmaster. Then he
became secretary-companion to his active mother until her
death.

Charles developed tuberculosis while at Harvard. His
greatest wish was to join Winslow in Europe, but on the way,
he died. During this period of Mercy Warren's life, there were

more deaths among those closest to her. James Otis, Mercy's brother, died in 1783, and her father died in Barnstable in 1784.

Ms. Warren returned to writing plays, seemingly the way she could most effectively vent her desolate feelings. For Winslow she wrote *The Ladies of Castille*, full of romance, women, and drama. Alexander Hamilton, in 1791, commented, "It is certain that in *The Ladies of Castille*, the sex will find a new occasion of triumph. Not being a poet myself, I am in the less danger of feeling mortification at the idea that in the career of dramatic composition at least, female genius in the United States has out-stripped the male." Later she wrote *The Sack of Rome*. Both plays were full of patriotic spirit. Not even grief could still that in Mercy Otis Warren.

Warren began her *History of the Rise, Progress and Termination of the American Revolution, Interspersed with Biographical and Moral Observations* in 1775. It was to take over a quarter of a century to complete, a total of three volumes; concurrently, she worked on plays, poetry, and correspondence. And she involved herself in politics once again. Two postwar conflicts inspired her; the first was the plight of poverty-stricken war survivors, who were faced with high taxes, lack of hard money, and debtor's prison. A rebellion led by veteran Daniel Shays demanded a halt to the debtor's prison system. The militia was ordered out against Shays's men, but since there was no money to pay the militia, they refused to move. Finally, General Benjamin Lincoln used his own funds to pay their salaries, about which James Warren remarked, "For fear that Captain Shays should destroy the Constitution, they violated it themselves." But the reimbursed militia managed to scatter Shays's rebels.

This led to the second conflict, a split in the ruling Federalist party. One faction in this party, led by John Adams, demanded a government strong enough to squelch any riots and to protect all private property. The opposition, or Anti-Federalists, wanted first to protect the civil rights

they had fought a war for. It was inevitable that James and
Mercy Warren would join the Anti-Federalists, along with
Thomas Jefferson and Elbridge Gerry.

It was also inevitable that a political division this basic
would destroy the old Adams-Warren friendship. The
Federalists were in power, and the Warren faction fell into
disrepute. Mercy was bitter about the lack of respect accorded
her husband, feeling James had been neglected after his
dedication to the Revolution. This disfavor included their son
George, who found himself sitting in an empty new law office
in Milton. The scarcity of clients finally drove him to try his
luck in Maine.

The division between the two factions became wider
when the federal Constitution came up for passage. Mercy
Warren objected to the elimination of a guarantee of
individual rights, which, she felt, was what the war had been
fought for. She wrote a ponderous article, expressing her
views, entitled, *Observations on the New Constitution and on
the Federal and State Conventions. By A Columbian Patriot.
Sic Transit Gloria Americana.* It was finally the threat of a
nationwide division that brought the two sides together and a
set of amendments was agreed upon, the first ten of which
were to be a Bill of Rights. Warren, victorious, went back to
work on her *History*, taking time out in 1790 to publish a
collection of her writings, *Poems Dramatic and Miscellaneous*,
under her own name at last. She willed the copyright to
Winslow as "the only thing she could properly call her own"—
ironically said, because a married woman was not legally
permitted to call anything "her own" at that time. She
dedicated the volume to George Washington, new president of
the United States, and sent a copy to John Adams, though
their relationship was tenuous.

Her argument with Adams intensified when Winslow
wrote the vice-president for a recommendation for a job.
Adams turned him down. Mercy Warren accused the vice-
president of boosting his own popularity at the expense of the
Warrens. Abigail Adams turned around to denounce her old

friend as having "unbridled ambition." It was shortly after
this that disaster struck Winslow. In 1791, after the Warrens
had moved back to the old Plymouth house, their Milton
venture acknowledged a failure, Winslow was found bankrupt
by the courts and sent to common jail with the harsh sentence
of no exercise in the prison yard. At the same time, he
enlisted in the army, a move which dismayed his mother, and
after his jail sentence, was sent to fight Indians on the
frontier. Winslow was killed in a surprise Indian attack on
his first mission into the wilderness.

Mercy Warren expressed her grief in poetry:

Oh, when I weep my hapless child
And contemplate his bleeding breast
His graceful form, a breathless shade
My grief's too great to be expressed.

The first volume of the *History* was published the same
year. In this last decade before the new century, John Adams
became president, and Mercy Warren sent a lonely letter of
congratulation to Abigail Adams (brooding James remained
silent). She was encouraged when Adams sent a peace
commission to France in an attempt to avoid a second war,
and included in the commission her old friend Elbridge Gerry.
But she was soon disillusioned when Adams passed the Alien
and Sedition Acts, designed to oust imaginary French
subversives from the land and clamp down on the anti-
Federalist press. Both bills were blatant violations of liberty,
and the Warrens dedicated themselves to successfully
removing President Adams after one term. The next
president, Thomas Jefferson, thanked James Warren for his
support in the campaign, adding, "I pray you to present my
homage of my great respect to Mrs. Warren. I have long
possessed evidence of her high station in the ranks of genius
and have considered her silence [during Adams's term] a
proof that she did not go with the current."

Shortly thereafter, George, the youngest Warren, died alone in Maine, and James, Jr., returned to Plymouth to be postmaster. More important, he stepped in to help his mother with her *History*, since her eyesight was fast failing ("wounded optics" was how she put it). The three volumes were finally published by 1805.

The *History* was not impartial; that was not Warren's style. Her political principles, like her religious ideals, were not to be questioned. She skimmed over the battle scenes of the war and concentrated on the philosophies involved and, even more pointedly, on the characters. Her knowledge was firsthand. Of John Adams, Warren wrote: "His prejudices and his passions were sometimes too strong for his sagacity and judgement." This seems especially true when one reads a series of ten letters, written in July and August of 1807, in which Adams replied to Warren's indictment. He often leaves the topic of the actual *History* entirely, going back to justify his own life and accomplishments, writing, in effect, a furious, feverish mini-autobiography.

Adams was very bitter, and refused even to sympathize when Mercy Warren lost her cherished husband in 1808. It was only through a mutual friend, Elbridge Gerry, that Adams and Mercy Warren were reconciled in 1813. Abigail sent a ring, formed from a lock of her hair entwined with a lock of John's hair, as a peace offering. Mercy Warren accepted it, and sent along a lock of her own hair. A grudging peace was made.

Ms. Warren was eighty-four when the War of 1812 threatened. John Adams joined her in opposition to the war, and the town of Plymouth sent a memorandum to the president declaring their refusal to fight. At one point, her sons James, Jr., and Henry were attacked by angry Federalist seamen who were out of work because of the war. Warren remained a staunch Anti-Federalist and continued to write her vitriolic letters, aimed even at her nephew, Federalist Harrison Gray Otis, who became her most bitter opponent.

Mercy Warren's last action was a fight for her own identity. In August 1814, *The Group* was claimed by another writer. Warren asked her old friend, John Adams, to corroborate the fact that she wrote *The Group*. The politician, bereaved by the death of his daughter, went to the Boston Atheneum and found the old pamphlet. On one leaf he scribbled that *The Group* was indeed written by Ms. Mercy Warren. And on the back, he added, "Whose energies and abilities were exerted by the use of her pen on all occasions and in various shapes in promoting the principles that resulted in the Independence of America." Obviously, John Adams, though hurt and disappointed by his old friend's opinion of his political achievements, never doubted her genius in pursuing the goals they both fought for.

Two months later, Mercy Otis Warren died, having seen the British once more shedding blood on American soil, burning the Capitol itself. She remained undaunted in her last days, refusing to give in to what she called, "womanish fears or the weakness of old age." Death came to her quietly in the Plymouth house during the still hours of an October night after a long and busy day.

3

Emma Hart Willard

In the early 1800s, the arbiter of an American woman's education was a Frenchman, Jean Jacques Rousseau: "The whole education of women," he advised, "ought to be relative to men. To please them, to be useful to them, to make themselves loved and honored by them, to educate them when young, to care for them when grown, to counsel them, to console them, and to make life sweet and agreeable to them— these are the duties of women at all times, and what should be taught them from their infancy."

To fulfill these "duties," a girl had only to master her catechism, to be able to run tiny stitches along a hem, and to make a graceful curtsy. The few schools available to her offered instruction in glass painting, music, fancy needle-work, and ornamental handwriting.

Academic study, in post-Revolutionary America, was for "strong minds," which meant *male* minds. If "delicate" females exposed themselves to challenging education, experts warned, madness, witchcraft, or heresy might result. A female's physiology best suited her for waiting with patience for a beau to court, marry, and give her the chance to provide him with a "full quiver of children." Doses of mathematics, science, or geography might only upset a wife's "natural submissive duty" to her husband.

It was commonly accepted that "all the higher mathematics any girl had to know was how many places to set at table. And no mother needed trigonometry to count twelve or fourteen children.... Chemistry enough to keep the pot boiling and geography enough to know the location of the different rooms in her house—these were learning sufficient for any woman."

To have the luxury of the most meager instruction, it was necessary that a girl be the fortunate property of a wealthy and indulgent father. Those parents who went further and provided their daughters with advanced tutoring were later forced to encourage them to hide the results of their work or risk society's scorn and male rejection.

Some nonconformist women wouldn't betray their intelligence: Judith Sargent Murray, Abigail Adams, Mercy Otis Warren. There were a few men who disagreed with Rousseau's restrictive educational theories. Such a man was Dr. Benjamin Rush of Philadelphia, who once spoke to a group of students and guests, declaring that female education "should be accommodated to the state of society, manners and government of the country in which it is conducted." And since the American republic was newborn, "the equal share that every citizen has in the liberty and the equal share he may have in the government of our country, make it necessary that our ladies should be qualified to a certain degree by a peculiar and suitable education, to concur in instructing their sons in the principles of liberty and government."

He spoke these "liberal" words in 1787, the year Emma Hart Willard was born.

Willard slipped into educational revolution as gracefully as her contemporaries might slip into a silk dressing gown. A mixture of the traditional and the radical, she believed that while a woman was by nature humble, her mind was strong and could withstand an academic education. She felt that a woman needed such training so she could be utilized for the good of the new republic. Schooling would form her into a better wife, mother, teacher, and missionary, and men would benefit from their wives' developed minds.

With this philosophy, Willard guided the country into its gradual acceptance of various revolutionary ideas. She introduced to women such subjects as trigonometry, geometry, history, zoology, botany, geography, and anatomy, and she was the first woman to write textbooks on advanced subjects. Willard opened the first teachers' college. She was the first woman to train teachers, and the first to offer scholarships to women. And on her way to these accomplishments, she became the first known female lobbyist.

Because of Willard's faith in the ability of the female mind, an educational web was spun across the country. And as Willard rebelled against the deficient, all-male educational hierarchy, she created new, exciting methods of teaching, and wrote stimulating texts to invoke student creativity.

The infant United States was readying itself for Willard's changes as it moved into the nineteenth century. As Willard was advancing opportunities for women, the country was moving into a new era of machines. Despite their puritanical background, women were working outside the home in factories. When President Jefferson purchased the Louisiana Territory, vast new lands beckoned settlers. With towns springing up throughout the continent, teachers were needed in growing numbers. Women were anxious to teach, but they had to be encouraged first and trained next.

Young Emma Hart received encouragement enough. She was born in a small Connecticut town. Her family supported her strong curiosity, but she had to teach herself many of the subjects that fascinated her, such as geometry.

The Hart home was electric with intellectualism. Samuel Hart, descendant of one of the earliest settlers in that state, told and retold stories of the birth of the Declaration of Independence, the founding of the American republic, and the

heroism of Washington, Lafayette, and John Paul Jones. He
had fought in the Revolutionary War, and after returning to
farm his land, had represented his neighbors in Connecticut's
General Assembly.

Lydia Hinsdale was Hart's second wife—young, well-
read, and vigorous. She bore Samuel his sixteenth child,
Emma. Besides the usual farmwife chores, Lydia Hart kept
up with her reading, and she taught her large brood the
thoughts of Chaucer, Milton, and Shakespeare.

Because of this parentage, Emma was enveloped by
history and literature. By herself she discovered the joys of
science and mathematics. And the many family members
argued with each other about morals, religion, government,
philosophy, and the drama being acted out in France, and its
protagonist, Napoleon Bonaparte.

Emma Hart Willard's biographer, Alma Lutz, wrote:
"Her father had instilled in her both idealism and courage.
Her mother's influence had added practicality and executive
ability." From this basis, she grew up to be affectionate,
opinionated, and realistic, seeing the world as an open,
welcoming, and challenging arena.

The Harts had their physical work as well as their
mental exercises; they wove flax grown on their land into
linen, and then sewed it into clothing (the best quality going
into father's clothes, the next best for the other men, and the
poorest quality for the women). They cured food and stored it
for the icy New England winter, against which even the
sturdy square wooden house, with its tall center chimney
stretching through three floors of rooms, could not act as
adequate protection.

If it were not for her vibrant family, Emma Hart
probably would not have pursued an education. Although
Connecticut was one of the first states to provide public
primary education, the district school was dull. Schoolwork
was tucked like bits of drudgery between house and farm
chores. At fifteen, Ms. Hart was sent to a nearby academy and
became interested in school, but by the time she was

seventeen years old, she knew a college education would not
be available to her, a woman. So Emma Hart became a
teacher.

She was assigned to the village school. This was to be
difficult for two reasons. The first was her youth, which was
pitted against the wide age span of the students. Second, she
was attractive in appearance, with sparkling blue eyes and
fair hair. In later years, one of Willard's students, Elizabeth
Cady Stanton, was to describe her as "a splendid looking
woman . . . [who] fully realized my idea of a queen. . . . She
had a finely developed figure, well-shaped head, classic
features, most genial manners, and a profound self-respect (a
rare quality in woman) that gave her a dignity truly
regal. . . ."

Predictably, the new teacher's career began with
frustration. Ms. Hart's idea was to arrange the students
according to advancement rather than size and age. However,
they were so unruly that sporadically a pupil would leap
through the window or dash out the door, others would talk
out at her, and many would just run around to let off steam.
The arts of reason and discussion, Emma Hart learned on her
first day of teaching, were unknown in the village school.

Hart had been advised by an experienced colleague to
make use of the hickory stick, but she had rejected this idea.
That afternoon, however, she was desperate enough to give it
a try. As she recalled, "I spent most of the afternoon in
alternate whippings and exhortations. The former always
increasing in intensity, until at last, finding the difference
between capricious anger and steadfast determination, they
submitted. This was the first and last of corporal punishment
in that school. The next morning, and ever after, I had docile
and orderly scholars!"

Emma Hart's teaching method, which evolved and
developed through the years, was a combination of recreation,
interesting subjects, and deserved praise. Because her well-
behaved students displayed intellectual progress, the new
teacher's reputation spread throughout the village, and

Emma Hart savored success in her first professional experiment. But stronger than her ego was her recognition of her own teaching limitations, so when her brother offered to finance further schooling, Hart accepted and moved to Hartford, where she studied needlework and primary education. She did not attend a college, but a small, private, traditional academy for young ladies.

She returned to her hometown the following summer and opened a select school for older children in the upstairs rooms of her father's home. In the winter, she returned to the village school and thus she continued teaching, taking spring and autumn off for her own schooling in Hartford.

Hartford was an educational experience, outside as well as inside the schoolroom. Emma lived with her cousin, Dr. Sylvester Wells, and his family. Wells was a liberal Anti-Federalist, and his wife was an ideal mixture of beauty, refinement, and wit. Together they presented a picture of intellectualism and elegance.

But even as a young woman under twenty, Emma Hart did not benignly absorb her relatives' beliefs. Her own father was a liberal Unitarian and Dr. Wells was influenced more by reason than by religion: Hart could not accept the idea of salvation of the few and damnation for the rest, but she was not a religious skeptic either. After a period of soul-searching, she joined the Episcopal church and remained a devoted member throughout her life.

Despite her uncommon educational environment, her religiously unorthodox relatives, and her radical beliefs about female education, Emma Hart tried to lead a conventional life. In later years, she was to veer from her ideal of the humble, quiet woman, who did not need to exercise political power and who should not speak out in public or create controversy. Basically, she strove to remain traditional in appearance and behavior. This, combined with her genuine talent for teaching, was one reason why her educational reforms took root.

By the time she was twenty, Ms. Hart was well known

throughout the state and was receiving other teaching offers. After a brief stay at Westfield Academy in Massachusetts, where she was disappointed with her menial, assistant's duties, she moved on to Middlebury, Vermont.

Like Hartford, Middlebury offered an environment of cultural and social activity, which attracted Emma Hart. She was put in full charge of the girls' school and had her first taste of administrative challenges.

"To please the greatest number of people," she wrote to her parents, "I must attend all the meetings Sunday, go to conference one or two afternoons a week, profess to belief, among other articles of the creed, that mankind, generally speaking, will be damned." She found it impossible to be conventional all the time.

Young Ms. Hart was an exuberant teacher. When her classrooms became unbearably cold in the winter of 1807, she had her students take dancing breaks to warm up. Her enthusiasm infected her students so quickly that the word got around, and after several months the school contained sixty young girls, aged twelve to fifteen, from all over Vermont.

Her scarce free time was spent writing poetry and visiting her new friends, but when Emma Hart fell in love, it was with a man twenty-eight years her senior. She had always had serious interests beneath her gregarious surface and was attracted to Dr. John Willard's maturity and poise. He, in turn, was enchanted by her friendly yet demure demeanor, her handsome carriage, and her intelligence and curiosity about politics and philosophy, which were also his interests.

They were married on August 10, 1809. At first, there were problems with the children of Dr. Willard's previous marriage, who suspected the twenty-two-year-old bride of marrying their father for his wealth and social position. Their attitude hurt Emma, for she recalled how her own mother's many stepchildren had loved her. She finally realized that it would take time, patience, and kindness to win them over.

Despite this difficult beginning, the Willards' marriage

became a fairly equal partnership. The doctor enjoyed
showing off his bright young wife to the neighbors. He was
well established in Vermont, with a large house and several
farms. As expected, Ms. Willard quit her teaching when she
married. But she soon found herself thoroughly bored,
especially when her husband was away on business. John
encouraged her interest in his medical books, but even after
her only child, John Hart Willard, was born in 1810, Emma
longed for the stimulation of working outside the home.

When Dr. Willard's nephew came to live with the
Willards while he attended Middlebury College, Emma found
a new interest. She questioned him about his classes, his
studies, his teachers. She began reading his textbooks and
taking his examinations. Alone, she went from subject to
subject this way. She felt deeply the inequity in boys'
receiving a free education while girls were deprived of this
benefit.

It took a financial disaster to finally get Ms. Willard
permanently out of the house and into the schoolroom again.
Her husband was director of a bank, and three years after
their marriage, his bank was robbed. All the directors were
asked to make up the loss, and although they were later
vindicated, John Willard temporarily lost his money and his
reputation. At first, Emma Willard limited herself to
comforting her husband, but after two years, she opened a
school for girls in her home. The Middlebury Female
Seminary was born, and Emma Willard was never to leave
teaching again.

It was 1814 and the country was in turmoil. The War of
1812 had plunged Americans into discouragement, while the
publicized debates of Clay, Webster, and Calhoun stirred
intellectuals into violent discussion. In this social climate,
Ms. Willard tread delicately with her new school. She began
with superficial studies, stressing penmanship, which she
believed to be important to a fine education. Then she
included subjects as she taught them to herself. Gradually she
added mathematics, history, and modern languages to the

syllabus. She was determined to prove that the female mind could master these subjects, and she succeeded. The girls were interested; parents were surprised at their daughters' mental acumen and their refined behavior. It wasn't long before seventy students had enrolled, and a housekeeper and an assistant teacher were hired.

Willard's teaching was dynamic. She had two aims: to stimulate women's minds and to produce female teachers. From the start, Willard encouraged her girls to consider teaching as a profession. Those interested became assistant teachers, learning the Willard method while continuing to study their courses.

The principle behind her technique was learning by understanding rather than by rote. In geography, she had her students compare the various attributes of different countries, such as population and topography, instead of merely memorizing maps. She later organized lessons in history, geography, and literature by eras for greater clarity. Original compositions were stressed, and always penmanship had to be precise. Shakespeare was introduced for oral reading and dramatics. Gymnastics, walking, and dancing were necessary for exercise. As Alma Lutz pointed out, "At a time when weak, delicate, fainting women were the fashion, [Willard's] girls were vigorous, proving that education did not undermine their health."

Ms. Willard employed graphic techniques in mathematics. She carved shapes out of potatoes and turnips and snipped flat figures from paper. She believed that math, more than any other subject, would develop the mind and clarify thinking. This was particularly important for women, who were conditioned to react emotionally rather than rationally. She wanted to stimulate her students to look at problems objectively and to deal with situations with reason.

Ms. Willard described her method in this way: "During the first part of the process, I talked much more than the pupils were required to do, keeping their attention awake by frequent questions, requiring short answers from the whole

class—for it was my maxim, if attention fails, the teacher
fails. Then, in the second stage of my teaching, I made each
scholar recite, in order that she might remember, paying
special attention to the meaning of words, and to discern
whether the subject was indeed understood without mistake.
Then the third process was to make the pupil capable of
communicating. And doing this in a right manner was to
prepare her for examination. At this time, I personally
examined all my classes." Willard invited the Middlebury
College professors to these examinations so they might
witness the strength and development of her students' minds.

It was not long before Emma Willard was committed to
an ambitious educational project—but she had little money.
She knew she needed more teachers and qualified professors
to teach advanced subjects to herself and to the students. She
had no funds to hire them and could not ask her students'
parents to pay any more tuition. Once again, she felt
personally and acutely the financial discrimination against
women's education. This time she decided to do something
about it.

The program that resulted was published in 1819 and
was called "An Address to the Public, Particularly to the
Members of the Legislature of New York, proposing a Plan for
Improving Female Education."

Emma Willard's plan would make her headmistress of a
female institution of higher learning to be situated in the
busy, prosperous Hudson River Valley, where river
transportation was available to out-of-state students. This
institute would not be so advanced as to be called a college.
Rather, it would be called a seminary. Always proper, Willard
explained that this would prevent "a jealousy that we mean to
intrude upon the province of men." Most important, the school
was to be endorsed by prominent men and was to be funded
by the state.

Willard arranged to have her plan presented to New
York's governor, DeWitt Clinton, who was immediately
enthusiastic. Her next step was to convince the state

legislators, who would allot the funds. Reading her plan to various groups of legislators made Emma Willard the first female lobbyist.

It was an exhausting period. Stately, well dressed, and always appropriately modest, Willard would explain over and over what she wanted to accomplish. She arranged her plan in four parts: The first section pointed out the defects in the female schools, which existed primarily to make money for the owners. They had inadequate facilities, taught only those subjects which would attract the most students, and stressed those accomplishments which could be displayed like after-dinner mints. As a result, women were regarded as "pampered, wayward babies of society."

Part two discussed the regulation of her proposed educational system. State aid was just as necessary for women as for men and would prove to the citizens "the justice, the policy, and the magnanimity of such an undertaking." Trustees would manage the school. There would be a large building housing a library, a laboratory, rooms for "philosophical apparatus," domestic arts equipment, dormitories, and classrooms, as well as an array of maps, globes, musical instruments, fine paintings, and qualified teachers—all this was necessary.

Part three was the curriculum, which included religion, morals, classical and modern languages, mathematics, science, literature (to understand the operations of the human mind), domestic instruction, and certain ornamental arts, but excluded needlework, which Willard found did not aid in forming character.

Section four considered society's benefits from such a school. The common schools would gain well-trained teachers. Men could go on to other work, since they looked upon teaching as temporary work anyway. And here, Willard pointed out that women teachers would accept lower salaries than men. She was later to regret this prediction.

When the published plan was circulated around the country and later the world, Willard received praise from various illustrious persons, including President Monroe and former Presidents Adams and Jefferson. However, the plan was so radical that the state legislators, who held the financial power, were hesitant. Eventually, they would grant her what was the first legislative charter to benefit education for women, but it would be fifteen years before the state promise for government funding would become a reality.

Emma Willard was thirty-four years old when the Willard family moved to Troy, a vital New York river port which boasted a citizen body willing to support an important women's school. While Willard awaited the promised government allotment, her Troy Female Academy began its life in Moulton's Coffee Shop, close to the city's business district.

The building was an ample wooden one of three stories, twenty-two rooms, and a large ballroom. The citizens had raised funds to purchase and to renovate it to Willard's instructions. "I expect the life of the school will be on the inside," she said, "and not on the out; and when the school wants to grow, you must enlarge its shell."

Since a married woman could not own property at that time, the school lease went to Dr. Willard, who became business manager and school physician. The yearly rent of four-hundred dollars was to be used by the Board of Trustees for repairs and loan interest, and the board would confer regularly with the Committee of Ladies on school matters. Willard learned very soon to depend on citizen support for her aims rather than the government.

The seminary opened in 1821, with ninety pupils from seven states, a staff of Willard-trained teachers, and one professor to teach modern languages, painting, and music. Here, Willard would develop the methods she had initiated in the Middlebury School and prove her theory that education for women would benefit society. The Troy Female Academy was to become the prototype for most American women's boarding schools.

The following year, Willard published her first textbook,

A System of Universal Geography on the Principles of Comparison and Classification. She next published a history text, *Republic of America.* Like the geography book, this was well received. Daniel Webster wrote Willard, "I cannot better express my sense of the value of your history of the United States than by saying I keep it near me as a book of reference, accurate in facts and dates."

In 1837, another Willard textbook was printed, *A System of Universal History in Perspective, Accompanied by an Atlas, Exhibiting Chronology in a Picture of Nations and Progressive Geography in a Series of Maps.* Willard sensed that America was at a testing point, and the next ten years would tell if its citizens truly could govern themselves. This book was acclaimed for its "vivacity, lucidness, and intelligent mode of arrangement," but never had the popular success of the earlier *History.* Still later, Willard's *Temple of Time* won a gold medal at the 1850 World's Fair in London for its originality in presenting history in chart form, with pillars, representing various centuries, standing on a floor that was sectioned to represent different nations.

Other textbooks written later in her life concerned astronomy, the Mexican War and California, and John C. Fremont. By the time she was in her sixties, Emma Willard was considered to be an authority on history and freely voiced her opinions on current American issues.

Willard continued the self-education she had begun in childhood. As she progressed through mathematics, she turned to science and hired Professor Amos Eaton to teach herself, the other teachers, and the students. He rated the syllabus at the Troy school as being far more advanced than those of men's colleges. It was Eaton who trained Willard's younger sister, Almira Hart Lincoln, who eventually became the outstanding woman science educator in America. (She wrote books on botany and chemistry which were to become standard college texts.)

Willard preferred to have a warm, friendly relationship with her students. Yet she made it clear that she was their superior and had final authority. From all accounts, the girls adored her, especially those whom she took into her own home to comfort because of homesickness and those to whom she loaned travel and clothing money. In her lifetime, Willard was to give out some seventy-five thousand dollars in educational aid, including financial aid and free tuition.

Emma Willard felt that the girls would be more comfortable in small rooms than in the customary large, crowded dormitories, and she insisted that these rooms be kept in perfect order, assigning monitors to check them and to administer necessary demerits. The girls were to dress simply and to wear very little jewelry; graciousness and social amenities were important. She also insisted that all students attend the nonsectarian chapel, and every Saturday, she gathered the girls around her to talk to them about the "peculiar duties" of their sex.

Willard removed all sense of competition from her school, especially in educational achievements. No grades or honors were awarded. If a student fell behind in any area, social or academic, Willard would take her aside and reprimand or advise her in private.

The students, however, were not so regimented that they became decorous, studious automatons. They enjoyed the recreational area, sometimes playing on swings like young children, and at other times shrieking and waving handkerchiefs at young men. And in the music room, they sang the popular songs, even though their teachers tried to substitute the more beautiful melodies of an earlier day.

The Troy Female Academy examinations were held in February and late July and soon became popular civic events, drawing crowds of parents, friends, prominent educators, legislators, and clergymen. They were held in the large second-floor examination room, which had ascending rows of seats on both sides. The spectators sat opposite the girls, who wore dainty white dresses with bright sashes.

In the center sat Emma Willard, the examiners, and the teachers of the classes to be tested. The educators who were to test the girls had not met them before this day. Two students stood together at the long table, but each girl was questioned individually. The examination included solving geometry problems, analyzing philosophical theses, drawing maps, and relating historical events and illustrating them with maps. Between recitations, other students would entertain by singing or playing the harp or piano.

Despite her innovative methods, Willard clung to decorum. If a composition were judged excellent it would be read aloud to the examiners, but not by the student who wrote it, since this was considered immodest. At the end of each day's examination session, the students sang a hymn of gratitude to God for giving them strong, able minds.

As Ms. Willard observed: "The very pupils who excel most in these studies which men have been apt to think would unsex us, such as mathematics and natural philosophy, are the most apt to possess the elegant simplicity of truly fine manners, without mannerisms. Even personal beauty is advanced; for as a woman improves in taste, and as her will gains efficiency in every species of self-control, she rarely fails to improve herself in symmetry of form. . . . Genuine learning has ever been said to give polish to man; why then should it not bestow added charms on women?"

Willard did not forget about traditional skills either. Part of the first floor of the school served as laundry and kitchen; the girls baked pies for Sunday dessert. And one favorite handicraft was painting "mourning pictures." It was a custom in the early part of the nineteenth century that when a relative or close friend died, their likeness, or sometimes the death scene, was painted with watercolors on China silk. This artwork was not useless dabbling, Willard felt, but an activity that helped young women to become more contemplative about death.

One of Willard's childhood heroes from her father's Revolutionary War stories was Lafayette. In 1824, she was thrilled to learn of his forthcoming visit to the United States. With tremendous enthusiasm and patriotism, she invited him

to visit her school, and when he agreed, she prepared her
students to receive him in a dramatic fashion.

She wrote a welcoming song for him and prepared a
flowered arbor with a banner reading: "America commands
her daughters to welcome their Deliverer, Lafayette." When
he finally arrived, he was greeted by an assembly of girls
garbed in white dresses with blue sashes. Each wore a satin
badge with Lafayette's face painted on it. Guns boomed, the
band played, and the girls sang the song composed by Emma
Willard, which ended with these words:

Then deep and dear thy welcome be;
Nor think thy daughters far from thee;
Daughters of human kind we bend,
And claim to call thee Father, Friend!

Understandably, Lafayette left Troy with tears of
gratitude and became Willard's lifelong friend and
correspondent. Later, when she visited Europe, Lafayette
dedicated himself to making her stay in Paris memorable.

By the late 1820s, Troy had fulfilled the Willards'
prophesy that it would become an important city. The Erie
Canal had opened. More students now arrived from the West,
while more teachers went out West with a Willard diploma.
Paved avenues lighted by oil lamps and houses marked with
numbers gave a civilized air to the city. A steamboat traveled
to New York City twice a week, while the stagecoach came
through regularly. By 1828, a wing had been added to the
Troy Academy and an extra building had been constructed on
the property.

Emma Willard, at forty-three, had known steady success
and fulfillment in her work. Her husband had died in 1825,
and she had added his duties to her own schedule of studying
and teaching. By 1830, she was tired. So Ms. Willard decided
to travel through Europe to see what educational methods
were in use there, and she took her son with her.

It was a dangerous undertaking to sail the Atlantic in

1830. The voyage took twenty-four days in rough October
weather. (Willard wrote that she did not get seasick.) From
Le Havre and Paris to London and Scotland, Willard noted
every detail—the thatched huts, the ornate hotels, the British
boarding houses, theatre costumes, and the "outrageous"
nude statues exposed for all to see in the Louvre. The
highlight, of course, was seeing Lafayette again. He escorted
her around Paris, to the House of Deputies and to the opera,
and she reveled in the adulation shown him by the French
people.

After studying the European schools, Willard concluded
that her own institution in Troy was far superior to the finest
in either France or England. She found she had more
suggestions to give European school directors than they could
give her.

In England, Willard was particularly disturbed by the
disdainful attitude shown Americans, especially American
women. Before this, Willard had not been intrigued by the
emerging American women's rights movement; she had felt
that rights without education would just be abused. Now,
however, she resolved to work harder for the general
betterment of her sex.

When they returned to LeHavre from the British Isles,
Emma and twenty-year-old John, Jr., were joined by a
Parisienne who was to teach French in the Troy school, an
Englishwoman who was to teach music, and a young French
orphan girl who was to study music at the academy.

When she returned to Troy after seven months abroad,
Willard found that the Troy Female Academy had fared well
under the care of her sister, Almira. Furthermore, through
Willard's example and advice, other avenues for advanced
female education were opening up. In 1823, Catherine
Beecher had started a seminary; the first public high schools
for girls opened (and quickly closed) in Boston and New York;
in 1833, Oberlin College was to admit women along with
men, though in a more restricted curriculum; Wheaton
Seminary followed in Massachusetts; and in 1837, due to the

Troy Academy's success, Mount Holyoke Female Seminary welcomed women to the first *endowed,* permanent school of female higher education.

Emma Willard lived comfortably on her book royalties in a campus house furnished with the objects and paintings she acquired in Europe. She was aided by servants and visited by students and teachers. Her school's student body had reached three hundred, and the school was considered fashionable as well as educational. Willard reigned over all, soft-spoken and majestic in her rich black gown and white turban wrapped around her head.

Willard began to move away from teaching now. She published a book of her poems, *The Fulfillment of a Promise, by Which Poems by Emma Willard Are Published, and Affectionately Inscribed to her Past and Present Pupils,* and a volume called *Journal and Letters from France and Great Britain.* The latter was printed to raise money for a women's school in Athens, Greece. Willard felt that just as more teachers were needed in the American West, female education was necessary around the world, especially in Greece, which had just won its independence from Turkey. The money for the Athens school was raised, and Willard continued to send money each year until it was financially solvent.

Willard's son and his wife, a former Troy student, took charge of the Academy, and Emma concentrated on advancing the school curricula and improving teaching techniques. She added the teaching of physiology and human anatomy, and when parents objected, she agreed to paste heavy paper over those pages in the text which detailed the human body. In 1846, she published "A Treatise on the Motive Powers Which Produce the Circulation of the Blood." This was one year before Elizabeth Blackwell became the first woman admitted into a medical school. Public opinion was firmly against women studying anatomy; even Emma's friends referred to her interest as an "unfortunate mania." Yet Willard eventually received recognition for her work in this area, particularly the effects of respiration on circulation, although her ideas were known as the "American" rather than the "Willard" theory. She became one of the few women admitted into the Association for the Advancement of Science.

As Willard approached her fiftieth birthday, she formed two alliances. One turned out to be a mistake; this was her marriage to a Boston physician, which lasted nine months and ended in divorce. Although going through a divorce was a humiliating experience for the conventional Emma Willard, she at least managed to retain her own material belongings. After this experience, Willard became more at ease with the unconventional side of her nature.

The second alliance was aimed at improving teaching methods and the teacher's situation. Willard formed and became first president of the Willard Association for the Mutual Improvement of Female Teachers. The Association was to keep in touch with teachers throughout the country, informing them of new teaching methods, airing problems, and offering advice and encouragement. By this time, a teaching certificate signed "Emma Willard" was considered the highest recommendation any teacher could have, and Willard felt free to make suggestions to her former students. She reminded them that education continues in all fields of life, not merely in the classroom. She urged her teachers not to stop studying while raising children, citing her own daughter-in-law as an example: "Mrs. John Willard, with five children, performs well the duties of principal of this school."

She stressed also the well-educated woman's responsibilities to her husband and children, advising that a child should be taught discipline, but not so his will is broken. A child's will, she once wrote, is the strength of his mind.

Willard became a familiar figure as she traveled around the country dressed in her black gown with lace trim, and a lace cap over her gray curls. Besides meeting with former students, she visited schools and commented on the general educational experiments and reforms taking place. At the same time, she urged state funding for a teachers' school, and she complained about the dollar-a-week salary female teachers were earning, suggesting a minimal two hundred fifty dollar annual wage. She was now regretting her earlier statement on low salaries for women teachers.

After her divorce, Willard temporarily retired to her Connecticut hometown, but once there, she realized that work was her best cure. She set up teacher workshops and drew up outlines regarding local school schedules, textbooks, and teaching methods. This lasted only until she felt emotionally strong enough to return to Troy and her own seminary. By 1846, this school had several additions, steam heat, and gas lighting; more important, it was considered the female equivalent of Harvard or Yale.

Although as she grew older education continued to be Emma Willard's main concern, she became less inhibited about voicing her beliefs about other issues. In the 1820s, Willard had refused to involve herself in heated controversies, such as the one between John Quincy Adams and Andrew Jackson. Twenty years later, she published a letter urging the new French government to consult their women when drafting their constitution.

She had turned from the docile ideal of womanhood to stating that, "It is certainly questionable how far we have a right to sacrifice ourselves. . . . To *have right,* as well as to *do right,* seems to be the duty of each individual."

Willard worried about the immigrants crowded into the cities and about the "peculiar" institutions of the Mormons, and she urged the construction of a trans-American railroad. Slavery, Willard felt, was morally wrong, but she understood the Southerners' dilemma; her widely publicized solution was to establish an African republic for freed American Negroes. Although she was against war, she strongly supported President Abraham Lincoln's actions once battle was inevitable. She helped organize groups to provide hospital supplies and clothing to soldiers, and when the fighting was over, Willard decided to dedicate the rest of her life to peace.

In 1864, Emma Willard published *Universal Peace,* which prophesied the League of Nations, World Court, United

Nations, and the Jewish state of Israel. This idea had burned within her since 1820, but at that time she had felt it was too bold to be printed. Her plan called for a unity of nations; representatives of these nations were to meet regularly in Jerusalem. Disputes could be discussed and wars possibly averted. Ms. Willard felt that since the Bible foresaw the return of the Jews to Jerusalem, gentiles of the world should aid in the Jewish migration to the Holy Land, which would be purchased from the controlling power, Turkey. Of course, she did not live to see aspects of her plan become reality.

Willard died April 15, 1870, at eighty-three, a bridge between traditional supportive women and the Victorian suffragists. Passionate, yet controlled, she recognized that she was more than merely "a visionary enthusiast, who has speculated in solitude without practical knowledge of her subject."

Willard's activism was directed toward one aim, female education. This, to her, was the only base that could support female advancement. It would take her descendants in spirit to build on that foundation.

4

Margaret Fuller

Margaret Fuller was a misfit. In the American age of which Alexis de Tocqueville wrote, "I know no country in which there is so little freedom of discussion or independence of mind," Margaret Fuller spoke out boldly and brilliantly. While New Englanders were following the leaders of Unitarianism, Fuller based her religion on Germanic mystical transcendentalism. To Margaret Fuller, femininity lay in having a passion for life rather than in fan fluttering. And because she could not flower in the rarefied Boston atmosphere, she transplanted herself to the rowdy activism of New York City.

But even in New York City Fuller remained a misfit. Finally, like the Brownings, Byron, Shelley, and Keats, she sailed to Italy. In the Latin milieu, she found satisfaction, a home, and love. But those years in Rome were few, and when she was forced to leave, Margaret Fuller's life was over.

Why was she a misfit? First, any woman with an ego "mountainous" enough to state, "I know all the people worth knowing in America, and I find no intellect comparable to my own," was not a typical lady of the 1830s. Furthermore, she was probably right; the "people worth knowing" composed an impressive roll. She alternately fascinated and repelled Henry David Thoreau, George Ripley, Julia Ward Howe, Oliver Wendell Holmes, Nathaniel Hawthorne, Henry Wadsworth Longfellow, Elizabeth Peabody, Horace Greeley, Edgar Allan Poe, and James Russell Lowell. But Fuller shared the most exciting of her love-hate relationships with the dean of American intelligentsia, Ralph Waldo Emerson.

Emerson, like the others, was drawn to her "man's mind" and supreme ego, wit, stimulating criticism, and humor. She was one of the few people who could make the somber Emerson laugh, but his prudish, self-contained nature recoiled from her plunges and soarings of mood, her search for romantic love, and her self-centered sarcasm. It was to him that she scrawled, "Farewell, O Grecian sage. Your excellence never shames me. You are intellect—but I am life." And it was Emerson who later recorded and interpreted her life, asserting that her abilities were but a quirk of feminine nature.

Fuller recognized early that she could electrify others with her brain if not her beauty. Though attractive, she was not the picture of femininity for her time. Her blue eyes were too steely to be gentle; her hair, flaxen and fine, could not be coaxed to remain in fashionable, soft, thick curls. Her long neck, said William Henry Channing, was swanlike when she was tender, but "when she was scornful or indignant, it contracted, and made swift turns like that of a bird of prey." Ms. Fuller was full-bosomed to the point of plumpness, and her posture was too majestic to be dainty.

In oratory, Margaret Fuller excelled, even though Emerson thought her voice nasal. Her refusal to chat mindlessly was threatening to men and women alike. For many years she was a scholar without a university, an intellect without a following, and a woman without a man. Nevertheless, she managed to become America's first female literary critic and foreign correspondent; and as a legacy, she left her thoughts as America's first feminist philosopher in

Women in the Nineteenth Century, the genesis of the feminist bible.

Emerson once wrote that Margaret Fuller was "a foreigner from some more sultry and expansive climate." Actually, she was born in Cambridgeport, Massachusetts, the first of nine children, on May 23, 1810. Her father, Timothy, had longed for a boy, but upon Sarah Margaret's birth, he dedicated himself to her education. Since the next Fuller child died in infancy, Margaret was for many years the sole object of her father's direction. This direction aimed straight for the ancient Roman ideal of perfection through will. "Mediocrity is obscurity," said her father.

Fuller quickly bypassed mediocrity; by the age of ten, she was reciting and reading Latin and Greek, organizing her own education, and rising at dawn to do it. At least one bright schoolmate, Oliver Wendell Holmes, was amazed by her vocabulary. He admitted that it was Margaret who taught him the meaning of the word *trite.*

Timothy Fuller led a life of political ups and downs. He had earned first place in his class at his Harvard commencement but was denied this honor after he participated in student riots. His political ideas were Jeffersonian, which irritated the Federalist fiber of many New Englanders.

Timothy served as a representative and speaker of the house in Massachusetts. He won and lost in the battles of politics, and his family went from top to bottom with him. He had married young "fair and flower-like" Margaret Crane when he was thirty; she immediately became pregnant and for the rest of her life she was immersed in childbearing and child raising, illness, and dependency.

Since his wife had no time or energy to spare, Timothy heard young Margaret recite her lessons every night, regardless of the hour. He was domineering almost to the point of tyranny, but Timothy loved Margaret and took great pride in her educational progress.

In adolescence, Margaret Fuller settled into a schedule of

rising before five, walking for an hour, and practising on the piano until seven, when the family breakfasted together. Then she would read French and philosophy, and at half-past nine, go to school to study Greek until noon. From noon until two, she read at home and then dined. Italian followed, and at six, she would walk or take a carriage ride. At eleven, she would write in one of her notebooks.

Ms. Fuller admitted later that not having a normal childhood bore consequences. She was a nervous, sensitive, self-confident, and overly assertive child. She suffered from migraines and insomnia, and when sleep came, it was often interrupted by nightmares.

Being raised with books rather than friends denied Margaret the benefits of relating to her contemporaries. Her classmates responded to her self-confidence and superiority by calling her "fat." It wasn't until mid-adolescence that she found contentment; her father moved the family to a beautiful house in Cambridge. Here, for the first time, Margaret made friends, primarily with the Harvard scholars who appreciated her intellect. She was determined to become the American Madame de Stael, bringing culture to her world through salons and bright conversation. By now, she was aware of her talents.

It was at this time that her father, hoping for a diplomatic post, decided to give a party in his elegant home for President John Quincy Adams. Sixteen-year-old Margaret would be presented. Mr. Fuller chose her dress, a pink satin gown that fit too snugly, and had her hair curled tightly. Energetic, romantic Margaret danced too long, laughed too loudly, and, her cheeks flushed with excitement, appeared totally unladylike. In society's eyes, she was a disaster.

And so was Timothy. The President arrived just in time for dinner and left immediately after. He didn't even receive the guests. From this point on, Timothy Fuller's political career plummeted. Several years later, Timothy left Cambridge and moved the family to a farm in rural Groton.

Ms. Fuller was despondent. She missed her friends, and

she was burdened with much of the housekeeping, since her mother was now a semi-invalid. She also taught her sister and brothers reading, history, geography, and languages, and still she was constantly driven by her own self-improvement goals. So, she began a translation of Goethe and planned a biography of his life. A short article by her was published unsigned in the Boston *Daily Advertiser*. But the household chores were tiring. At twenty-four, physically and emotionally exhausted, Fuller fell ill with a raging fever and hallucinations. She cried out for her father.

Timothy soothed her, and Margaret soon recovered. Shortly thereafter, Timothy came down with Asian cholera. Within days, he was dead. His daughter, desolate, was left to care for her sick mother and her young brothers and sister, who were totally dependent on her. She resolved that the three boys would continue their education, and that she would see her sister settled and her mother cared for. So burdened, she tried to console herself with Goethe's advice, "Enjoy the present and leave the future to God." But for the present, she could not hope for enjoyment; she had to concentrate on survival.

"Never had I such reason to regret my sex," she wrote. "If I were eldest *son* I could be guardian to my brothers and sister, administer the estate and be the *real* head of my family." She had to fight the family's legal head, her uncle Abraham Fuller, who was opposed to all her ambitious plans.

Fuller's greatest disappointment came when she had to pass up a chance to go to Europe. It was especially frustrating because the man she had fallen in love with, Samuel Grey Ward, was going. She had met Samuel when she was twenty-five and he was entering his last year at Harvard. She called him "Raffaelo," after the young, sensuous artist; he called her "Mother." Burdened with her responsibilities, Fuller had to watch him sail away to the Europe she longed to see.

Ms. Fuller visited Cambridge often after her father's death, first to visit Samuel Ward and later to see her old friends. She had heard about Ralph Waldo Emerson and finally met him. She felt insecure, intellectually superficial, and lacked the self-definition she had known before; she wanted someone to help her understand herself again and believed Emerson could do this.

If Emerson could not help Fuller define herself just then, he did introduce her to a progressive young educator, Bronson Alcott, head of the Temple School in Boston. Alcott invited Margaret Fuller to join his teaching staff, and she agreed. This was a turning point in her life. By teaching, Fuller learned that her voice, rather than her pen, was her most effective means of communication.

The Temple School was sunny, open, and comfortable, with carpeting on the floor and bright maps coloring the walls. Each child had his own desk, but the students all gathered around the teacher for frequent discussions. Gymnastics, singing, and games were included in the activities, as were visits by artists and poets, including Emerson. It was a welcomed step forward from the traditional solemnity of hard oak floors and long wooden benches.

Margaret Fuller loved Boston. If New York was the nation's business capital and Philadelphia America's historical base, Boston claimed cultural supremacy. The citizens kept the museums well stocked, and the Academy of Music brought Beethoven to these shores. Fuller accepted the job of teaching evening classes in German and Italian to the daughters of Boston society.

She was earning money and gaining contentment. Alcott considered Margaret Fuller "the most brilliant talker of the day," but she soon grew disenchanted with the school. She disapproved of her employer's abstract nature; she felt he neglected the value of experience in favor of intuition. Still, she remained there until 1837, when the school became the focus of depression-time criticism and was labeled "heretical." When students ceased coming, Fuller had to leave.

Her next job was in Providence, Rhode Island, a place she hated. She missed Boston but had no choice but to stay in Providence, since she needed the salary. Anyway, she felt she

could do her work on Goethe in that undemanding atmosphere.

She continued to enjoy visiting Boston, especially its
theaters and museums. She described the ballet performance
of Fanny Elssler as a religious experience. She spent hours
with Sam Ward when he returned from Europe, but now their
time together lacked passion, for Sam's ardor had cooled.

Finally, she realized that she could not serve two
masters, teaching and writing, so she said goodbye to her
students and moved back to Boston. Boston became the
center of her existence; she moved the entire Fuller family
there. The controversial new group of intellectuals, the
Transcendentalists, who stood against orthodoxy in religion,
accepted her. She had agreed to the idea that all the world's
parts were interdependent, forming an organic unity; she
believed that human duty was to interpret nature. Fuller also
adopted the idea of moral freedom as an inherent sense that
would direct the human will and mind.

In spring 1839, Margaret Fuller's first book was
published, a translation of Eckermann's *Conversations With
Goethe*. Still, not enough money was coming in, so once again
she began looking for a job. She had the idea of bringing
together for conversation the city's educated women. The
purpose of these conversations, she wrote, would be to
ascertain "what pursuits are best suited to us, in our time and
state of society, and how we may make best use of our means
for building up the life of thought upon the life of action."

With the help of Mrs. George Ripley, Fuller began setting
up her plan, and the year that young Victoria was crowned
Queen of England and George Sand became queen of literary
France, Margaret Fuller became queen of Boston's educated
women. Her famed conversations began with a group of
twenty-five ladies on November 6, 1839, in the rooms of her
friend, Elizabeth Peabody. The thirteen-week course cost
twenty dollars, and each session lasted for two hours. One
subject was to be discussed for an entire course.

Fuller chose to begin with Greek mythology, particularly

popular that year because of Byron and the Greek war for independence. She would introduce the topic, offer some ideas, and moderate the conversation, urging each woman to take part. That was often difficult since the era was not one in which women were encouraged to air their views in public.

The following year, the women discussed fine arts. Those who joined her classes came from the top strata of Boston society: Mrs. Josiah Quincy, Mrs. George Bancroft, the Peabody sisters, Maria White, Lydia Child, and young Elizabeth Cady, who was to become the creative force of the suffragist movement within ten years.

The conversations became so popular that men, too, began to come, and Fuller started an evening class for both sexes. If the attendance of men intimidated some of the ladies, it did not daunt Fuller, who felt confident even when Emerson himself sat in on her classes.

Boston was revitalized through these conversations; bright women shifted into gear for the first time since Anne Hutchinson had conducted her own classes two centuries before. And Margaret, as well, was stimulated. Many of the ideas she aired were eventually put down in a book which she called *Woman in the Nineteenth Century*, and her groups became a school for the coming generation of abolitionists, temperance workers, and suffragists.

At this time, Margaret Fuller was invited to move into the publishing world as editor of *The Dial*. Although she was still plagued with headaches, she accepted the job. She was to earn two hundred dollars a year, but as it turned out, she never received that much. Her business manager was George Ripley; her co-editor, Ralph Waldo Emerson.

The Dial was a quarterly magazine that aimed to stimulate thinking. The first issue came out on July 1, 1840. This was a time of reforms. There were cries to abolish slavery, banks, tariffs, hereditary property, government by force, war, and labor exploitation, and there were pleas for peace, a congress of nations, fairness to Indians, and changes in marriage laws, trade laws, prisons, hospitals, and education. The groups were split, one side arguing against the other. It was an exciting era.

It was during these years that Fuller watched the formation of Brooke Farm—a new country community which predicted "a more pure, more lovely, more divine state of society than was ever realized on earth." It was to be a self-supporting union of labor and culture, a severing of man's slavery to the new machines. It was utopian, but, as Emerson said, "We were all a little mad that winter. Not a man of us that did not have a plan for some new utopia in his pocket."

Brooke Farm was not destined to become Fuller's utopia, although she was interested enough in the experiment to enroll her dull-witted brother, Lloyd, there. She visited the farm for evening discussions, enjoying the adulation shown her by the young communists. As for heavy labor and lack of privacy and individuality, she'd had enough of that at the old Groton farm.

Meanwhile, editing the magazine became more and more strenuous for Ms. Fuller, despite her joy in publishing her own essays. (One such essay was "The Great Lawsuit: Man versus Men and Woman versus Women," later expanded in *Woman in the Nineteenth Century*.) There was no money to pay writers, high standards fell, deadlines were ignored, and circulation was miniscule. Fuller found it difficult to reject works by friends such as Thoreau, even if the pieces were not really good enough. When she finally quit, Emerson agreed to succeed her, commenting, "Let there be rotation in martyrdom."

In May 1843, Fuller finally got her chance to travel. A close friend, James Clarke, invited her to join his sister and himself "out West." They began in Niagara Falls and took the steamer to Chicago, where James's brother, William Clarke, joined the group. He guided them through northern Illinois and Wisconsin, where they looked at wilderness, prairie lands, and fertile meadows. When visiting an Indian settlement, Fuller noted the women's work and she later wrote that men seemed to protect their women only against excitement, certainly not from hard labor. She was impressed, too, by the difficulties Eastern ladies had as they tried to adjust to the savage new land.

Moving back into the civilized world, Ms. Fuller sensed the tarnish there. In Boston, she began to develop her travel journal into a book, *Summer On The Lakes*. When it was published, this book attracted the attention of Horace Greeley, editor of the New York *Daily Tribune*. He not only offered her the job of literary critic, but agreed to publish her feminist writings, *Woman in the Nineteenth Century,* requesting that Emerson write the introduction.

Emerson agreed to do it, but as Fuller prepared to leave Boston, she saw no signs of any progress by her friend. It finally came out that the fastidious, though sympathetic, philosopher could not come to terms with women's rights. To him, the finest lady was a "docile daughter" of God, "helpful and admirable to all." He begged Fuller's forgiveness. She was deeply hurt, but admitted that their ideas were basically incompatible.

Minus Emerson's introduction, *Woman in the Nineteenth Century* came out in February 1845 to fairly good reviews. Edgar Allan Poe was one critic who called it a curiosity in "independence and unmitigated radicalism," and Greeley said, "If not the clearest and most logical, it was the loftiest and most commanding assertion yet made of the right of Woman to be regarded as an independent, intelligent rational being, entitled to an equal voice in framing and modifying the laws she is required to obey, and in controlling and disposing of the property she has inherited or aided to acquire."

Most agreed that the book was verbose and poorly organized; some claimed it was a showcase for Fuller's own erudition. But the message was there, and it became the intellectual charge for the women's revolution.

In her book, Margaret Fuller did not quarrel with the domestic role women have traditionally held, but she argued that men place barriers against women leaving that role. Regarding the male-female relationship, she pointed out that men were encouraging women to become overgrown children rather than stimulating individuals.

As reluctant as Fuller was to leave Boston, on December 1, 1844, she stepped energetically into her new prestigious position in New York. The *Tribune* had flourished during the four years under Greeley's editorship. Fuller's job was to write three columns a week. One was a social commentary, which sent her delving into the city hospitals, charities, jails, and homes. The other two columns were literary, including reviews of the foreign press and of science books; she introduced Balzac and the Brownings to America. Fuller's most popular pieces were her evaluations of current American literature. She felt strongly that American writers should reflect the free, open spirit of the frontier, with original ideas and "fresh currents of life." Fuller quickly became an influential critic, sharing the spotlight only with her rival critic, Poe.

Fuller was invited to move into the Greeley "farm," near the East River and Forty-ninth Street. She was surrounded by admiring, thinking women and wrote only in spurts (the transcendental idea was to let the unconscious create). This irritated Greeley, but he continued to believe that she was the most remarkable woman in this country.

Then Margaret fell in love with James Nathan—a foreigner and a Jew. Neither of the Greeleys approved of the match. Nathan wanted to be a writer and admired Fuller's talent and position; Fuller was attracted by all things German. As it turned out, this romance, too, ended sadly for Margaret when James sailed back to Germany, where he later married another woman.

Fuller moved out of the Greeley home and took an apartment in Brooklyn Heights, the New York City literary encampment. It wasn't long after Nathan left that a wealthy couple, Marcus and Rebecca Spring, asked Fuller to accompany them to Europe.

Europe. Fuller was tempted, but her total savings amounted to only a thousand dollars. She decided to turn to her old beau, Samuel Ward, who now worked for a banking firm. She reminded him that ten years before, she had watched him sail for Europe and now she had her chance. Greeley had given her permission to correspond from Europe; her promise concerning her brothers' and sister's welfare had been fulfilled. (Two of her brothers had Harvard degrees; one was established in New Orleans while the other lived with their mother. A third brother, Lloyd, was under professional care. Margaret's sister was married and lived in Cincinnati.) Samuel sent her the money she needed.

In July 1846, Fuller went to Cambridge to bid her mother farewell and to see her old friends. Emerson wished her luck and gave her a letter of introduction to Thomas Carlyle. Back in New York, she wrote in her column that the twenty months spent in that city "have presented me with a richer and more varied exercise for thought and life than twenty years could in any other part of these United States." She boarded the *Cambria* for England. She would never set foot in America again.

During the ten day voyage, Fuller filled her notebook with descriptions, people, and places that would interest her New York readers. (Many of these were later selected by her brother for publication in a volume called *At Home and Abroad*.)

In England, Fuller met with great respect. She visited the intellectuals of the day—Harriet Martineau, Wordsworth, De Quincey. Busy though she was, Fuller still hoped eventually to find James Nathan in Germany. But before she could get there, she spent one night alone and lost in the mountains of Scotland. It was a harrowing experience. She decided on that night that her own individual fulfillment was more important than her great love for Nathan.

Margaret Fuller was thrilled to meet Carlyle, found him witty though arrogant, and she wrote Emerson that Carlyle laughed more than he did. To Carlyle, Fuller had "a true heroic mind; altogether unique so far as I know among the Writing Women of this generation; rare enough too, God knows, among the writing Men."

But her great joy was an introduction to Giuseppe

Mazzini, who became her hero. She was caught up by his patriotism and his commitment to liberate Italy from Austria's grip and unify it as a socialist republic, but she did not then suspect how personally enmeshed she would become in that cause.

Fuller moved on to Paris in November and met the same admiration. Her *Woman in the Nineteenth Century* was due for publication in France, and she was asked to work as a correspondent for a French publication when she returned home. To her delight, Fuller visited George Sand ("I never liked a woman better") and Chopin. But most important, she met the exiled Polish poet Adam Mickiewicz. He was preparing to go to Rome and urged her to become involved in Italian liberation, to express her views and feelings by her actions, as well as intellectually. They planned to meet in Italy.

Fuller began the long journey to Italy. She had a great fear of boat travel and the trip from Pisa to Naples was particularly frightful since her ship almost collided with a mail boat. Stepping foot on Italian soil at last, Fuller exclaimed with relief, "Italy receives me as a long-lost child!"

It was April when she reached Rome, and the impending revolution clouded the spring air. She began researching a book on Italy but became more interested in the people and their spirit.

While troops were forming, Fuller traveled to Florence and Venice, visiting American expatriots and enjoying the country. Observing the activity, she felt somewhat guilty because she had not been more active in the abolition cause or the movement for the annexation of Texas in her own country. And then she met Marchese Giovanni Angelo Ossoli. He was almost ten years her junior, vital, considerate, gallant, uneducated yet cultured. Margaret Fuller fell in love with him.

At first she was hesitant, recalling the hurt she had felt with James Nathan. But Ossoli and Fuller were soon inseparable. He came from a conservative and aristocratic Catholic family, but she inspired him to join the revolution.

Ossoli later served as a spy, reporting to Mazzini what the
conservatives were planning. Ossoli was devoted to Fuller,
and she bloomed in his love. And then she became pregnant.

It was December, grim and gray, when she found out. She
was despondent. She was no longer young, and she brooded
over her lack of funds and a husband. She felt alone in a
strange land. Apparently, she and Ossoli married that winter,
although there are no papers of certification.

With the coming of spring, Fuller's spirits rose. She loved
Ossoli, and the gains Mazzini and his revolutionaries made
comforted her. Prince Metternich of Austria resigned, Louis
Philippe of France abdicated, and Naples revolted. Italians
swarmed to volunteer, hoisting the Italian flag and cheering
Mazzini home after seventeen years. Margaret was
disappointed only in Pope Pius IX, whom she felt lacked
courage because he did not support the revolution.

Margaret Fuller moved to Rieti in Abruzzi to have her
baby, and in September, Angelo Eugene Philip was born. Two
months later she returned to Rome, leaving her son with a
nurse. She was pressed for money now, and Greeley's
advances could not get past the endless mail tie-ups, so the
couple lived frugally.

In February 1849, the Roman Republic was declared, and
Mazzini became a member of the Assembly. But, by now, the
European Catholic powers decided to step in and restore papal
sovereignty. Louis Napoleon sent a force into Italy and
surrounded the capital. Garibaldi's troops entrenched
themselves to keep the French out, becoming prisoners in
their own city. At the front was Ossoli, guarding the walls.
His wife worked endless hours at the Hospital of the Fate
Bene Fratelli, where the patients saw her as a "mild saint
and a ministering angel," quite a change from the haughty,
critical Bostonian Emerson knew.

The French finally broke through the Italian barriers
and entered Rome in July, and Garibaldi's forces fled. Fuller
and all other foreigners who had aided the republic were
given twenty-four hours to leave the city. Fuller went to
Rieti, where she found that her baby was suffering from

malnutrition. She cared for him until he was stronger, then Margaret, Ossoli, and the baby traveled to Florence and then to America. There was nothing left for the Ossolis in Italy now.

With a feeling of trepidation, the family boarded the *Elizabeth* on May 17. Fuller had hired a nurse to care for the baby while she tried to finish her book; the family needed money to survive in America. She was fearful that her friends would not accept her husband and that the intelligentsia of Boston would scorn the young, illiterate man. How liberal were they? she wondered.

The future appeared more cheerful as they caught sight of the Jersey shore. It was a bright, breezy July 18, and the next day, they would disembark in New York. But that night, a gale whipped up, and by four in the morning, the ship was aground off Fire Island. A shipment of marble stored in the hold broke through the bottom, and one hundred yards off shore, the *Elizabeth* began to go down. The body of Margaret's infant son washed ashore, but Margaret Fuller and her husband were lost forever.

Fuller's friends were shocked. Thoreau rushed to the scene, and some of her letters and journals were found, but not the book. Silently they wondered if Fuller had ever reached her goal: "The freedom, the religious, the intellectual freedom of the universe to use its means, to learn its secret, as far as Nature has enabled them, with God alone for their guide and their judge."

Ralph Waldo Emerson later wrote, "All that can be said of Margaret is that she represents an interesting hour in American culture. She was a fine, generous, inspiring talker who did not outlive her influence."

That, of course, is not all that can be said of Margaret Fuller, who was only forty years old when she died. Not only did she not "outlive her influence," but she did not live to see her full influence. It took a fiery new generation of females to latch on to her philosophy of what womanhood can be and to carry it to the goal of suffrage.

5

The Bettmann Archive

Susan B. Anthony

It was 1823, in the Quaker town of Adams, nestled against the Berkshire Mountains, when Lucy Anthony prepared to give birth to her third child. She sent Susan, then three, and Guelma, a year and a half older, to stay with Grandmother Anthony for six weeks. The girls returned home bursting with excitement. They had learned to read during that visit, but, according to Susan, "the first thing mother noticed was that my eyes both turned toward my nose." It was then that Susan Brownell Anthony learned that the value of attractiveness was higher than that of intelligence, and a feeling of self-deprecation came over her which would continue to nag at her throughout life.

It meant little to the three-year-old child that Lucy was under heavy strain and grief because her new baby was stillborn. Susan Anthony believed her appearance was inferior, even when the left eye straightened itself. At twenty, she sought an operation to repair the right eye; this turned out to be a disaster, for the doctor "cut the muscle too much, and that threw the eye the other way." She tried concealing the defect with spectacles, although she had excellent vision

until her death at eighty-six. In middle age, she insisted her
photographs be taken in profile. Ms. Anthony's concern about
her eyes increased as she grew older, and the sad truth is that
her closest friends stopped noticing the out-turned eye very
quickly.

When we think of Susan B. Anthony today, we often
conjure up the image of a testy, pinched spinster, clutching a
red shawl about her shoulders, and shouting invectives
against marriage, discrimination, and other aspects of society.
In a way this is true—Ms. Anthony was often testy, remained
a spinster, did indeed wrap a red (for "revolutionary") shawl
around her, and certainly did attack society. Throughout the
nineteenth century she joined with the most creative minds of
her day and then left them behind when they wearied of her
relentless drive for the rights of women.

The image leaves no room for a soft heart, yet that
was the strength of Susan Anthony's push—she was
compassionate enough to brave slander when a strange
woman with her child pleaded for help in escaping a
tyrannical husband, and later to take on the emotional
trauma of nursing her dying sister. She was generous enough
to dole out her limited finances for the feminist cause until
suddenly she was old with no material security at all. And
through all this, Susan B. Anthony was forever vulnerable to
the reflection in her looking glass.

Daniel Anthony was an inquiring, occasionally rebellious
Quaker, and Susan was her father's daughter. Daniel was a
reformer who inspired and prodded his daughter to work
against inequities such as slavery, and for social improvements such as temperance. He was one of the signers
of the Declaration of Women's Rights, written at the 1848
Seneca Falls convention while Susan Anthony was engrossed
in abolishing drunkenness.

Ms. Anthony also treasured the example of her aunt,
Avis Read, sister of pretty, feminine Lucy Read, Susan's
mother. Avis was, according to Susan, "beyond the ordinary.
She was a democrat; something of an invalid; smoked her

pipe, sat in a corner and read the papers. People used to come
from miles around to hear her talk politics; men, of course.
Women thought her strange and queer. What she had to say
at an election or a campaign was of vital interest to the voters
because she was informed, and information in those days was
gained by concentrated attention on whatever news was
available."

Young Susan recognized the difference between
intelligent, brusque Avis and resigned, lovely Lucy and
realized that mere physical beauty dissolved in the hardships
of a nineteenth-century marriage. While Susan was growing
up, she never saw her mother as the once merry, adventurous
bride who had persuaded her beau to take her to a dance on
the night before their wedding. He, a Quaker, sat back,
watching Lucy whirl from partner to partner until four in the
morning. This was her last fling. Susan Anthony knew Lucy
only as the work-bent mother of eight children in sixteen
years, with no time for thinking, much less gaiety.

Susan Anthony watched all this, and decided that to
achieve her own fulfillment, she must have a busy life outside
the home, even at the cost of a family hearth, husband, and
children. She had a strong sense of inner worth. She would
never be a beauty, that was sure, but she could be as socially
active as her father and as intellectually independent as her
Aunt Avis.

Susan Anthony later explained her fierce dedication: "I
had my own thanks by retaining my self-respect." This self-
respect was tied in strongly with participation in government,
and since women did not have the vote or any power in
government, Susan B. Anthony became one of the few hard-
core feminists of her day, and probably the most determined.
Her colleagues often strayed to other reforms—temperance,
abolition, or peace—but Ms. Anthony felt everything must
come second to women's rights. Once, speaking before the
Daughters of the Revolution on the subject of peace, she
snapped, "It does seem very strange to me that you should be
more interested in peace and arbitration between nations

than in the enfranchisement of the women of this so-called
republic. It is evident that if the women of our nation had
been counted among the constituencies of every State
Legislature, and of the Congress of the United States, the
butchery of the Spanish-American War would never have
been perpetrated."

Women's rights, in Ms. Anthony's day, were nonexistent.
"A girl needed to know how to read her Bible and count her
egg money, nothing more," was how one teacher put it.
Women were legal minors; they were inching into education,
writing, factories, even medicine, but all their wages belonged
to their husbands, or, if unmarried, to male guardians.
Women had no rights to property, nor did they have
guardianship of their children. They were, in legal fact,
properties themselves. Susan B. Anthony worked hard to
change these conditions and lived to see 154 universities and
colleges become coeducational; the number of women teachers
rise from twenty-five to eighty percent; and women enter the
fields of art, theology, and law. She saw women given the
right to take their pleas to the Supreme Court, to own and
control their own property, to sue and be sued. They could
make their own contracts and keep their earnings. But
probably most important was their new sharing in
guardianship over their children.

Susan B. Anthony never lived to see her main goal
achieved, however. "While women still suffer countless minor
disadvantages, the fundamental rights have largely been
secured except the suffrage," she admitted toward the end of
her life. She put tremendous importance on the vote; one
story tells how she rejected several proposals of marriage, and
when asked why, she replied that she could not allow any
man she loved, who would have the constitutional right of
self-government and eligibility to the office of president, to be
united with a political slave, which was her status as a
woman.

In her crusade for the vote, Susan B. Anthony, the small-
town Quaker girl, evolved into an indefatigable traveler.

While she was still young, the Anthonys moved from Adams to Upper New York State, where Daniel opened a mill. It prospered and the family bought a commodious tavern which they converted into a home. When she reached the right age, Susan was sent away to Deborah Moulson's School in Philadelphia, a traumatic step, for not only was she leaving her father but she felt Miss Moulson was cold and unfriendly toward her.

During these years, Daniel Anthony's business failed and he went bankrupt, losing his house, belongings, everything. And then, to Susan Anthony's shock, all her mother's inheritance was confiscated, since it automatically belonged to her husband.

Bankruptcy, rather than dividing the family, brought it closer together. The children were happy to come home from school, and Susan Anthony moved nearby to teach. Her spirits picked up and she even corresponded with two young townsmen for awhile, sensing that she might possess some qualities appealing to men. She wrote of one of these men: "May he know that he has found in me a spirit congenial to his own and not suffer the glare of beauty to attract both eye and heart."

Ms. Anthony enjoyed periodic spurts of carefree gaiety, but something always steered her back to social reform. When she saw so many wives chained to drunken husbands with no recourse but to live it through, she embraced the cause of temperance. Discrimination in wages hit her when she was hired to teach school for $2.50 a week while her male companions earned $10.00. Throughout her twenties, Ms. Anthony found herself teaching, arguing, joining, and leading. "What an absurd notion that women have not intellectual and moral faculties sufficient for anything but domestic concerns!" she scoffed.

There were setbacks, but Susan B. Anthony cultivated the ability to salvage some thread of hope and repair reversals with new optimism, as when Daniel went bankrupt again, and the family moved to a farm near Rochester, New

York. Lucy Anthony's brother held the lease, so Daniel's creditors could not grab the property. Susan Anthony got a job teaching in nearby Canajoharie and sent her wages home until Daniel got on his feet again. This accomplished, Susan Anthony, living for a time with non-Quaker relatives, decided for the first time to enjoy her earnings. She bought colorful shawls and fashionable dresses, wrapped her thick chestnut hair about her head, and even went dancing. But if Ms. Anthony was decorative outside, she was still the reformer within, and in 1849, she became president of the local Daughters of Temperance.

It was now that her organizational talents were loosed; she arranged an elaborate and successful fund-raising fair at which she made her first speech. She became very popular with the local citizens, but that lasted only until she aired her feelings against slavery. Temperance was acceptable; abolition was controversial. So, she left Canajoharie and went back to live with her family in Rochester. She was through with teaching and would devote her time to social reform, and it was for the Daughters of Temperance in Rochester that Susan B. Anthony began her peripatetic life.

Traveling to temperance conventions opened her eyes to a new avenue, the rights of women. In 1848, a convention had been held in the nearby town of Seneca Falls, where a matronly radical named Elizabeth Cady Stanton read her Declaration of Rights of Women, going so far as to recommend that alcoholism be grounds for divorce and to demand that this be included in the resolutions.

It was this woman that Ms. Anthony wanted to meet, and her chance came when the Daughters of Temperance sent her to Seneca Falls for the 1851 convention. She boarded with Amelia Bloomer, publisher of the temperance magazine *The Lily,* and Ms. Bloomer introduced her to Ms. Stanton. The relationship which resulted was more than a partnership and more than a friendship; it helped two capable people accomplish extraordinary feats.

On the surface they seemed direct opposites—Ms.

Anthony was long and lean, while Ms. Stanton was short and ample—but creatively, they nourished each other. Elizabeth Stanton was the fiery orator and eloquent penswoman; Susan Anthony was the relentless fact-finder and organizer. Susan once described her relationship with her friend: "Mrs. Stanton makes the bullets and Miss Anthony fires them." They had immense respect for each other, but while Elizabeth called Susan by her first name from the start, Susan could never bring herself to call Elizabeth anything but "Mrs. Stanton," even when they had known each other for fifty years.

Elizabeth Stanton was thirty-five, five years older than Susan Anthony, when they met. The daughter of a wealthy lawyer from Johnstown, New York, Elizabeth studied at Emma Willard's Seminary in Troy. There were five girls in the family, and one son who died, causing an anguished father to cry to his favorite, Elizabeth, "Oh, my daughter, would that you were a boy!" He recognized her aptitude, but saw only marriage for her sex. Elizabeth wanted to prove she could take her brother's place, so she studied Latin, Greek, and math with a boy's class. When she won first prize in Greek, she rushed home to show her father, who kissed her with a sigh. "Oh, you should have been a boy."

Although Judge Cady was resigned to his daughter's ambition, and Daniel Anthony encouraged activism, both girls learned when they were very young that to be female was to live a second-class life—and they were both determined to escape that mold.

At twenty-five, Ms. Cady married Henry B. Stanton of the American Anti-Slavery Society. Their honeymoon took place at the World Anti-Slavery Convention in London, where the bride joined Lucretia Mott as a delegate. To their astonishment, they were told to remove themselves to the gallery behind a screen, for females were not to sit in serious discussion with men. Ms. Stanton and Ms. Mott vowed then to work toward abolishing such discrimination, beginning with a women's rights convention in Seneca Falls, New York.

Susan B. Anthony was personally introduced to women's

rights in much the same way. She was sent to Albany as a
Daughters of Temperance delegate to the Sons of Temperance
meeting, but upon rising to make a motion, she was informed
that Daughters did not speak; they were there to listen and
learn. Anthony indignantly stalked out, a handful of women
following. She set about forming a women's state temperance
society to meet that spring, and called on her new friend,
Elizabeth Cady Stanton, to be the main speaker and first
president. Ms. Anthony would be secretary. This was to be
their pattern as long as they lived.

They turned their attention from temperance to feminism
when the other members of the Daughters of Temperance
could not agree that they must fight for women's rights if
they hoped to be effective in other reforms. Stanton and
Anthony quit the Daughters and went on their own. Women's
rights became priority number one, and Amelia Bloomer with
The Lily went with them.

It was in *The Lily* that the country saw a shocking new
costume for women. It featured a knee-length skirt over pants
which were gathered at the ankle. It was dubbed "The
Bloomer Look." The women who adopted it, Ms. Stanton
among the first, were ridiculed. Still, it gave physical relief
from the traditional dress, which consisted of a concentric
girdling of hoopskirts over petticoats, fitted over tightly
drawn stays and pinching whalebones, and a train to sweep
the muddy streets. This traditional dress weighed over ten
pounds, explaining why fainting spells were epidemic among
well-dressed ladies of the day.

Ms. Anthony was hesitant to follow the style, having
already returned to simple Quaker garb, but Ms. Stanton
persuaded her to cut her hair and don the bloomer costume.
When she did, Ms. Anthony was reluctant to wear anything
else, even when Stanton saw that onlookers focused on the
bloomers rather than on the message. Stanton decided to
switch back to more conventional dress so more women would
identify with her, and although Ms. Anthony saw the point, it
bothered her to yield in this or in any battle.

It was Anthony who did most of the public speaking in those days, for Stanton was tied down at home with her children, eventually numbering seven. Anthony did not approve of marriage, especially when Stanton wrote after having her sixth child, who weighed twelve and a half pounds at birth: "I never suffered so much before. I was sick all the time before he was born, and I have been very weak ever since. He seemed to take up every particle of my vitality, soul, and body." Susan B. Anthony preferred to save her vitality, soul, and body for her cause.

Ms. Anthony was depressed during this period, just as she was when Lucy Stone and Antoinette Brown married, for the burden of preaching fell on her, and her efforts were often superhuman. Anthony was strong, but she was sometimes incapacitated with melancholia. Still, she would always snap back because, as her biographer Katherine Anthony noted, "A well-balanced realist, Susan did not play with her emotions. She was capable of profound despondency but not of the play-acting that would superficially relieve it. No one in the world was less of a sentimentalist. The habit of facing the truth, confirmed by long practice, came to her aid and the bondage of depression passed."

One of Anthony's and Stanton's first joint ventures was aimed at easing women's poverty. Women were dependent upon their men, not only for subsistence and social standing, but also for their private, traditionally feminine causes like temperance and church work. They had to beg for or wheedle funds and permission to promote projects, and Susan Anthony had witnessed the frustrations of this herself many times in her temperance work.

In 1848, women were given the right to retain their own real estate inheritances, and at that time, Lucy Anthony's brother handed over to her the deed to her farm. However, in 1854, Susan Anthony wanted this right expanded to allow women rights over all their belongings, guardianship over their children, equal wages, and suffrage. She and Stanton set out to collect signatures to back such a petition, which would

be read by Stanton before the New York state legislature.
They got six thousand names, presented their resolves, and
were denied. A survey of married men on the Judiciary
Committee showed that they believed women had enough
rights, including "the best seat in the cars, carriages, and
sleighs . . . their choice on which side of the bed they will lie,
front or back."

Such a privileged life was unknown to Susan Anthony,
whose routine was the hard, physical labor of door-to-door
petitioning, tramping across the state and later across the
country, from village to city and back. At one time, her sleigh
stuck in the snow and her feet were frostbitten, requiring that
she be carried on stage to deliver her talk. Episodes like this
were not uncommon. In her first year of lecturing, she covered
fifty-four out of the sixty counties in New York.

The second petition for these resolutions was presented
six years later. Stanton orated before the state legislature for
two hours, and this time the bill was passed, although the
vital inclusion of suffrage was denied. Stanton and Anthony
were elated. This was a revolution for women—they could
control their own money, make contracts, sue and be sued,
and best of all, they had some say over the raising of their
children. It was a happy time, but a short one, for one year
later, the Civil War broke out.

In one way, the Civil War recharged the batteries of the
women's movement. It gave many American women the
incentive to expand their traditionally narrow environs of
home and church and move into what was always the
masculine sphere. This resulted in such actions as women
giving medical assistance on the battlefields as well as in
more subtle maneuverings such as encouraging their men to
fight for the cause, Union or Confederate. The Civil War
aroused anything but apathy, in women as well as men. And
when the war was over, women were established in
schoolhouses and offices to stay.

In another way, the Civil War slowed down the
momentum of the feminist cause. Anthony and Stanton had

always admired the abolitionist leaders, partly because they were so supportive of the women's rights cause, but also because such leaders as William Lloyd Garrison and Wendell Phillips were so charismatic. Anthony joined the Anti-Slavery Society, and after Fort Sumter, she doubled her efforts and her traveling for feminism and abolition. It was for the abolitionists that she made her most eloquent speeches, but as was the case with all her other side causes, this was temporary. While it lasted, her zeal for abolition was fiery. Ms. Anthony was not facing mere jeering men but hostile Democrats and Republicans, some of whom went so far as to burn her in effigy in the public square of Syracuse, New York. Threats only stiffened Susan Anthony's back, and when John Brown was executed, she boldly organized a memorial service and strode through the streets to lead it, although the killing had shaken many of the Northern liberals, who feared for their own lives.

Ms. Anthony was definitely against slavery. The war, however, was a different matter. She hated to watch women desert feminism for the war effort. "I have not yet seen one good reason," she once complained, "for the abandonment of all our meetings." She could not see her way to support the war, although her father, just as ardent a Quaker, had accepted his sons' enlistment.

Ms. Anthony decided to work off her frustration by doing heavy farm labor and joined her parents at their farm. She tried to read; novels made her feel that she was wasting time, so she concentrated on books which could inspire her occasional anti-slavery speeches. Toward the end of the summer, she forced herself to return to the lecture circuit. Stanton convinced her that slavery was the topic of the day, and they'd better go along with the tide while it lasted. This was in 1862. And then, suddenly, Susan Anthony's father died.

With the death of Daniel Anthony, Susan lost her primary moral and financial support. Her biographer, Katherine Anthony, remarked, "Fortunately for her, his

guidance had endured until her feet were well planted on the
ground of the future and her vision of her place in life was
definitely outlined."

Susan Anthony buried her grief in the cause closest to
her heart, the women's movement. She moved to New York
with the Stantons, and, with Elizabeth, drew up an "Appeal"
for all women to enter politics as well as charity work. Next,
she and Stanton issued a "Call" for a National Loyal League.
Ms. Stanton, as usual, was elected president and Ms.
Anthony, secretary. Susan Anthony made an impassioned
plea to "forget what the world will say, whether you are in
your place or out of it." Probably the most outstanding
resolution from this meeting insisted upon equal rights, not
only for Negroes but also for women. This is what caused
Susan B. Anthony's eventual split from her old abolitionist
allies.

There were already small tears in the alliance. The first
came at the twelfth anniversary of the Seneca Falls
convention, when Stanton, during a brilliant oration,
proclaimed the need for more liberal marriage and divorce
laws. The abolitionists protested. Anthony defended Stanton's
right to speak, and the two sides parted on less than friendly
terms.

The next rip came when the Civil War began. Some
abolitionists wanted to support the government while others
remained vehemently anti-Lincoln. Ms. Anthony, for
instance, felt Abraham Lincoln was lackadaisical about
slavery when he merely advocated a ban on the institution
for the emerging western states rather than erasing slavery
from the entire country. Even when Lincoln issued his
Emancipation Proclamation and public sentiment swung to
his side, Susan Anthony was busy pointing out its
deficiencies.

After the war, Ms. Anthony traveled to Kansas to visit
her brother, a journalist. A small news item in his office
caught her eye. It mentioned a proposed Fourteenth
Amendment to the Constitution which would prohibit the

denial of vote to "any of the male inhabitants of such State,
being twenty-one years of age. . . ." *Male* was the word that
choked her. She packed her bags and headed back to New
York, and once there, she rounded up the old reformers—
Elizabeth Stanton, Antoinette Brown, Lucy Stone, and
Lucretia Mott. They were to start a new petition for women's
suffrage. Here was where they ran against the old-line
abolitionists, who were determined to focus their attentions
on Negro suffrage alone. Horace Greeley of the *New York
Tribune* tried to reason with Ms. Anthony, telling her that
this was the Negro's hour. Her turn would come next, he
promised, but Susan B. Anthony was not one to wait. She
would fight her own battles in her own time.

She ran into Mr. Greeley again at the state constitutional
convention in New York. He asked her, "Miss Anthony, you
know the bullet and the ballot go together. If you vote, are
you ready to fight?"

"Yes, Mr. Greeley," retorted Anthony, "just as you fought
in the late war—at the point of a goose quill." Later, knowing
his support was gone and she had nothing to lose, Susan
Anthony publicly displayed the petition for women's suffrage,
drawing attention to the first name, Mrs. Horace Greeley.
The laughter in response was probably not equal to the loss of
an ally, but it must have been some comfort to Ms. Anthony.

The final split came in 1869. Anthony and Stanton
resigned from the Equal Rights Association and formed their
own National Woman's Suffrage Association. Meanwhile, the
less radical, more "respectable" female segment of the old
abolitionist group formed the American Woman's Suffrage
Association to continue the fight for the universal vote. Lucy
Stone led this group, and Julia Ward Howe and Antoinette
Brown joined her. For twenty years, the suffragists were thus
divided.

Anthony and Stanton traveled around the country,
promoting their new suffrage amendment. On one of these
trips, they ran into the notorious George Francis Train, as
controversial as he was wealthy. This aggressive, money-

making entrepreneur spotted the two disillusioned crusaders
in Kansas, nearly destitute, with hardly enough money to get
back to New York. He not only offered to escort them back in
style, but proposed financing a feminist publication to be run
by Susan B. Anthony!

Anthony's newspaper, *Revolution,* was first issued in
January 1868, and to her it was as dear as any child. The
aims of the paper were defined as: The True Republic—Men,
their rights, and nothing more; women, their rights, and
nothing less. After the first issue, the *New York Times*
snidely suggested that Anthony get herself a husband and
children, and that Stanton go home where she belonged.

From the start, Susan Anthony had trouble keeping the
paper financed. George Train had sailed for England, and no
one would lend Ms. Anthony money unless she disavowed her
connection with him, which Anthony, stubborn and loyal,
refused to do. By now she was almost fifty, wiry and youthful,
but cantankerous, while weary Stanton was feeling her years.
Both were anxious to let younger women move in as standard
bearers, but not even talented Anna Dickinson could keep up
their pace and initiative. Only one, Victoria Woodhull, came
close, for her ambitions were lofty enough: she wanted to be
president of the United States. Woodhull's few years in the
public eye were enough to slash any ties remaining between
the two suffragist groups, for her philosophy ran with free
love, abortion, birth control, and legalized prostitution, along
with the less sensational but just as radical goals of world
government and public housing.

Ms. Anthony could not follow the Woodhull life style any
more than Lucy Stone could, but she wouldn't disavow
Woodhull completely, since they both agreed on female
suffrage. When Anthony stood next to Woodhull before the
women's convention, they were linked together in the eyes of
the delegates, and were cast aside together by the
"respectables." It took many years for the public to break the
association.

Revolution lived until May 1870, keeping the women's

suffrage issue before the public with Stanton's brilliant articles. Susan Anthony wrote editorials on the working woman's problems, and arranged for a Working Woman's Association to meet weekly in the newspaper office. But bankruptcy was the final, fatal illness, and when the newspaper succumbed, Anthony grieved. She took little comfort in the fact that the message of feminism would continue to be carried by her rival Lucy Stone in her new publication, *Woman's Journal,* which ran for fifty years after the death of *Revolution.*

Though Ms. Anthony mourned her paper, she did not weep in a corner. With Stanton, she took off for California, a special dream ever since 1849, when Ms. Anthony watched young men leave the East to seek their fortunes in the gold rush. The journey by stage and train was dusty and halting, but the atmosphere was ripe for their cause, and from Chicago on, Anthony and Stanton found themselves in friendly country. The trip was one of the successes of their careers except for one incident. Ms. Anthony made a statement, in San Francisco, defending an alleged murderess and prostitute, Laura Fair. San Franciscans were incensed by this outsider poking her nose into their business. Invitations to speak were withdrawn and Susan Anthony was stunned by the whole reaction. Stanton, meanwhile, had gone off alone down the coast. She evidently did not want to taint her message by sticking near Ms. Anthony. This was an attitude Susan Anthony could accept. Later, when they left California, they were both well received once again.

Despite the enthusiastic response she received during her travels, Susan B. Anthony did not see any concrete results in her fight for the vote, so she decided to test the issue for herself. On November 1, 1872, she and fifteen other women marched into the Rochester registration office and demanded to be signed in as eligible voters. On November 5, they cast their ballots. On Thanksgiving Day, Anthony was arrested.

"Susan B. Anthony of Rochester (being then and there a person of the female sex)," decided a grand jury, "contrary to

the form of the statute and against the peace of the United
States of America and their dignity" was to be turned over for
custody, and her trial was scheduled for summer.

She had no money at all. She was burdened with a ten-
thousand-dollar debt for *Revolution* which she resolved to pay.
Her mother and sister Mary had sold the farm and bought a
house in Rochester; her sister Guelma was dying of "a serious
lung difficulty," and it was up to Susan to tend her until her
death. Preparing her defense, toiling to repay her debt,
trudging through the icy winter to lecture, and facing the
grief in her home, Susan Anthony steeled herself, in mind
and body, just to keep going.

On May 23, 1893, "not Susan B. Anthony but the
government of the United States" went on trial. The site of
the occasion was Canandaigua, a quiet, conservative
community, and the judge was Ward Hunt. Justice Hunt had
been recently appointed to the Supreme Court by Senator
Roscoe Conkling, who now wanted to get rid of this
embarrassing Anthony case as fast and as inconspicuously as
possible. This trial, therefore, goes down in American law
annals as one of the most prejudiced and unorthodox
proceedings in our country's history, for after each side had
presented its case, Justice Hunt cleared his throat and spoke
to the jury: "I have decided . . . that under the Fourteenth
Amendment, which Miss Anthony claims protects her, she
was not protected in a right to vote. And I have decided also
that her belief and the advice which she took do not protect
her in the act which she committed. If I am right in this, the
result must be a verdict on your part of guilty, and I therefore
direct that you find a verdict of guilty."

With these few swift words, the jury was dismissed
without rendering a decision.

Susan Anthony sat in shocked silence as she awaited
sentence, but she sprang to life quickly enough when Justice
Hunt unexpectedly offered her a chance to speak. "I am
degraded from the status of citizen to that of a subject," she
insisted, "and not only myself individually but all of my sex,

are, by Your Honor's verdict, doomed to political subjection
under this so-called Republican government."

When she was finished, Hunt fined her one hundred
dollars and the costs of the prosecution. Ms. Anthony's reply
was immediate. "May it please Your Honor, I shall never pay
a dollar of your unjust penalty. . . . I shall work with might
and main to pay every debt of [the *Revolution*], but not a
penny will go to this unjust claim."

She did not go to jail for this refusal, for Judge Hunt was
clever enough not to stipulate that she be imprisoned until
the fine was paid. If Ms. Anthony had gone to jail, she could
have appealed the decision and perhaps won a reversal, for
there was clear denial of a jury trial.

Despite the inequities, the notorious trial faded and Ms.
Anthony continued with dedication to pay off the *Revolution*
debt. Consequently, 1876 was a year of double celebration for
her; not only was her indebtedness ended, it was also the
nation's one hundredth birthday and the party was in
Philadelphia. The suffragists could not let such an occasion
pass without some advertisement of their cause. Although
they were refused permission to present a declaration of
women's rights at the July Fourth celebration, several of
them were granted passes. That was enough; as the
ceremonial reading of the Declaration of Independence ended,
Susan B. Anthony and her companions rose silently and
moved forward to place their own document in the hands of
Vice-President Ferry. They then continued out of the hall,
passing copies to the right and left, and marched to a
bandstand, where Susan read the entire declaration aloud. A
woman's center was set up in the city where they could greet
and inform visitors from all over the country. Through
shrewd maneuvering, fifty-six-year-old Susan B. Anthony had
stamped her mark on the historic occasion.

Her sister Guelma, meanwhile, had died, and younger
Mary and old Mrs. Anthony lived on in the Rochester house.
Susan Anthony had moved to New Jersey with Stanton to
begin their three-volume *History of Woman Suffrage*. It had

taken them ten years to get the literary wheels whirling, but this time Anthony sternly kept Stanton tied to her desk and pen, and the writing progressed at superhuman speed. Since Stanton was as articulate on paper as in speech, it was Anthony's job to scour the libraries doing the necessary research. And because the writers had to pay part of the publishing costs, Anthony took the summers off to lecture across the country, living on her fees and saving as much as she could.

By this time, the women's movement was beginning to have an aura of respectability. One reason was the public dismay over Anthony's unfair trial; there was also great admiration for her paying off the *Revolution* debt in full. In addition, the movement had achieved a certain accreditation by having been publicized for over thirty years. But the firm stamp of acceptance was probably secured when the *History*'s first volume appeared in May 1881 to good reviews and occasional praise.

Respectability accompanied the women to Europe, where Anthony and Stanton were treated as celebrities. Stanton had decided to travel with her daughter, who later married and settled in England. Anthony followed only because she was bequeathed a sum of money from a wealthy supporter. Lucy Anthony had died, and Susan, probably sensing her own mortality and admitting that her tenacious third-of-a-century's work quite reasonably called for a rest, agreed to the "Grand Tour."

Ms. Anthony was very impressed with the European feminists, and before sailing home, she arranged for an International Women's Rights Council to be called every five years. It was at the first of these councils that Susan Anthony spontaneously donned the red silk shawl that became her trademark. As one newspaper noted, "Spring is not heralded in Washington by the approach of the robin redbreast but by the appearance of Miss Anthony's red shawl."

In the flush of approval, Susan Anthony continued her tour for the Sixteenth Amendment, which would give them

suffrage. She saw Wyoming as her first success, followed by
Colorado, Utah, and Idaho. This was far from national
popularity, but enough to give Anthony and her cause a spurt
forward.

Perhaps the ultimate proof of Ms. Anthony's acceptability
was an invitation for a meeting with Lucy Stone. This had
been Susan Anthony's dream—the reunion of the two
divisions of the women's movement—and she jumped at it. On
January 21, 1889, the two endorsed the formation of a
National-American Association, with Elizabeth Stanton as
president, although she was now seventy-five and her heart
was in England with her daughter. In fact, right after the
election, she was off again to Europe, and soon it was obvious
that Ms. Stanton should be exchanged for a more dedicated
president.

Susan B. Anthony, now seventy, decided to put down
roots. She had been feted with a birthday party, and was
horrified when she learned that all the guests had been asked
to contribute four dollars. Her answer was to give out dozens
of complimentary tickets before enjoying the honor. Soon
after, she moved to the Rochester house, paying her sister
Mary twenty-five dollars a month rent and taking over the
housekeeping herself. These two remaining sisters eventually
grew very close, enjoying not only their blood tie but a
kinship in the cause of feminism.

But Ms. Anthony was not one to remain stationary for
long. In one year she traveled three times between New York
and Kansas. Another year, she rode as many as one hundred
miles in one day, crossing New York State countless times.
Before she was seventy-five, she toured the South, attended
annual women's conventions, became a member of the
heretofore all-male State Industrial School Board, and
enjoyed another birthday celebration. She was given five
thousand dollars, invested with an insurance company so that
she would have an annual income. This arrangement was
made so that the capital would not be spent on feminism but
would provide financial security for Susan. That same year,

on a trip to California, she met Ida Harper, who agreed to
help her write her autobiography. Harper and the two
Anthony sisters shared the Rochester house.

The next five years were hectic for Anthony, traveling
again to London for the International Council of Women,
organizing a family reunion in the old town of Adams,
producing two volumes of her biography, and defending Ms.
Stanton, who was rewriting what she considered a sexist
Bible, much to the shock of the other feminists. At the end of
that decade, Anthony announced that she wanted to begin her
largest fund-raising campaign and establish a standing
account for the women's organization so they would not
always be begging for money.

It never got off the ground, for the next year, Susan B.
Anthony fell ill. She had made an agreement with Rochester
University to collect one hundred thousand dollars to pay the
costs of admitting girls as students. Close to the deadline, she
was still eight thousand dollars short. She worked frantically
to collect the rest, persuading Mary Anthony to donate two
thousand dollars from her will and calling on people day and
night to collect as much as she could.

She succeeded—Rochester University became coeducational. But Susan Anthony took to her bed and could not
speak for a week. The diagnosis was stroke. Nearing her
eighty-first birthday, she was urged to rest. This enforced
recovery period was discouragingly slow for Anthony, for she
was not really incapacitated once her ability to speak
returned. Eventually, she gathered enough strength to attend
a suffrage convention in New York. Once again, Susan B.
Anthony was back in action.

Then, in October 1902, she received the dreaded telegram
announcing Elizabeth Stanton's death. She was desolate and
devoted all her energy to obituary requests in her friend's
memory. She turned to young Anna Shaw, her latest
protégée, for consolation and two years later Shaw was
elected president of the women's association.

Anthony was elderly but she traveled as extensively as

ever, even to Germany for an international council meeting.
Here Susan's pace tired her younger sister Mary, who sailed
home early. The two clung together these last years, for their
youngest brother had died, and when Susan returned from
Europe, she was called to Kansas to see her beloved Daniel,
Jr., on his deathbed. When only the two sisters were left, they
journeyed through California and Oregon together, speaking
for the vote.

Early in the new century, Susan B. Anthony was invited
to the White House to visit President Theodore Roosevelt. She
is reputed to have cautioned him, "Now, Mr. President, we
don't intend to trouble you during the campaign, but after you
are elected, then look out for us." At the White House, she
asked for his recommendation to Congress for a suffrage
amendment and added, with her famous candor, "And I hope
you will not be a candidate for office again." Apparently, the
office of president was not awesome to this old lady.

Susan Anthony, on her last birthday, was inundated with
congratulations. There was first a celebration at the women's
convention in Baltimore. The winter was cruel, and she lay ill
in her quarters, but as the evening of the tribute appeared, so
did Anthony, garbed in a new crepe de Chine gown, and
sitting erect on the stage, attentive to the countless speeches.
Here, she learned that the women were rededicated to
establishing the standing fund which she had deemed so vital
but which had been abandoned due to her illness. After the
celebration, she went back to bed, her spirits raised.

Ms. Anthony continued on to Washington and heard
more speeches in her honor. Sitting before Congress, as she
neared the end of her life, Susan Anthony doubtless felt the
wasting of minutes, and finally she interrupted the talking
with, "When will men do something besides extend
congratulations? I would rather have President Roosevelt say
one word to Congress in favor of amending the Constitution to
give women the suffrage than to praise me endlessly!"

Somehow, Anthony, now ill with pneumonia, made it
home to Rochester where she advised Ida Harper of her

obituary wishes and ordered her will changed to leave
everything to the new women's fund.

When the ravage of her body overcame the resolve of her
mind, Susan Anthony lapsed into a coma, and on March 13,
1906, she was dead. Her Quaker funeral, a celebration of her
life, was filled with sunshine and violets. There was an honor
guard of young university women dressed in white, and Anna
Shaw gave the final tribute. Around the country, flags
fluttered at half-mast and journalists mourned the passing of
the "Champion of a lost cause."

But the cause was not lost, and if Susan Anthony did not
live to see women's suffrage, she always believed that the day
of her amendment would eventually come. During that last
public appearance in Washington, she had left her audience
with these words, "Failure is impossible." For Susan B.
Anthony, failure was never even a consideration.

6

Dorothea Lynde Dix

It was an icy Sunday morning in March, 1841. Dorothea Lynde Dix stood still, the snow and slush wet around her feet. She stared ahead at a sign above a door. The sign read "Middlesex County House of Correction." She knew it as the East Cambridge Jail. Dix had come to teach a Sunday School lesson to the female prisoners.

Have I taken on more than I can handle? she may have been thinking, as the cold March wind whistled around her. She was weak, barely recovered from a complete physical breakdown. She could no longer teach school, which had been her profession. She was in her thirty-ninth year and somewhat resigned to spending her remaining years as a decorous mid-Victorian spinster should, existing on her moderate inheritance.

But she knew the reason she was there. Despite lung deterioration, the intense pain in her side, and overwhelming fatigue, Dix had learned early that in order to respect herself, she had to work. New England in the middle of the nineteenth century had a social climate of productive labor and of contribution to the general good. She could not exist without giving of herself in some way. So, when a young

Harvard divinity student told her of the need for a Sunday
School teacher for twenty young female inmates, Dix
spontaneously volunteered. Though he felt it was unwise for
her to undertake the task because of her ill health, she
insisted she would be at the jail the following Sunday. And
there she was. She sighed, pushed open the heavy door, and
walked in.

The religious instruction took place uneventfully. What
was to drastically alter Dorothea Dix's life was her descent
afterwards into the basement where the insane were kept.
When she emerged, she was determined to change from a
genteel schoolteacher to one of the most effective reformers of
an era of reform. As her first biographer, Francis Tiffany, put
it in 1890, "To find her parallel in this respect, it is necessary
to go back to the lives of such memorable Roman Catholic
women as St. Theresa of Spain or Santa Chiara of Assisi."

When Dorothea Dix visited the basement jail, she found
four pathetic victims of mental derangement. Their cell was
dark and bare. The air was stagnant from lack of ventilation
and so foul smelling that she could hardly breathe. The cold
was intense; the walls were covered with a sparkling blanket
of frost. When she asked the jail-keeper why there was no
stove to provide heat, he replied that the insane could not feel
the cold, even when the temperature hovered near zero.

Dix was stunned. That night she could not sleep. She was
horrified and shocked. Was this jail an exception or did it
typify conditions throughout the Commonwealth of
Massachusetts?

Dorothea Dix lived another forty-six years, and during
this time she drove herself, relentlessly, crusading for the
mentally ill. She began the first prison and mental asylum
reforms in this country. She set aside her fatigue and illness
to singlehandedly uncover and publicize the appalling
conditions in prisons and mental asylums. She was directly
responsible for establishing 32 mental hospitals in the United
States as well as several in Europe and Japan. She was an
inspiration for most of the 123 mental institutions which had

come into existence by the time she died. Dorothea Dix, beginning on that Sunday in March 1841, turned aside the tradition of restraining and hiding the mentally ill and successfully converted the nation to a new theory of therapeutic, sympathetic treatment.

She refused to consider the recording of her accomplishments while she was alive, and there was no way to chronicle her early years after she died. Dix never talked about her early life. "I never knew any childhood," she explained. What is surmised, however, is that the first twelve years of Dix's life were intensely painful. Apparently, her later strength and dedication came from her grandparents. Dr. Elijah Dix, her grandfather, was born into a poor family. Through his own efforts, he became a physician, apothecary, and investor. He was physically strong, aggressive, tyrannical, and unpopular.

Her grandmother, Dorothy Lynde, was the very stereotype of the New England puritanic lady—dignified, precise, responsible, unimaginative, and unemotional. Duty led her to provide her neglected granddaughter with a decent education and material security. If Dorothea Dix inherited purposeful ambition and courage from her grandfather, she gained diligence and a commitment to perfection from her grandmother. From nobody did she receive tenderness, love, or affection.

Her father, Joseph Dix, was a drifter and a drunkard who had religious delusions. He would take off from time to time to spread the gospel to the people in the streets. He married Mary Bigelow, eighteen years older than he, an uneducated farm woman. Perhaps to him she symbolized maternal affection and understanding. However, Mary was chronically sick and very nervous. Obviously, neither one helped the other.

Old Dr. Dix bought land in Maine and sent his son and daughter-in-law to live there, hopefully in obscurity. Dorothea was the first of their three children. She was born in a wilderness village called Hampton on April 4, 1802.

Often when her father was off on his gospel-spreading missions, and her mother was sick in bed, Dorothea was shuttled to Boston to stay with her grandparents in the Dix mansion. Here she settled upon the goal of getting her brothers and herself out of their parents' hopeless situation.

The Dix family eventually moved from Hampton, Maine, to Worcester, Massachusetts, the birthplace of Dorothea's grandmother. Apparently, both Joseph and Mary were now completely unable to care for themselves or their children, for a great-aunt placed them with relatives for a fee, and sent the children to Boston and the Dix mansion.

Elijah Dix had died several years before, and his widow was nearing seventy. She felt she could prepare her grandchildren for a hard life by teaching them discipline and perseverence. Dorothea Dix drew from this rigid training for her later precise investigations into mental hospitals, but the ideal of uncompromising thoroughness was to work against her in her Civil War position of superintendent of nurses.

The unfeeling atmosphere of her grandmother's home must have been preferable to the slovenly lack of attention in her parents' home. But Dorothea was approaching adolescence and had her moments of frustration and rebelliousness. When she tried to assert herself, her grandmother would silence her. When her grandmother attempted to prepare Dorothea for the social life of a young early-Victorian lady, Dorothea was hostile. Finally, Madame Dix wrote her sister in Worcester that she was sending Dorothea back. The girl was just too headstrong for the old woman to handle.

Dix decided that to reach her goal of independence, she would have to gain financial security. The best way to do this was to become a teacher. Teaching would bring her social respect and would fulfill her desire for knowledge. Therefore, at fourteen years of age, Dorothea Dix set up her first school in Worcester.

To look older than she was, she wore long skirts and long sleeves to cover her arms. She drew back her dark brown hair. As one of the students was to later describe her: "The child-teacher was tall for her age, easily blushing, at once beautiful and imposing in manner, but inexorably strict in discipline."

This description fit her throughout her life. Dorothea Dix was certainly attractive—tall and willowy, with sharp blue eyes and rich wavy hair. But she disguised these assets with somber clothes, a severe hair style, and a stern expression. She always tried to be austere and was helped to this goal by an iron will.

In her first school, Dix enthralled her young pupils with stories of everyday life and objects. She told them about rocks, flowers, and the sky. She loved natural phenomena, particularly plants. She wrote down these discussions and later published them as *Conversations on Common Things*.

In 1817, Ms. Dix returned to Boston. For four years she studied and read in preparation for opening a school for older pupils. This was also the year that Emma Willard's Academy opened in Troy, but Dorothea Dix's school was not as scholastically ambitious as Willard's. Dix had no aim of uplifting the female mind; her goals were to make a life for herself, to help her brothers, and to take care of her elderly grandmother and her pupils.

Just beneath her somber surface, however, smoldered a strong passion. She had already turned down a marriage proposal from her cousin Edward Banks, recalling the despairing life her parents had led and the frigid atmosphere of the Dix mansion. During her life she made many close friends. To one in particular, Anne Heath, she could freely unburden her feelings: "I was early taught to sorrow, to shed tears, and now when sudden joy lights up or any unexpected sorrow strikes my heart, I find it difficult to repress the full and swelling tide of feeling."

To ease the poetic and spiritual longing within her, Dix turned to religion. Boston, in the early nineteenth century, had a population of under fifty thousand, but it was quickly emerging as the country's philosophical nucleus. Intellectuals

were turning away from traditional religion and toward a
more humanitarian spiritualism. Responding to this change,
Dix was drawn to the Unitarian church and Dr. William
Ellery Channing, and it was the Channings who rescued her
when she collapsed.

Her sensitivity to suffering had led Dix to set up a school
for poor children in the rooms over the estate stables. Out of
this school grew the Warren Street Chapel, which was
renowned for its work with children. Dix rose before dawn
and went to bed after midnight. Her mind was incapable of
resting. She had no outlets for relaxation. There was no
happy home environment where she could unwind. Dorothea
Dix, in her early twenties, was wrapped up in books and
study. She taught herself subjects and then wrote about them.
She drove herself and her students relentlessly.

Because of her two schools, her long days, her
responsibilities in the mansion, her compulsion to make
something of her life, and her lonely environment, Dix
became seriously ill. Her lungs were congested and already
hemorrhaging. Her voice grew weak and scratchy. Her tall
frame became stooped, and in one side she felt a relentlessly
stabbing knife of pain. Her body had become the enemy of her
goals.

By the time she finally collapsed, Dix had won the
respect of several prominent Bostonians, especially the
Channings. To get her out of the city, Dr. Channing asked
her to tutor his children in the spring and summer at
Narragansett Bay. During this period of partial recuperation,
and under Channing's influence, Dix's spirituality and
intellect grew. She read poetry, science, and biographies. She
wrote stories and published several children's and nature
books, as her old love of nature and particularly of botany was
developed. Solaced by the beauty of nature, she acquired a
sense of Deity. Dix began to believe that her illness served a
purpose—to bring her spiritual joy.

With the Channings, she sailed one winter to St. Croix.
Here she relished the lush tropical foliage and sea animals.

But she was also overwhelmed by a bewildering languor. For the first time, Dix could not rouse herself to study and write; and for the first time she came in contact with people, the natives of the island, who seemed so free and so musical, and who loved to dance. At first she was fascinated with their grace, their physical beauty, and their musical voices. But her ingrained moral attitude reasserted itself before long, and she began to worry about their souls. However, by the end of that winter, she had grown accustomed to their ways, and had stretched her narrow ideals for humanity to allow for some imperfection in other people—though not in herself. In judging her own life, Dorothea Dix clung to her personal, austere laws.

Dix was now managing to spend most of her winters away from the wet, freezing weather of Boston. With renewed health, she returned from St. Croix to reopen her schools with the same drive as before. She was dedicated to her pupils but could never fully appreciate and accept their irresponsible attitudes. She felt children should prepare themselves for some lofty mission in adulthood. The school lasted five years, and then Dorothea Dix collapsed completely. At thirty-three, she was told by doctors to give up teaching, go abroad for a rest, and accept the life of an invalid.

Dix sailed for England on April 2, 1836, planning to land in Liverpool, travel to London, and then go on to Italy to recuperate. She never went beyond Liverpool, where she remained for a year and a half.

Dix carried a letter of introduction to the Rathbones, a prominent philanthropic family in Liverpool. Upon landing, she was so ill that the Rathbones transported her to their estate so that she could regain her strength. She called this the most peaceful period of her life; for the first time she was receiving rather than giving. Her compassion was ignited as Rathbone introduced her to other humanitarians, and she learned about the horrors of slum living and child labor, the primitive prison conditions, and the inhuman treatment of the insane. During this period of regaining her health, Dix was informed that both her mother and grandmother had died. Her father had died earlier, so she was left with no family except her brothers, now leading their own lives. Sensing a new feeling of release and freedom, Dorothea Dix prepared to return home.

Dix had her inheritance to maintain her. She spent the winters in Virginia, studying but with no goals, restless and bored. For the first time she was directionless. She was a spinster in an age when spinsterhood was unacceptable. And then, in March 1841, she was asked to teach the female prisoners' Sunday School.

Dix's first step after witnessing the East Cambridge Jail treatment of the mentally ill was to bring to court a demand for a prison stove. She presented her argument and she won. The inmates finally had heat. But Dix suspected that conditions at this jail were not an isolated instance of inhumanity and began an investigation of the state's treatment of the insane and a study into theories of insanity.

In 1841, there were only six state or community hospitals in the United States which recognized in the mentally ill person a human being. The general attitude was that the insane were born depraved and had to be confined, either at home or in jail-like institutions. The American Puritan tradition saw anyone who veered from the accepted morality as an outcast, not only from society but also from God. This led to an emotional revulsion toward prisoners and, even more so, toward the mentally ill. It was believed that in an insane person, the evil elements of the human soul had gained control over the higher attributes. To combat these murderous "invaders," iron cages, clubs, and chains were used for restraining, and starvation, purging, and bleeding were the "medical treatment."

Though these beliefs had been somewhat liberalized in the nineteenth century, they were still widely accepted. What Dix was taking on, therefore, was strongly ingrained superstition and apathy.

After having the stove installed in the East Cambridge

Jail, and supervising some attempts at sanitation, Dix turned to the most enlightened men she knew for advice on how to accomplish real, lasting reforms: Dr. Channing; educator Horace Mann; statesman Charles Sumner; and Dr. Samuel Gridley Howe, head of the Perkins Institute for the Blind. They all told her that before the legislators would allot funds for more institutions, someone had to visit all the jails and almshouses in Massachusetts and present a detailed report. Dix decided to take on this job herself—alone and without financial backing.

For the next year and a half, Dix found enough abuses of the mentally handicapped to significantly tarnish Massachusetts' reputation as an "enlightened" state. From Cape Cod to the western Berkshires, she investigated and wrote down the endless details of maltreatment. Finally, in January 1843, she stood before the Massachusetts legislature to recite what has been called her "catalogue of horrors."

In a low voice and with clipped words, she began: "I shall be obliged to speak with great plainness, and to reveal many things revolting to the taste, and from which my woman's nature shrinks with peculiar sensitiveness. But truth is the highest consideration. I tell what I have seen, painful and shocking as the details often are, that from them you may feel more deeply the imperative obligation which lies upon you to prevent the possibility of a repetition or continuance of such outrages upon humanity."

Discussing the conditions of inmates whom she saw "in cages, closets, stalls, pens; chained, naked, beaten with rods, and lashed into obedience!" Dix brought out many examples:

In Groton, she found a youth, declared harmless but nevertheless locked in a wooden shack with a strong, heavy chain leading from the floor to the iron collar around his neck.

In an almshouse in Danvers, a young woman who was suffering from depression had become violent and was caged. She was unwashed, producing such an odor that Dix could not remain near her more than a few moments at a time.

"Irritation of body, produced by utter filth and exposure, incited her to the horrid process of tearing off her skin by inches: her face, neck, and person were thus disfigured to hideousness."

Dix saw a young woman in Worcester holding an infant of which she was "the unconscious parent."

In Newton, an old woman was chained in her room, which was virtually a toilet.

Dix ended her "memorial" with a plea for adequate provisions for the mentally ill, both for reasons of humanity and to erase the blot on the reputation of the state.

The memorial was harsh, and it was received with disbelief. Newspapers accused Dorothea Dix of having an overactive imagination; jail-keepers called her a liar; incredulous citizens said the report was "sensational." But the respected men who had encouraged her investigation— Channing, Howe, Mann, and others—again backed her. At their insistence, a committee was chosen to investigate further, and when Dix's plea for action was seconded by this committee, a resolution was finally passed. Provisions for one hundred additional patients were allotted to the state lunatic hospital at Worcester. This was the first victory in Dix's crusade.

Meanwhile, Dix was studying the new scientific theories of insanity, speaking to doctors and teachers, and planning her next investigation into neighboring Rhode Island.

As she traveled, Dix concluded that inhumane treatment of the insane prevailed all over the United States. In Rhode Island, she visited one inmate chained in a thick-walled stone cell with no openings for light or air. The keeper's wife revealed that it was so cold in winter they often shoveled out a bushel of frost at a time. Yet, the inmate had survived there for three years. Dix wrote of this ordeal, calling it "Astonishing Tenacity of Life."

To raise money for hospital aid in Rhode Island, Dix paid a visit to wealthy Cyrus Butler in Providence despite warnings that he was a confirmed miser. To keep her from

asking for money, Butler tried to discuss one extraneous topic
after another, but she finally got her story told. Then she said
that her responsibility was over; it was up to Butler now to
use the facts she had given him and do something about
rectifying matters. Cyrus Butler surprised everyone by
donating forty thousand dollars to enlarge the hospital in
Providence.

Her next attack was on New Jersey. Here Dix veered
from her earlier aims of simply enlarging existing institutions. She wanted to set up an entirely new hospital for
the mentally ill. To finance this, citizens would have to be
taxed, so Dix realized she must begin changing citizens' as
well as legislators' attitudes about the insane.

Quietly and alone, Dorothea Dix moved into New Jersey.
Her methods of work were now defined: her job was to get
facts and prepare the report. She would antagonize no one
and thus gain help from all sides. She would enlist legislators
to get her "memorial" before the state legislature, so she
made it a point to know every legislator, his sensibilities, and
his sensitivity to the desires of his constituency. (She
privately learned to distrust the slick, polished, wealthy
legislators, but did not let her prejudices be known.)

Ms. Dix's work was done in a special room given her for
her use in the state building. Here the legislators could come
to visit her, and her traditional feminine image did not have
to be sacrificed by her appearing aggressive. Dorothea Dix
tried in every way to be efficient and inoffensive.

When Dix's report was read to a state legislature, the
newspapers would place it before the people. Each memorial
was well organized, specific to that state, and containing local
examples. Dorothea would then follow up with more articles,
written either by her or by talented writers sympathetic to
her cause.

Through this method, a bill establishing a state mental
hospital was passed in New Jersey in March 1845. Simul-
taneously, a similar bill was passed in Harrisburg for a
state asylum in Pennsylvania. The Trenton hospital, which

she called her "first-born child," always held a special place in her heart, and when Ms. Dix was too old and feeble to move around, it was to this institution that she retired and it was there that she died.

Now satisfied with her efforts, Dorothea Dix took off around the country. In her first four years of investigating, she visited over eight hundred institutions housing the mentally ill. In the next three years, she traveled thirty thousand miles, reciting memorials before numerous legislatures and receiving sympathetic publicity. She became well known. Railroads and steamship lines gave her travel passes as she moved from New Orleans to Nova Scotia, and westward past the Mississippi and Missouri rivers.

Travel in the mid-1800s was usually precarious and always an adventure. Once, when she was traveling by stagecoach in Michigan, the coach was suddenly stopped by robbers. Dix immediately turned to the nearest holdup man and began to scold him. "I recognize that voice!" the robber exclaimed. He said he had heard her lecture while he was in a Philadelphia jail. He convinced his companions to return all the stolen property and let the stagecoach continue. Dix, however, insisted he take some money from her so he would not go on to rob someone else.

Steamships were no less hazardous, for the captains liked to have a hearty, if reckless, race whenever they met another boat. Carriage drivers were equally reckless, drunk, or both. Dix learned that stagecoach and carriage breakdowns were common and that repair ability was rare among the drivers, so in her satchel she carried wrenches, rope, hammers, and nails so she could cope with a broken wheel or axle.

Summer droughts, autumn rains, winter blizzards, and spring mud and floods were routine parts of her journeys, and Dix contracted malaria, which added to her other lifelong afflictions. Again and again, she seemed close to death, yet each time she sprang back with even more spiritual strength and dedication. Hemorrhages, malarial attacks, and pain were her constant companions, but she had trained herself as

a perfectionist and nothing diverted her. To preserve her
strength, she took advantage of the events which stopped her
vehicle. During storms or floods, she would sleep as much as
sixteen hours; this was to tide her over the next few days of
traveling. Eventually, she did her work in the South during
fall and winter and moved north for summer.

Every year, a new state asylum was named, and honor
was heaped upon Dorothea Dix. She was particularly loved in
the ante-bellum South, for she kept her resolution to not
become political, controversial, or antagonistic. She never
attacked slavery, which was a favorite cause for her fellow
crusaders. Dorothea Dix's first concern was the humane
treatment of the insane, and by concentrating on this, she
was the first New England reformer to make concrete gains
in the South. Nine states there set up mental hospitals
because of her memorials.

Gradually, her responsibilities extended beyond the
allocation of hospital funds. It was up to her to select the
proper site, to decide upon the types of buildings, to solicit the
county to yield its land, and to arrange proper landscaping so
that the occupational therapy of farming and gardening could
take place. She also demanded colorful rooms, cheery
pictures, and evidence of human caring. With strict criteria in
mind, she appointed head physicians, superintendents, and
other personnel.

Despite the burdensome work, Dix recognized the
hazards of ignorance. The fruits of her hard work could be
smashed later if her planning were careless. She felt it was
her duty to make certain all details were settled.

Through all this prevailed a double image of Dorothea
Dix. One was the shy, respectable, sweet-voiced lady in a
plain grey dress with snowy collar and cuffs. The other was
the gifted reformer with a winning demand for perfection and
a tenacious drive, whose motto seemed to be, "The tonic I
need is the tonic of opposition. That always sets me on my
feet."

Dorothea Dix had progressed from soliciting for hospital

extensions to creating new hospitals. In 1848, she went one
step further. She presented a national memorial to the federal
Congress in Washington, D.C. She wanted land, at first five
million acres, and when this was denied her, Dix raised her
request to over twelve million acres.

The federal government had given land to each state; this
land was to be used for schools, highways, railroads, canals,
and other public needs. Dorothea Dix felt that aid to the
mentally ill constituted just as strong a public need. She
calculated that millions of acres were still unspecified for use
and business interests were bidding for them. She had better
use for that land and was determined to get it. She planned to
sell the land and set the proceeds aside as a perpetual fund to
care for the needy insane.

During the period her memorial was under consideration,
Dix traveled around the country. At the same time, she tried
to keep in touch with the proceedings in Washington.
Sometimes her asylum work led her into alien fields. In
1853, for example, while she was working in St. John,
Newfoundland, a severe storm wrecked many ships. The
storm was particularly bad near Sable Island, off the east end
of Nova Scotia. The island was littered with wrecked vessels;
in fact, as Ms. Dix was visiting the island, another shipwreck
occurred. In response to the devastation she saw, she
arranged for a fleet of rescue boats to be permanently based
on the island to help ships in trouble.

For six years the memorial passed from one Congress to
the next. Finally, in 1854, her reputation was strong enough
to compel a final push through both houses. The bill called for
12,250,000 acres of land and also for the establishment of a
Washington, D.C., hospital for the mentally ill of the army
and navy. All the bill needed was the signature of President
Franklin Pierce.

Dorothea Dix was exhilarated. She was also tired. She
had spent almost fourteen years at her investigative crusade.
She received letters of congratulations from all corners and
felt great satisfaction with her efforts.

Then President Pierce vetoed the bill. Ms. Dix could hardly believe it; Mr. Pierce had personally told her how interested he was in her project. Pierce's argument was that Congress could make charitable provisions for the mentally ill only within the limits of the capital. If Congress helped all the indigent insane, it could be called upon to help the poor of all the states.

Dix considered this an arbitrary decision going against the majority opinion. Nevertheless, the veto stood, and once again, Dorothea Dix collapsed. Her reserves were depleted, and she returned to Europe to regain her strength.

She received one morale boost when she went to the American Steamship Lines to pick up her passage ticket. The owner of the steamship company told her that the nation owed her a great deal. He, as an individual, would do his part by giving her free passage in a private cabin!

Perhaps this extension of gratitude gave Dix the incentive to raise money on board ship when the chance came. She noted that some passengers placed bets on the steamer's run; Dix waited until all bets were placed and the winner chosen, and then she asked the winner for his proceeds. This she gave to the captain to keep for the Home for the Children of Indigent Sailors in New York.

She spent several weeks with the Rathbones and then she traveled in Ireland. She planned to visit Scotland and other countries in Europe, hopefully going as far as Palestine. She wanted to investigate the asylums of the Old World. In Scotland she found the private mental institutions were horrendous. She could not ignore their existence. Despite the fact that Dix was labeled an interfering stranger, she convinced Parliament to appoint a Royal Commission to look into the condition of Scotland's lunatic asylums. In two years, an act had passed which led to the establishment of new, humane asylums around Scotland to care for the mentally ill. (By this time, Dix was already back in the United States.)

After a similar investigation of the Channel Islands, Dix accepted an invitation from the Rathbones to vacation with them in Switzerland. She noted that this was one of the most pleasant sojourns of her life. It was followed by an investigative of Europe and parts of the Middle East.

In Paris, she found the charitable institutions satisfactory, although ventilation was poor and this seemed to contribute to a great many deaths. She also reported that the resident medical students used inmates in their medical experiments.

In Rome, she discovered just behind the Vatican a hospital so bad that she personally reported it to the Pope. She accepted his promise to look into the hospital conditions himself. The Pope corroborated her findings, and when he met her a second time, he thanked her.

From Italy, she visited Greece, Turkey, Austria, Bohemia, Germany, Sweden, Norway, Denmark, Holland, Belgium, and Russia, but she never got to Palestine. She did very little sightseeing or socializing, for nothing could lure her away from her mission. She would not be refused entry into any hospital and wrote back to friends that traveling by herself was perfectly easy. She ran into little difficulty, although she was not fluent in any foreign language.

Returning home in 1856, Dix was met with pleas for help —new extensions were needed, another hospital in one state, more money in another. Friends wanted her to write a book about her trip, but Dix felt her first priority was to utilize what she had learned abroad to improve conditions in the United States. Dorothea Dix was to raise more money for charity than any other individual up to that time.

The Cambridge jail episode directed Dorothea Dix into her life's work, and the Civil War steered her career into a new arena. It was her grandmother's perfectionist standards and her grandfather's tenacity that helped her become an "angel of mercy" to the outcasts of the world. But this inheritance brought her frustration when she became a government administrator.

Dix expected the war. She had heard that Abraham Lincoln's election in 1860 had stirred certain Southern elements to plan to seize Washington, D.C., cutting off all communication between the capital and the rest of the country. The Confederacy would then declare itself the legal government, and Lincoln would never be inaugurated.

Dix let influential leaders know of these plans, pointing out that Southern troops were already drilling. Because of this revelation, President-elect Lincoln was smuggled into the capital. After the inauguration, volunteer troops were called up to defend the city. Dorothea Dix, then sixty years old, joined these troops, knowing that once fighting broke out, wounded soldiers and disease would combine to present a serious problem. Soon after volunteering her services, Dorothea Dix was named superintendent of nurses, the first woman appointed to a federal administrative position in this country.

Since there was no military nursing service when the war broke out, Dorothea Dix was placed in a difficult and frustrating position. From the thousands of women volunteering, she had to set the standards, choose the most qualified for nursing, train them, and supervise them. Naturally, her standards were utopian. Recognizing the importance of her situation, Dix wanted only the best. To dissuade flighty romantics, she specified that the nurses be over thirty years old and plain in appearance. Overseeing the nurses at work, she was as precise as when she was investigating hospitals. Many dedicated nurses resented her —some openly. Motherly Jane Swisshelm thought Dix was cold and unsympathetic, and Louisa May Alcott, an admirer of Dix, considered her "a kind old soul, but queer and arbitrary."

Dix had other duties, such as handling and distributing clothing, bandages, and food to the sick and wounded. Since there were no facilities to store these provisions, Dix took it upon herself to find space, and she doled out the provisions herself. Because she had always worked alone and with her own plans, Dix found it difficult to operate within a bureaucratic framework. During the four years of war, she

tried to do everything alone, never resting a moment. She
inspected hospitals, terrorizing the negligent; distributed
supplies; set up Washington infirmaries and sewing circles;
wrote to widows and mothers; consoled and sat with the
critically wounded and dying; and collected and distributed
baskets of fruit when scurvy broke out among the troops.

She went without sleep and regular meals; her weight
plunged to ninety-five pounds. No one was more overworked
than she. But her perfectionism was more operable in times of
peace. In war, it was obvious that shortcomings had to be
tolerated when the best was not available. A bad medical
facility was often the only accommodation to be had; an
inexperienced surgeon had to be acceptable if no better
surgeon could be found. But Dix refused to lower her
standards and ran into relentless criticism and abuse. She
found her own self-control cracking under the weight of ill
health and mental pressure. Dix herself said of the situation,
"This is not the work I would have my life judged by."

Luckily, Sanitary Commissions were set up further along
in the war years, relieving Dix of many of her duties, but she
remained working until the fighting ended. Secretary of War
Edwin M. Stanton, though impatient at times, never lost his
awe of Dorothea Dix. He felt the fact that she had done *too*
much in the line of duty should bring her commendation, not
disgrace. When the war ended, he asked Dix how the country
could best repay her for her services—with money or public
acclamation? Dix asked only for a pair of flags, and these she
received.

After the war, Dix felt more must be done for the soldiers.
She worked to get pensions for the veterans and financial aid
for indigent nurses. And, though many Americans agreed
that a lasting monument should be erected for the Civil War
dead, no one wanted to tackle the job of fund-raising and
overseeing the task, so Dix took on this duty as well. She
personally searched the Maine quarries for the right piece of
impermeable granite and stayed with the project until the
monument at the National Cemetery in Virginia was finally

completed. And then she went back to her hospital work.

She stayed at this job until she was eighty, traveling as before from Maine to Texas to San Francisco and back again. She investigated carefully, turning over mattresses, tasting soup, choosing physicians, and talking with patients. She was dismayed over the state of mental hospitals after the war. She felt all her hard work was in vain, and the abuses she found were "monstrous."

Year by year she tackled each problem individually. She found she had a deep hatred for the South, which she tried to suppress. But the Southerners received her help so affectionately, she slowly overcame her hostility. Dorothea Dix was virtually the only Yankee who was welcomed in postwar Dixie.

The personal adulation Dix had known before the war was gone in other places, however. Her generation was dying, and her reputation as a "savior" was dying with it. Newer administrators and younger men ridiculed her, calling her an "old maid," or the "self-constituted lunacy commission." They resented the way she moved in and out of the mental hospitals at will, calling for fire drills and scolding the officials for anything she found amiss.

Like a candle, she burned steadily those last years, helping the victims of the great Chicago and Boston fires, setting up a drinking fountain for the overworked Boston draft horses, and so on. The candle burned out at last in 1881, when, feeble and overworked, Dorothea Dix returned to her "first-born child," the hospital in Trenton, New Jersey. She had known no other home for fifty years.

Mentally, she was still active, but physically, she was spent. Exhaustion, hardening of the arteries, malaria attacks, respiratory trouble, and increasing deafness and blindness plagued her for six more years. Yet, she never lost her drive. "I think even lying on my bed, I can still do something," she would tell visitors.

On July 18, 1887, Dorothea Dix died. Those she touched felt she was one of the most distinguished and least pretentious humanitarians ever produced in America. She may also be the most forgotten. One biographer, Helen Marshall, wrote, "Rather than emblazoned on monuments of stone, her name was written deep in the hearts of the generations that knew her, and with their passing, her place in social history has been overlooked."

7

Jane Addams

Laura Jane Addams was born on September 6, 1860, seven months before the first Civil War guns fired on Fort Sumter. Her birth bed stood in a wide, commodious house in the second-generation frontier town of Cedarville, Illinois, where her father owned two mills. (He also served sixteen years in the state senate, corresponded with Abraham Lincoln, cried at the death of Giuseppe Mazzini, and rose every morning at three to read in solitude.)

Seventy-four years later, when Jane Addams died, she had written ten books and presented innumerable lectures and essays, was honored with fifteen university degrees and the Greek medal of military merit, and in 1931, was the second American awarded the Nobel Peace Prize. She had also known derision as a pacifist and slander as a socialist, as an anarchist, as a pro-German when Americans were anti-German, and as a Red when Americans were anti-Russian. Hull House, her home for almost a half century, was situated in the slums of immigrant Chicago, where garbage carpeted the "streets of gold" and Old World farmers slaughtered sheep in the basements. Yet, this same Hull House was visited by dignitaries, including the crown prince of Belgium, American government officials, and a wide array of actors, writers, and musicians.

How did this slight and sickly prairie child evolve into "Saint Jane" of Chicago's "Cathedral of Compassion"? How did a Victorian female step out of the stereotyped framework of delicacy and decorum to become, along with Queen Victoria, the most famous and admired woman in the world?

The answer, of course, lies in Jane Addams herself; she was the embodiment of the contradictions of the late Victorian Age. The gravestone inscription which she herself ordered reads, simply and inadequately: JANE ADDAMS of HULL HOUSE and the WOMEN'S INTERNATIONAL LEAGUE FOR PEACE AND FREEDOM. Yet, Walter Lippmann lauded her as "Not only good but great." Prestigious *Nation* magazine read "compelling tragedy" in her face, while one of her closest friends insisted that Addams "was full of the love of life—of life as it is, not only as it might be."

Once, before making a speech, Jane Addams was described as: "A smallish, dark-faced woman, gentle of manner and soft of voice. . . . She is dressed in a tailor-made suit of grayish blue. . . . She is slightly stooped as she stands with her hands clasped behind her in a way touchingly childish, looking out at her audience. . . . Her face is sad, though the eyes are luminous, and the lips adapt themselves readily to smiles."

Jane Addams was a strong, manipulating organizer, an ivory goddess rearranging the lives of the poverty-stricken. *Christian Century* wrote, "She had no interest in descending to the poverty level. Her interest was in lifting the level all about her to new heights." A charismatic, brilliant intellectual and a legendary figure, she grabbed the country's spirit, whirled its imagination, and received as much fan mail as any contemporary music star. All this while her country was enduring the birth pangs of an industrial age. The farmland roots of thousands were being torn up and transplanted to hard urban turf; cities swelled with peasants, native and foreign, who were trying to become technological employees.

Jane Addams recognized this American dilemma when she moved to Chicago in 1889. This was the second largest city in the new nation, a microcosm of the whole land. In it was merged established immigrant power with new immigrant poverty; it waved "Happy Hooligans" off to hop freight cars and see the country; it seethed with anti-British prejudice and absorbed the British influences of Darwin, Huxley, and Spencer. The educated, restless middle-class Chicago women read Stephen Crane and organized a symphony orchestra, not knowing what else to do with their schooled individualism in a society which offered them no place to burn their flames. At the other end of the city, the region of Halsted and Polk streets teemed with new immigrants. Their quarter was a maze of stables and alleys and narrow streets without sewers, where women sorted rags and labored in sweatshops for pennies. It was in this lower world that Jane Addams bought Hull House and became a settlement worker.

Addams believed that character is formed in earliest childhood, where it settles into "definite lines of future development." Her father had a great influence on her. One description calls him kindly but not very approachable, courteous yet reserved. This could apply to his daughter as well. Sarah Addams had died when her eighth child, Jane, was not yet three, and the little girl formed a quick and touchingly close alliance with her tall, imposing father. Skinny and pigeon-toed, with a slightly curved spine, Jane grew up in utter awe of John H. Addams, even to the extent of rubbing miller's wheat between her fingers to develop "miller's thumb" as he had.

Mr. Addams was a non-church-supporting Quaker with such high moral ideals that, when he died, one newspaper editor mentioned that John Addams was the only man who had never been offered a bribe because bad men

were instinctively afraid of him. Young Jane was often
embarrassed to walk with her father, afraid people would
wonder how such a handsome gentleman could be related to
this ugly duckling. It wasn't until later that she was
convinced her father was not ashamed of her; she once met
him unexpectedly in the city and he swept off his hat, bowed
low, and to her astonishment, acknowledged her before the
Cedarville "world."

Jane was a serious child, who drove herself in spite of ill
health to become a serious woman. After her death, *Nation*
compared Ms. Addams to the physician who wears an
emotion-hiding mask "in the face of suffering and death lest
he be emotionally destroyed." In childhood, Jane had a
precocious sense of responsibility for carrying on the world's
affairs. In one repeating dream she found herself alone in the
world with the job of making the first wheel. At the same
early age, she confided to George Haldemann, a young
playmate whose mother later married Jane's father, that
someday she would establish a large house in the midst of
those "horrid little houses so close together" which she had
noticed near her father's mill.

Despite her curved spine and her solemn mien, young
Jane apparently led a happy life, romping in the country with
her brothers and sisters and friends. She often claimed a
country childhood far surpassed a city one. In the country,
children could devise endless games which could be played
without interruption, whereas city activities were constantly
broken up by cars, traffic, and passers-by.

When she was seventeen, Jane wanted very much to go
east to Smith College, but her father opted for school near
home followed by travel abroad, so Jane trailed after her
sisters to Rockville Seminary, called "The Mount Holyoke of
the West," even though it was not accredited as a college.
Here, Ms. Addams was one of the few students who resisted a
career in missionary work. She urged that Rockville
Seminary become accredited as a college. Addams and a
friend took extra courses to qualify for a bachelor's degree.

One year after she graduated, Rockville Seminary did become Rockville College, and she and her friend returned to collect their already earned bachelor's degrees.

Addams was very active intellectually and became totally involved in her studies. Once, in order to understand De Quincey's theory of dreams, she and some friends fed themselves opium at designated intervals. They were so excited about the experiment, however, that they did not even grow sleepy, and before they could complete the test a teacher confiscated the powder.

In her senior year, Jane Addams blossomed forth as class president, valedictorian, and editor of the school magazine. She also received a marriage proposal from a leading student at another college. She turned it down, having decided to go on to medical school and spend her life among the poor, treating their bodily ills.

The door to this career abruptly slammed shut when John Addams died; shock, combined with an aggravated spinal difficulty, caused Jane to drop out of Women's Medical College in Philadelphia after only seven months. She felt somewhat relieved, however, for though her first exams had gone well, Addams was finding out that a physician's work was not particularly to her liking. However, she was shattered by her beloved father's death. (Grief over the deaths of people close to her would physically enfeeble her at various points throughout her life.) Addams was told at this time that she could never bear children and was advised to travel to Europe for an extended rest. She thereupon began the only lethargic period of her life, and it lasted eight long years.

She was plagued with doubts and conflicting views of the meaning of life, but on each of two trips to Europe, there occurred an incident which helped reweave the tapestry of her existence. The first took place on a Saturday at midnight while she accompanied friends on a tour of squalid East London. There was an auction in progress: decaying fruits and vegetables were being sold before the Sunday ban on merchandising. She could never forget the horror she felt at the sight of human hands grasping for the food, hundreds of gnarled fingers straining upward, and whenever she saw hands in this gesture, even among school children in a classroom, Jane Addams remembered that London poverty. She sensed then that her educated life was being wasted.

From this point on, Addams vowed to learn life by living. Devoting one's life to the pursuit of culture, she decided, was just misdirecting energy which could bring solace or relief to others; she would somehow have to combine education, morals, philosophy, and the arts with the necessities of food and shelter, and she would have to induce the poverty stricken to seek a rounded life.

She went on to visit Germany and later Italy, never forgetting the sight of the grasping hands. Two years later, she spent a winter in Rome to study the catacombs, admitting that, "In spite of my distrust of 'advantages,' I was apparently not yet so cured but that I wanted more of them."

Between these two trips, Jane Addams spent the winters with relatives in Baltimore and the summers in Illinois. It was a confused, frustrating time for the sensitive girl, who was studying the United Italy movement and Mazzini and trying to avoid her stepmother's attempts to marry her off to her stepbrother, George. At one point, Addams embraced the Presbyterian religion, yearning for "an outward symbol of fellowship . . . some blessed spot where unity of spirit might claim right of way over all differences." She was groping her way through the position of the privileged and educated, to which she didn't want to yield; on the other hand, she was embracing a romantic vision of the poor, the Christian poverty ethic, the distrust of aristocracy. She was hoping to discover the meaning of Jane Addams, and how she could make some improvement in the civilization she found herself in.

The second European incident which solidified the direction of her life took place in Madrid on Easter Sunday, 1888. There, Jane Addams snapped out of her dreams. She was attending a bullfight with friends, watching the blood

and gore with indifference, pensively comparing the matador
to gladiators, martyrs, and knights, while her disgusted
friends were leaving the arena one by one. It wasn't until
later that night that her own revulsion about the bloodshed
hit her. "It was suddenly made quite clear to me that I was
lulling my conscience by a dreamer's scheme, that a mere
paper reform had become a defense for continued idleness and
that I was making it a raison d'être for going on indefinitely
with study and travel." The next day, the first concrete plans
for Hull House were made. It was to be the answer to
Addams's own dilemma, as well as a partial answer to that of
her country.

In January 1889, Jane Addams and her friend Ellen
Gates Starr found in Chicago a fine old house sitting back
from the street, with a wide porch running along three sides
and supported by wooden Corinthian-style pillars. It had been
the home of architect Charles J. Hull, and had known duty as
a furniture store, a factory, and a home for the aged. It had
also been the only house in the area to escape the great
Chicago fire of 1871, and this fact would provide sentimental
good fortune as far as Addams was concerned. The two young
women dubbed it Hull House, and thereupon joined the first
wave of the settlement flood.

As Addams put it several years later, the settlement
movement was based on emotion as well as conviction.
Young, well-educated people, cultivated into overly sensitive
idealists, were searching for an outlet. In settlement houses
such as Hull House, they could translate democracy into
terms the neighborhood could understand, and thereby
achieve "universal brotherhood," a realization of human-
itarianism. Most important of all, the settlement was a
grand experiment in healing the social ills of modern city life.

"All the misunderstandings we have in life," wrote
Addams, "are due to partial experience, and all life's fretting
comes of our limited intelligence." She urged understanding
of the cities, which offered an environment that people
created themselves and that they could control themselves.

She fought against the tearing down of human efforts by ignorance, poverty, bossism, and war. Quite an intoxicating challenge for a small-town girl to answer and to induce others to meet along with her.

The two friends set right in. Hull House, on the corner of Halsted and Polk, was part of Ward 19, an immigrant section with nineteen different nationalities, including Italians, Germans, Bohemians, Poles, and Russians. Addams noted that the streets were "inexpressibly dirty," the number of schools was inadequate, and the street lighting and paving were in very bad shape. There was no basement too dark, no stable too foul, no tenement room too small to be a sweatshop.

The houses around Hull House were mostly wooden, one-family structures that usually sheltered several families. Many had no water supply other than a faucet in the back yard, no fire escape, and inadequate garbage facilities. This was a vast change from the airy midwestern countryside which had nurtured Jane Addams.

Hull House sat with dignity between an undertaking parlor and a saloon, and Addams and Starr set out to furnish it as elegantly as possible, using many pieces they had collected in Europe. On September 18, 1889, Jane Addams, Ellen Starr, and Mary Keyser, a housekeeper, moved in to begin their new life.

The house on Halsted Street quickly became the center of community life, and like the sun, it radiated activity and improvement to its neighbors—a reading circle, a kindergarten, a boys' club, lessons for girls. Other young people, first only women and later men, joined the Hull House staff as residents to offer children what was omitted in the crowded schools and hopefully to encourage independence and initiative. They washed the newborn and held holiday parties for the aged; they were undertakers and they were nurses; they delivered an illegitimate child when local midwives refused to "touch the likes of" the young mother; they established the first public playground in Chicago; and they brought roses to an old Italian woman, who deduced that the

flowers must have been imported from Italy since she had
never seen fresh roses in Chicago!

Jane Addams had a realistic mind—she could adapt and
change; when the nutritious but unimaginative food she
offered her neighbors was rejected as too dull, she sought to
make it more palatable. This pragmatic inclination she
inherited from her father, who once altered his Quaker
pacifism to support the Civil War. Years later, Ms. Addams
must have remembered the necessity of compromise when she
allowed young militant Greeks to drill at Hull House. She
appreciated their sincere commitment to defend their native
land against the Turks. She was not one to stick fast to rules,
even her own; rather, she aimed to keep the settlement fluid
and her ideas adjustable, and to bend her idealism to find
concrete solutions to the problems that arose.

Yet, as deeply as Hull House was immersed in the
turbulence of the community, it took on the character of a
tower enclosing an ivory goddess. Some dubbed the
atmosphere "bracing" and "astringent," invigorating rather
than warm; Addams involved herself passionately with
people, but she still kept some reserve, even toward the Hull
House residents she worked with and genuinely loved. The
whole settlement movement, in fact, was characterized by
some as lacking the human touch which is so necessary to
friendship.

Hull House flourished. Addams's goal was to combine
recreation and education with nourishment and shelter, so
the first building to be added to the settlement was an art
gallery, which also contained an art studio and a reading
room. It was at this time that Addams discovered the abyss
developing between the immigrants and their Americanized
children, so she set aside Saturday evenings for family
gatherings to celebrate national holidays, preserving the folk
music, crafts, and literature of the old country. A labor
museum was established to exhibit the old skills; there, older
immigrants became teachers. Young factory workers learned
firsthand that the spinning wheel was a predecessor of

modern plant machinery. Eventually, the museum became a permanent, self-supporting workshop selling its own products.

Dancing, songs, and theatre were all used to bring the immigrants of many nationalities together. Outside Hull House, Addams encouraged bringing orchestras and festivals to public parks, spotlighting the various nationalities which made up the neighborhood. She felt a democratic state should respect variation and heritage and liked to remind the neighbors that Abraham Lincoln, her father's old friend, had never repudiated the customs of his forebears, but had retained and utilized them.

Children demanded a great deal of Jane Addams's attention and concern. From the start, she found herself asking why four-year-olds were put to work in sweatshops yanking basting threads while their mothers stitched trousers; why three thousand children in her ward were without classroom seats; why the only playground was a garbage-splattered alley (which was later found to be the spawning ground of a typhoid epidemic because a sewer line merged there with a water line). Addams set up a day-care center for the children of working mothers. It had been a custom in winter to lock children in tenement rooms. One crippled child was tied to the leg of a kitchen table so he wouldn't stray into trouble while his mother was at work. In summer, children were locked outside and often would wander into the cool halls of Hull House, clutching the penny they had for lunch.

Hull House cared for these children, first in a little cottage and later in a special children's house. Addams knew that children needed attention and love, and that babies in institutions had a high death rate because no one would take the time to simply inspire them to fight for life. Since poor mothers could not give their children the necessary time and loving care, she advocated state allowances to mothers to encourage them to stay home, especially during the early childhood years.

Adolescents, as well, demanded time and attention. "We

fail to understand what [youth] wants or even to see his
doings, although his acts are pregnant with meaning, and we
may either translate them into a sordid chronicle of petty vice
or turn them into a solemn school for civic righteousness," she
wrote in *Spirit of Youth and City Streets* in 1909.

Jane Addams's preoccupation with children led, in 1899,
to the establishment of the first juvenile court and to a 1907
law to stop the sale of cocaine to minors. It led to studies of
truancy in schools and of the scarcity of textbooks for her
district; it also led to investigations of tuberculosis in children
and of infant mortality and its relationship to national origin.
Addams also took up the cause of newsboys who, because they
were "merchants," were not protected by child labor laws.

New problems involving children and labor cropped up
like weeds. During the first Christmas season at Hull House,
residents wanted to give candy to a group of little girls. The
children refused the candy because they were working a six-
week pre-Christmas shift in a candy factory, seven in the
morning to nine at night, and they simply could not stand the
sight of any more candy!

For Addams, offering sympathy and kindness was not
enough. She was most effective drawing together her
organizational skills, so she instructed Florence Kelley, a
resident, to investigate Chicago's industrial conditions,
including child labor. The completed survey was presented in
1893. It proposed setting the age of employment at fourteen, a
list of sanitary regulations for sweatshops, and a limit of
eight hours of factory or workshop labor for women, since
women who worked nights or overtime were still faced with
household duties. Years later, these proposals were included
in the first factory laws of Illinois.

Hull House was a constant and effective battle force
against legal and civic inequities. Jane Addams's investigation of working conditions, for example, led her to
embrace the trade union movement. Unions, she felt, were
the only defenders of individual workers, assuming what
should really be a community responsibility. While she

admitted that there were many wrongs committed by the movement, Addams accepted the position of secretary of the Civic Federation's Industrial Arbitration Committee. In 1910, she brought about the precedent-setting agreement that ended the textile workers' strike when she insisted upon including the right of collective bargaining.

Long before this, in 1891, Jane Addams had founded the "Jane Club," a cooperative for working girls. The cooperative began as two apartments and in a few years expanded to fill an entire house. Girls could strike for higher wages without fear of being left without food and shelter. Addams encouraged scrubwomen, seamstresses, and factory workers to band together for better conditions and higher wages. She began reforms that led to the establishment of a free state-licensed employment office, and she provided a constant flow of information to the public, prodding factory owners and labor unions to take firm steps forward.

Labor involvement merged with civic involvement. Chicago was then called the city of "garbage, graft, and gangsters," and Addams's particular foe was the Irish "godfather" of Ward 19—Johnny Powers. Powers was famous for donating turkeys to the poor and sending wreaths to funerals, going so far as to supply a hearse if needed. However, his ward was infamous for having the third highest death rate in Chicago and the poorest refuse collection service. Huge wooden boxes tied to the pavement were filled with rotting garbage. They were also used by toddlers learning to climb, by kids scrambling in games, by young lovers talking into the night.

In Hull House's first years, Addams had installed a small incinerator and dutifully reported the filthy street conditions to Powers. Then, a Hull House women's club did a two-month investigation and uncovered 1,037 violations, leading to the transfer of three city investigators. Ms. Addams asked for and received one of these openings; this was the only paid job she ever held. The salary was one thousand dollars a year. At six each morning, she arose, hitched her horse to her buggy, and set forth following the garbage collector on his rounds. In one place she discovered eighteen inches of garbage hiding the pavement. Powers was furious with her poking and prying; garbage investigator was supposed to be a patronage job for one of his supporters, not for this spear in his side, Jane Addams. Eventually, he abolished the position, substituting a "ward superintendent" post to be open only to men.

But Powers very much wanted to be Addams's friend and dangled bribes before her. Bribes were nothing new to her, and she was more embarrassed than angry, remembering her father's reputation. Still, she didn't wage war against Johnny Powers until she knew she was ready.

The time came in 1898 when Powers was up for reelection. Jane Addams made a speech, innocuously titled *Some Ethical Survivals in Municipal Corruptions,* and in it she opened fire on Johnny Powers. Addams recognized two reasons why corrupt government flourished in the slums: the generous Dutch uncle image of Johnny Powers and the remembrance of corrupt Old World government that remained with the immigrants. Simon Armstrong was urged to run for Powers's post, backed by Hull House, the Municipal Voters League, the Independent Democrats, and the Cook County Republicans.

At first, Powers laughed it off. He had been entrenched too long; his people would not forget him. But the election was in April, and by January, Powers saw that Armstrong was gaining strength. The "kindly protector" applied pressure to the landlords, the Catholic church, the businessmen—all owed him money—and it worked. Powers was reelected.

By now, Powers appreciated the power of Hull House, and the next year he announced publicly that a truce had been signed with Jane Addams. Furious, she retorted: "It is needless to state that the protest of Hull House against a man who continually disregards the most fundamental rights of his constituents must be permanent!"

These "masculine" activities—garbage collecting, making statements to the newspapers, agitating for reform, engaging

in politics—did not always go over well with the neighbors of
Hull House, at least, not when perpetrated by women. But the
female residents continued their push into endeavors that
were traditionally male. Florence Kelley (who later organized
the National Consumers League), Julia Lathrop (who became
head of the United States Children's Bureau), and Dr. Alice
Hamilton (professor of industrial medicine at Harvard) all
began their careers with Jane Addams, writing about and
protesting social discrimination. But they also had to justify
their points of view to the immigrant women they were trying
to help.

Addams believed that it was indeed womanly to extend
the standards of the home to the neighborhood streets, and
the streets of Ward 19 were, to put it politely, unwholesome
and unsanitary. Immigrants tried to carry out their
traditional agricultural activities in the city tenements.
Women sorted soiled rags in the streets, and bakers used
dirty pavement spaces to mix the dough for the bread their
neighbors would eat. Midwives served maternity needs using
centuries-old, often cruelly primitive techniques, until
Addams joined the Chicago Medical Society and was able to
set some standards. She arranged for a post office and a
savings bank to be placed in Hull House; she founded the
Immigrants Protective League and set up baths in the
basement of Hull House. (This paved the way for the first
public bathhouse in Chicago under the Board of Health.)
Eventually, the death rate in Ward 19 dropped from third
place to seventh.

Jane Addams became a model for the ladies of the upper
middle class, who had been more involved in conspicuous
consumption than in constructive activities. She gave them
an identity and an active role to replace that of farm wife. She
pointed out that a healthy society called for "feminine"
attributes blending with the "masculine," and that the home
and the streets concerned women more than men, since it was
mothers who had to cope with that environment day after
day. To achieve the necessary changes, Addams urged

mothers to unite for clean milk and kindergartens; she rallied propertied women against unfair taxes and professional and university women against discriminatory wages. "None of these busy women," said Ms. Addams, "wished to take the place of men or to influence them in the direction of men's affairs, but they did seek an opportunity to cooperate directly in civic life through the use of the ballot in regard to their own affairs."

Yet, the way to better neighborhoods, better conditions for families, and more rights for women had to come through suffrage. Addams wryly accused males of prejudice when she wrote the turnabout called *If Men Were Seeking the Franchise*. It assumed that women already had the vote and were listing reasons why they had to reject male suffrage: for example, men like fighting too much, so society would lose its educational funds to battleships; men are careless about housekeeping, and they would tear down all the protective workshop legislation women had built up through the years; men possess savage instincts, so much money would be spent on jails and policemen because of the high male crime rate.

Addams felt these reasons were more logical for withholding the vote than those that men gave against suffrage for women (for example, women would find politics corrupting; they would vote as their fathers and husbands did; the vote would diminish men's respect for women; women didn't really want the vote).

Women, Jane Addams believed, *did* want to vote. They wanted to extend their concerns beyond the immediate family, not only to the neighborhood, but to all of humanity. She was traditional enough to feel that personal self-development was not justifiable if it meant surrendering the sanctity of the family, but progressive enough to feel that daughters as well as sons should be encouraged to contribute to the national and international good. In 1930, Jane Addams wrote a paper urging women to enter city government and assume some responsibility in civic affairs: "If one could connect the old maternal anxieties which are really the basis of family and tribal life, with the candidates who are seeking offices, it would never be necessary to look about for other motive powers, and if to this we could add maternal concern for the safety and defense of the industrial worker, we should have an increasing code of protective legislation."

Women, she felt, would learn on the job: "Woman has no right to allow what really belongs to her to drop away from her, so we contend that ability to perform an obligation comes very largely in proportion as that obligation is conscientiously assumed."

In these "innocent years," Addams was understandably considered radical by many people, but she would compromise if necessary: "Fanaticism is engendered only when men, finding no contradiction to their theories, at last believe that the very universe lends itself as an exemplification of one point of view." To counteract fanaticism, she held an open social hour every night at Hull House. With dusk, issues of garbage collecting, unwed mothers, disease, and the like were tucked away as talking and visiting took over.

Jane Addams almost always found herself on the side of socialists and anarchists, in fact, behind any "unsocial" viewpoint, although she rarely wavered in her own personal ethics. She admired the socialists because they seemed to understand the pressures of city living, but she resented their insistence that she conform to all their ideals. She allowed the anarchists to have their say, although the bitterness of the 1886 Haymarket riots and the resulting execution of four anarchists still lingered with the neighbors. At one point, she traveled thousands of miles to the Russian home of Tolstoy, a life-long idol. She came away impressed but doubtful that his methods of "bread labor"—and his recommendation that each morning she bake the daily bread—was practical for every society. It obviously would not work for Jane Addams, whose talents lay at the bargaining table rather than the baking oven, even if she was a miller's daughter.

Exposing people to ideas led to the establishment of Hull House college extension classes, which were very successful

with the neighbors. Addams discovered that simple people
craved complicated subjects such as world history. She found
also that they enjoyed art, for it served to lift their minds
above the monotony of their daytime labors and to connect
them with the larger world. Slum existence also called for
practical education, so Jane Addams provided training in
both domestic skills for the home and in millinery and
dressmaking for wage-earning possibilities. And finally, she
brought in athletics, but only as they conformed to the ideals
of the settlement: "That type of gymnastics which is at least
partly a matter of character for that training which
presupposes abstinence and curbing of impulse, as well as for
those athletic contests in which the mind of the contestant
must be vigilant to keep the body closely to the rules of the
game."

In 1912, Addams was invited to second the presidential
nomination of Theodore Roosevelt on his broad Progressive
party platform of social welfare. She received a larger ovation
than any other seconder and was the only one the audience
listened to with rapt attention. At the same convention, she
agreed to include the construction of two battleships in the
platform. Although Addams was a pacifist, she realized that
without the ships there might be no social reform passed. In
the campaign itself, Jane Addams was credited by some for
gaining one million votes for Roosevelt, and while she denied
this, she did admit that even though Roosevelt lost the
election, his campaign brought about more social reform
discussion than she had hoped for.

One million votes or not, Addams was obviously a great
campaigner, and in 1916, both the Republicans and
Democrats wooed her. However, she backed principles rather
than parties, and in 1916, she endorsed Wilson, a Democrat;
in 1920, Debs, a Socialist; and in 1924, LaFollette, a
Progressive. In 1928 and 1932, she backed Republican
Herbert Hoover, her ideal politician, who shared her belief in
individualism and nonviolence.

Jane Addams had become America's "Saint Jane," and

Hull House was her "cathedral." She rode the crest of admiration, often regretting that her own beacon was dimming the accomplishments of other women, even her own co-workers. She was an administrative genius, conferring constantly with the powerful and wealthy to finance her myriad projects, investing, gaining real estate, and earning publicity. At her peak, she was awarded degrees, the first woman to gain one from Yale; she was urged to run not only for a Senate seat but for the White House itself. But Addams was a moderate and a moderator in the midst of whirling ideas. She was always alert to the possibility of smashing into rocks while riding a crest, and at one point she ruefully remarked to a friend, "Woe unto you when all men speak well of you." It wasn't long before Addams's popularity plummeted, and she was branded offensive and un-American.

Jane Addams had stepped onto the unpopular path of pacifism. She was squarely against U.S. involvement in the First World War and set out to use her organizational prowess to prevent it. A life-long pragmatist, Addams could not believe that there was a problem that man could not solve peacefully. Humans are born aggressive, she felt, but the civilizing world should teach them to direct this aggression toward easing poverty, disease, and hunger. She pointed out that as long as the world was violent, women would be treated as inferiors, since they had less physical strength. For these reasons, she supported the American Union Against Militarism, emphasizing that since immigrants could live together in one city, nations could learn to live together on one earth.

In 1907, Jane Addams attended the first National Peace Conference and stated, "We believed that the nations in the past had gone to war with each other because there was no court they could use to settle their difficulties, but that after International Courts were established, they would use them more and more and so finally compose their difficulties without war." The same year she published *The Newer Ideals of Peace,* which became the bible of the women's pacifist movement.

In 1915, Addams traveled to Washington for a convention which led to the new Women's Peace party; three thousand women elected her chairwoman. They put forth an eleven-point program, including a call for a Neutral Conference for Continuous Mediation, limitation of arms, nationalization of the manufacture of arms (to eliminate private war profit), and a "concert of nations" to substitute law for war. Many of these ideas were later adopted by Woodrow Wilson for his Fourteen Points and the League of Nations.

Soon after, Jane Addams became president of the National Peace Federation and led a Women's Peace party delegation to Europe for an International Suffrage Alliance convention. This group was scorned and ridiculed by Americans, including the delegates' own families and personal friends and the government. Nevertheless, they persisted, and an International Committee of Women for Permanent Peace was born out of that meeting, with Jane Addams as its leader. By this time, it was obvious to Addams that all her energies and dedication would have to be focused on peace, and she undertook a European trip that spring, visiting heads of state, foreign officials, the Pope, and soldiers.

When she returned, she gave a speech at Carnegie Hall in New York and told some of the stories she had heard from soldiers, for example, that they were given intoxicants before going into battle. She ended with the declaration that war was an old man's game inflicted on the young, who were far from enthusiastic about fighting.

Addams's popularity fell to its nadir in March 1917 when she visited President Wilson with a final, desperate plea not to enter the war. She was told that fighting was now unavoidable, and just weeks later, on April 2, 1917, America declared war on Germany. The conservative press, the Daughters of the American Revolution, other women's clubs, and fellow social workers all attacked Addams, whom they cursed as pro-German. She was placed high on the Senate blacklist, although Secretary of War Newton Baker remarked that "the name of Jane Addams lends dignity to any list on which it appears."

Addams could do nothing but ride out the storm. She spent the war years and those that followed working at Hull House and devoting her energies to the American Civil Liberties Union (ACLU) and the Women's International League for Peace and Freedom (WIL). The motto of the latter group, which had developed out of the Women's Peace party, was: The dictators of the world will make you fight but the women of the world will make you free! Addams herself stated, "We therefore feel . . . that it is the sacred duty of every woman to claim her share with men in the government of the world." She joined Hoover in his Department of Food Administration to feed the starving in Europe; she traveled to war-torn countries to supervise rehabilitation; she attended the yearly WIL conferences, working to instill the necessity of peace in the minds of state leaders. She continued to be met with great hostility from certain groups, including the military, which opposed her statements against chemical warfare, and the Ku Klux Klan, which threatened to attack her 1924 peace train.

The ACLU was born in 1920 out of the Union Against Militarism into the midst of a Bolshevik scare, which brought all social reform to a screeching halt; so Addams was blocked on her two passionate projects—pacifism and social aid. Her popularity was renewed, however, in these last years. Her experiences were summed up in *Peace and Bread in Time of War*, published in 1922, and widely acclaimed, and by the end of that decade, she had been awarded numerous honors. In 1929, for example, Hull House was feted on its fortieth birthday. Its annual income was now ninety-five thousand dollars, although Ms. Addams had been earning just over one thousand dollars per year for the previous fifteen years. The following year, she celebrated her seventieth birthday

at a party attended by such influential people as the
Morganthaus, the Peabodys, and the Rockefellers.

Years before, Addams had allowed Greek boys to drill in
the courtyard at Hull House, so in 1930, the Greek
government presented her with a medal of military merit.
The same year, she commented: "I believed that peace was
not merely an absence of war but the nurture of human life,
and that in time this nurture would do away with war as a
natural process." This philosophy led to the 1931 Nobel Peace
Prize, which she shared with Nicholas Murray Butler,
president of Columbia University. Jane Addams donated
her portion of the money, approximately sixteen thousand
dollars, to WIL, explaining, "The real cause of war is
misunderstanding. Let this money be spent in the cause of
international understanding."

Jane Addams was too ill to travel to Oslo for her award.
Over the years she had undergone six major operations and
suffered recurrences of spinal trouble. She had survived
typhoid fever, pleuropneumonia, hemorrhaging, angina
pectoris, tuberculosis of the kidney and removal of one
kidney, and appendicitis. She had been ill with bronchitis and
heart trouble, compounded by grief at the deaths of close
friends.

Jane Addams lived four more years, enjoying her
blooming popularity during the New Deal era of concern
about adequate food, justice, and human dignity for all. At
seventy-four, she was honored with a special reception in
Washington, where Eleanor Roosevelt applauded her role in
peace leadership. That spring, she felt a sharp pain in her
abdomen, underwent surgery, and a malignant tumor was
found. Four days later, on May 21, 1935, Jane Addams was
dead.

Fifty thousand people—from Italian laborers to
government heads—paid their respects as Jane Addams lay
in state in Hull House. Messages from all over, from the
president, European leaders, and the "king of the hoboes,"
poured in. A place beside Woodrow Wilson in the national

cathedral was offered for her burial site, but the family grave site in Cedarville, Illinois, was the place Ms. Adams had chosen.

Her massive funeral proved she was a woman for all seasons. She tackled problems a hundred years ago which are still being grappled with today—the situation of women; the discrimination against blacks (she was a founder of the NAACP in 1909); the problems of child care; comprehension of youth; security and prestige for the elderly; the necessity of trade unions; the endless battle with poverty; the obscenity of war.

Yet, there remained traces of that self-effacing little girl who was awed by a handsome father. At one lecture toward the end of her life, a chairman introduced her as "the first citizen of Chicago, the first citizen of America, the first citizen of the world." Jane Addams rose, smiled, and shook her head. "I'm sorry," she replied, "but your chairman must have meant someone else."

But, of course, he didn't. In a provincial world without airplanes or in a world blasé about space explorations, Jane Addams would always be "the first citizen," dedicated to humanity.

8

Ruth St. Denis

Ruth St. Denis, "first lady of American dance," was a theatre revolutionary—a matriarch of modern dance. She instituted an imaginative new philosophy of dance and introduced bold new production techniques. As a result, the American stage received a new face and fresh meaning. "Ruth St. Denis is an amazing woman," wrote dance critic Walter Terry before her death in 1968, "by all odds the most amazing dancer ever produced in this country and certainly the most colorful and interesting of women."

Before St. Denis, American dance had two "personalities" —vigorous, hand-clapping, fun-loving, sex-oriented entertainment for carnival and vaudeville and "culture" imported from Europe.

For a long period of time, America dampened the rise of its own theatre. First, puritanism frowned upon recreation. Next, the hardship of mere existence, the scarcity of people for an audience, and the lack of leisure time and spare energy discouraged theatre entertainment.

When cities began to grow, a demand for amusement grew also, and the more culturally developed countries,

137

England, France, and Italy, were expected to supply it. In 1787, an antitheatre law discouraged European dance troupes from making the treacherous Atlantic Ocean voyage to entertain in the United States. Although this ban was eventually lifted, the new Constitution was written without provision for a minister or a department of fine arts. It was unique for a civilized nation to ignore totally the training, protection, and patronage of art. And since there was no group of wealthy citizens willing to finance private theatre, America was born into an almost total official neglect of the arts.

Outside of New Orleans, no opera companies or ballet troupes were formed. No distinction developed between entertainment and artistry. A citizen craving theatre was usually offered a mélange of Shakespeare, tumbling acrobats, a ballerina, and an animal act to close the show. Yet, the demand existed, so the foreign dancers kept coming, many of them remaining here to teach.

In the 1820s, French ballet took the lead in popularity: "Parisian ballet" amused the American audiences with its acrobatic performances, *pirouettes, pointes,* high leaps, and dizzying spins. When French prima ballerina Fanny Elssler appeared in America, she captured the entire country's spirit. She was everything Americans loved in a performer— dynamic, versatile, and charismatic.

Unfortunately, while Elssler introduced true talent to the United States, she also stifled American creativity. Talented Americans, such as Augusta Maynard, Mary Ann Lee, and one of the few male dancers, George Washington Smith, all mimicked her style. Husband-and-wife dance acts became common during this peak of ballet interest, and often the children were included. Dancing acquired a reputable image.

With the Civil War, however, interest in ballet waned and the status of dancing plunged. Male dancers were ridiculed into oblivion; female dancers were ignored unless they wore scanty clothing, bared their legs, and undulated their bodies. Theatre billboards advertised handsome ballet girls with pseudo-French names to intimate loose morals.

They appeared in elaborate productions with names like "Nymph of the Rainbow" and "The Twelve Temptations." These shows were gaudy and expensive, yet the dancers were paid almost nothing, and they were generally ostracized by polite society. Ironically, low reputation was borne only by dancers; talented singers and actresses enjoyed a higher status.

Also emerging was a contradiction in Victorian morals. Although dancing on the stage was considered depraved, virtually all upper-class girls were given ballet lessons, stressing the rigid classic positions. Dancing teachers became the ultimate arbiters of social grace.

All this was turned upside down by two women, each born around 1877 but on opposite coasts of the United States. They resembled each other in their philosophy and ambition, although they never met. As children, both were instinctive dancers, swaying like the flowers and imitating the ocean's roll. They let nature invade their souls and grew up to seek spirituality from nature in order to express it through their bodies in dance.

They were both to eschew classic dance, which they considered unnatural and distorted. Eventually, they influenced even the trend of traditional ballet, replacing the stilted, individual movements with passion, drama, and continuity. They both insisted upon freedom, and they succeeded in elevating dancing from the level of frivolity to one almost on a par with religion. Both became teachers; both were influenced by the teachings of a Frenchman whom neither met, Francois Delsarte. His theory was that the body is divided into three basic areas: the lower abdomen is the physical zone; the rest of the torso is the spiritual zone; the head is the mental zone.

Both of these women revolutionized dance, not only in their native country but throughout the world. One was Ruth Dennis; she changed her name to Ruth St. Denis. The other was Dora Angela Duncan, whose first name became Isadora.

Isadora Duncan, born in San Francisco, bequeathed a legend as her major legacy. She left no school of technique,

few characteristic movements, no repertoire. But she injected
a new dignity into dancing. She swept away all the stilted
artificiality and restored the basic movements of running,
walking, and skipping.

Yet, sentimentality clouds the significant heritage of
Isadora Duncan. Her belief in free love masked her
contributions to dance in conservative America. So she
received her greatest acceptance and had more influence
elsewhere, particularly Germany and Russia. Ruth St. Denis
was less romanticized, and thus had a more direct influence
in America, inspiring an American tradition in modern
dance.

Ruth St. Denis had a commanding presence on stage,
wearing elaborate, exciting costumes in a dramatic setting.
She was tall and strong, yet elegant and supple even when
well into her eighties. Her hair turned white, prematurely.
Usually she wore a wig when performing, but when her hair
could be used as an effective prop for a dance, St. Denis would
let it hang free.

Walter Terry recalled in his biography of Ruth St. Denis
how electric her stage presence remained all through her
ninety-one years. Once, when she was well into her sixties,
she was marking out movements in rehearsal, walking about
on the stage. She was absorbed in thought; her body looked
loose, flabby, graceless, almost pathetic. Suddenly her music
began, and St. Denis started a low fast turn which spiraled up
and up, until she held still at the end, her body stretched high
and taut. She was as breathtaking as she had always been.

In contrast to her dramatic stage presence, St. Denis
looked almost dowdy in street clothes. While she exuded a
dynamic personality and could hypnotize her companions'
attention, she poured all of her creative energy into her stage
image. She was notoriously absent-minded, which probably
contributed to her lack of concern about her off-stage
appearance. She was known to stroll out of her house in full
exotic costume, head for the theater, and then run back for
her shoes. She could never remember names, so, she called

everyone Dear; yet St. Denis loved being around people and
regaling them with stories about herself, her experiences, and
her plans for the future.

She was also a bit eccentric. While she lived in
California, she moved into the kitchen of her large house. All
her drawings, costumes, programs, makeup, files, poetry,
even her bed, were crammed into the kitchen, where, to her
eyes, everything was organized.

Ruth St. Denis claimed an allegiance to three gods—
physical love, art, and her religion. Yet, she admitted, "I am a
faithless wench, faithless to the three of them. . . . I have
vacillated, turning first to one and then to the other."

Her feelings about physical love were made particularly
clear when St. Denis, close to ninety, made a "personal
pilgrimage" to Perth Amboy, New Jersey, the place where she
was conceived. "Where you were born is unimportant. You're
born in labor, in pain, in considerable messiness. What is
there to celebrate about that? But you are conceived in love,
in passion, in ecstacy. *That* is when it all begins."

Although she remained a virgin until her marriage, at
thirty-three, to Ted Shawn, St. Denis was not shy about her
body; she once posed nude for a photographer, and she
admitted being unfaithful to Shawn many times. Yet, with
her dance troupe, she was a strict, moralistic mother figure,
insisting upon their respectability, virtue, and loyalty.

She appreciated her own worth. Her husband once
commented that St. Denis placed her faith in herself, and if
that failed, in her God, adding, "Sometimes she confuses the
two."

Religion was important in her life. She studied yoga and
the writings of Mary Baker Eddy. She experienced religion in
nature, not in churches, and felt that her body was as
important as her soul in expressing religion. As a child she
would pose in the crucifixion position, trying to understand
more fully the pain of Christ's death. She was also open to
other religions and philosophies, and spent much of her life
expressing herself through Oriental mysticism rather than

Western methodism. Still, religion, like physical love, always
gave way to art. Her brother once claimed that while Ruth St.
Denis was sincerely spiritual, show business came first.

Ruth Dennis was born in Newark, New Jersey, and spent
most of her childhood on a farm near Somerville. Her father,
Thomas, was trained as an electrical engineer, but worked as
an inventor. St. Denis once wrote to him, "Go on building
castles, Father dear. We have to build them first in thoughts
always, only don't stop there. Try not to bite off more than
you can chew, but having taken the bite, chew it!"

His daughter was not to be an improvident dreamer. His
wife saw to that. Ruth Hall Dennis was one of the first female
licensed physicians in the United States, but she ended her
medical practice early. Her primary career was helping her
daughter, whom she considered a genius.

Ruth Hall Dennis was young Ruth's first teacher. She
had Delsarte's book and taught her daughter his theories. She
also instilled in the child her own ideas about natural health
and beauty, stressing the hazards of long skirts and wasp
waists, which were then the fashion. Ruth Hall Dennis also
championed personal freedom, arguing with friends, relatives,
and often her husband for her daughter's right of expression
in an era of restrictions. At a time when dancers were held in
low esteem, Ruth Hall Dennis encouraged her daughter to
develop her talent and was her chief companion until St.
Denis married.

Ruth Hall Dennis was also her daughter's disciplinarian,
for Ruth St. Denis was often an unmanageable, self-centered,
temperamental prodigy. There were times when St. Denis
would be so exasperating in her demands that Mother would
be called in to handle the star. Ruth Hall Dennis never
indulged her daughter.

The second important person in Ruth St. Denis's early
life was her brother, who was rarely called anything but
Brother. He and his mother eventually changed their names
from Dennis to St. Denis, too.

Ruth St. Denis was an intuitive dancer. She had little formal training; in fact, she was once expelled from a ballet school by her teacher, Maria Bonfanti. In her childhood, St. Denis had sporadic lessons, but she learned most by watching traveling shows. Three performances greatly influenced her: When she was nine, she saw a Barnum and Bailey circus finale called "The Burning of Rome," and later she watched a show called "Egypt Through the Ages." Both of these productions were highly theatrical and had a theme of antiquity. The third performance was by Genevieve Stebbins; young Ruth saw how a dancer could move with coordination and spirituality. Later, St. Denis would fuse circuslike sparkle and stagecraft with spirituality and ethnicity, using concepts of both movement and nonmovement.

Ruth St. Denis was a vivacious young girl. She was also enterprising; when she was given a chance to study dancing in New York and needed travel money, she picked and packaged watercress, then sold it to neighbors. This was the start of a lifetime of finding ways to finance some aspect of her career. Once, she entered a marathon bicycle race at Madison Square Garden hoping to win the prize money; she came in sixth. She entered the next race and this time, she won.

Her first job dancing came when her father's farm had to be sold. St. Denis auditioned impromptu in the lobby of a New York vaudeville house-monster museum. She got the job because she was very flexible and could copy any dance movement, including the high kicks so popular in vaudeville.

She was also brilliantly innovative, but in the first ten years of her professional life, St. Denis was busy performing vaudeville dances: "I took an activity and made an art." She had not yet discovered her mission in dance, which was to expand her abilities into three areas—performing, creating, and teaching.

Her first break came as a minor role in a David Belasco show in London. More important to St. Denis's later career

was a side trip to Paris, where the American dancer Loie
Fuller was performing with her Japanese troupe. Fuller was
famous for her use of fabrics, and the delicate Japanese
movements impressed St. Denis. This was stored in her mind,
waiting for the catalyst that would combine the elements into
the giant of the dance world that Ruth St. Denis became.

The catalyst appeared five years later in the form of a
cigarette poster. St. Denis had returned to New York. One
dismal, rainy day, she and a girl friend went to a drugstore
for an ice-cream soda. Perched on a seat, St. Denis glanced up
at an advertisement for Egyptian Deities cigarettes. Pictured
was a temple, flanked by two columns, with a pond of lotus
blossoms in front. In the center sat Isis, mother goddess of
ancient Egypt, contemplative, mysterious, and regal on her
throne.

Suddenly, Ruth St. Denis knew what her dancing must
reflect, and it was not the technicalities of ballet or the
gymnastics of vaudeville. She was going to dance Egypt as a
nation, from its birth to its death. She didn't know how, but
her first step was to get that poster for inspiration, and her
next was to find out as much about ancient Egypt as she
could.

This was the period when St. Denis expanded from a
talented dancer to a creator of dances (the word *choreographer*
had not yet been invented). She later explained her feeling
about dance to Walter Terry: "All I can say is that with my
theory of the androgyne, . . . every artist is both male and
female, and . . . sometimes, the two great elements are in
conjunction within him, so that all by himself he suddenly
gets the melody and the burst of feeling of a great symphony
without any external stimuli." *Egypta* was growing and
developing inside Ruth; it would be her symphony. "In other
words, he has to have that quality of soil which can be
impregnated by the external. And this is what happened to
me—the soil of Egypt must, unconsciously, have lain within
me because my dance not only went to Egypt, but it spread to
the other countries of the Orient."

St. Denis finished out the rest of her Belasco tour, three plays in all—*Zaza, The Auctioneer,* and *Mme. Du Barry.* Belasco was enchanted with her. He had changed her name from Ruth Dennis to Ruth St. Denis; he promised to create a musical for her if she would stay as his star and comedian, but Ruth St. Denis wanted only to dance.

When she finished her tour, she explained to her family what *Egypta* meant to her. Although it was obvious that the production would be too expensive to put together at that time, her family supported her dream. And it was not much more than a dream, for the Western world had never seen anything like what Ruth St. Denis had in mind. Once she began her plan she made sure that the production would be authentic to the final stage prop and smallest hand gesture.

Rather than start with *Egypta,* St. Denis decided to first produce the story of Krishna's beloved *Radha,* using it as an example of the human search for contact with the divine. St. Denis identified with *Radha;* they both possessed spiritual chastity within physical sexuality. She made *Radha* an extremely dramatic production. The setting was the interior of a temple, with a dim light illuminating the bronze figure of *Radha.* As the music started, the statue slowly began to move. *Radha,* danced by Ruth St. Denis, experienced intensely each of the five senses: jewels were savored by her eyes; she listened to beautiful sounds; she inhaled the heady fragrance of flowers; she moved her hands over her body; and she tasted wine. The stimulation of her senses inspired her and she moved into a wildly sensuous dance, her gold skirt swirling about her body. Finally she fell, spent. Then, rising slowly, she returned to her original immobile position in the temple. *Radha* had renounced her senses.

St. Denis and her troupe, a group of Oriental dancers, rehearsed *Radha* in whatever cramped quarters St. Denis could find. She lived with her mother and brother, scraping together money from neighbors, a former boarder at the old family farm, and ultimately from society patronesses.

Radha was planned as a series of scenes, combining

dancing with acting and ceremony. It took seventeen minutes
to perform. For the first performance, St. Denis had to rent
her own space. She invited theatre managers, but none came,
and *Radha* was performed for one cleaning woman. Then, St.
Denis cajoled one manager to pay for a matinee, and he
persuaded other managers to attend. That was Henry Harris,
who became her personal manager until his death on the
Titanic.

St. Denis was booked for several engagements after that
appearance. Once she performed between a monkey act and a
boxing match! *Radha's* selling point, printed in bold letters on
the program, was, "The entire dance will be done in bare
feet."

A group of society women became intrigued with this
exotic newcomer, and they decided to sponsor a matinee
performance. St. Denis put on what would become three of her
most popular dances—*Radha, The Incense,* and *The Cobras.*
That show, on March 22, 1906, was unlike anything the
ladies had ever experienced. Incense burned in the lobby,
ushers were dressed as Orientals, and Ruth St. Denis danced
in her Far East costume of bare midriff and diaphanous
materials. (She once said her costumes made her the
grandmother of the bikini.)

What the audience saw on stage was not an imitation but
an interpretation of the Oriental spirit, bringing to New York
poetic examples of a very old culture. In performing, St. Denis
used no distracting movements; every action was joined to the
next in motions which seemed to ripple down her body into
the earth or up into the air. (Her arm motions once so
fascinated several European physicians that they went
backstage to examine her arm to determine whether or not it
was a normal human arm.)

In *The Incense,* she moved her arms to accompany the
curling smoke of burning incense. She was dressed in a gray
sari and surrounded with gray curtains. When the end of the
dance came, she, like the smoke, disappeared into the setting.

The Cobras was performed in a busy Indian bazaar

setting. St. Denis was the snake charmer. After she settled herself amid the chatter and bustle, her arms and hands appeared, representing the deadly snakes. Huge emerald rings were the cobras' glaring eyes. The "snakes" moved back and forth threateningly. The snake charmer watched every movement, always cautious, always attentive. The snakes glided over her body and, at the climax, they attacked and killed each other. The snake charmer rose, turned her back to the audience, and left—the snakes hanging down her back, their eyes still glaring at the viewers.

It was a provocative afternoon for the society women. Many were shocked, but many praised Ruth St. Denis. She became a minor celebrity at social gatherings. Some years later, even after performing in auditoriums as large as the Hollywood Bowl, St. Denis never denigrated small audiences, distinguishing between "performing" and "dancing." She once said, "It doesn't matter about the size of the audience. I have *performed* for thousands when they found me exotic, the vogue, daring, but I have *danced,* at any given time, for about ten people. They are the ones that saw something more than a novelty, something more than surface. They were the ones I reached. They were the ones that left the theatre forever different from the way they were when they came in. All of my long, long life, I have danced for those ten."

From the beginning of her creative phase, Ruth St. Denis invented many production devices now commonly used in the theatre. She wanted to utilize light, to combine it with color and music to evoke certain moods, so a simple pinwheel device was created which effected a change from one colored light to another. St. Denis also used fabrics to create a mood; the materials were "an extension of the movements of the body into space." Sometimes her ideas were bizarre, as when she danced *The Spirit of the Sea;* the stage was covered with filmy green gauze representing waves and her own white hair was the foam.

Soon after this first success, Harris booked St. Denis and her troupe through Europe and, of course, Mother and

Brother St. Denis went along. They shared her excitement at
her tremendous acclaim. In London, she danced before King
Edward VII; in Paris, she was sketched and adored by Rodin;
and, like Duncan, St. Denis found her greatest audience in
Berlin.

Although St. Denis was recognized as a chaste, though
sensuous, spirit, her costumes remained controversial. In
Berlin, she had a brief encounter with police when they
protested her scanty attire. Years later, an American mayor
threatened to arrest her if she appeared without "fleshlings."
St. Denis knew that fleshlings looked like skin from a
distance and she could not see why she should bother wearing
them. When she saw the mayor in her audience, she
performed wearing her street clothing over her costume. At
certain moments during her performance she tossed an article
of her clothing down to him—her fur, a shoe, gloves. When
she got down to her costume, she repeated the whole dance.
She often claimed she gave birth to the striptease.

While in Europe, St. Denis developed two dances which
became staples in her repertoire: *The Nautsch* and *The Yogi*.
The first interpreted the provocative twirling dances
performed by girls of the East at markets, outside temples,
and before rulers. *Nautsch* dances became so important in
American modern dance that they were routinely learned and
practiced by all serious dance students.

The Yogi was the first dance focusing on the inner being.
It had very little action, the dancer holding the audience's
attention by posing or slowly moving an arm or a leg.

When Ruth St. Denis returned to America in 1909, she
had reached the status of major performer and faced a series
of sold-out performances; she was the first dancer to have a
solo evening series on Broadway. She inspired the hiring of
dance critics for various publications. And, six years after the
cigarette poster episode, *Egypta* was produced.

St. Denis assembled elaborate sets, a huge cast, lavish
costumes, imaginative scenes and lights. Walter Meyerowitz
wrote the score. Every aspect of ancient Egypt was researched

by St. Denis. *Egypta* played to receptive New York and
Boston audiences and then toured the country.

On one such trip, St. Denis made a stop in Denver.
There, a divinity student came to her performance, and as
he watched, he wept. He called her work "a religious
experience," and claimed, "I date my own artistic birth from
that night."

The student's name was Ted Shawn. He was tall, husky,
handsome, and about thirteen years younger than St. Denis.
He had been attending college when diphtheria hit him, and
an overdose of antitoxin caused paralysis in his left leg. He
took up dancing for therapy and never left it. He learned
ballet techniques, flamenco, and pantomime, but for Oriental
dance, he wanted to study with the "unchallenged star in the
field," and that was Ruth St. Denis.

Shawn moved to California where he survived a hectic
routine of working at a full-time job, teaching dance, studying
dance, and performing at afternoon shows. Then he moved
East where he met Brother St. Denis and managed an
introduction to Ruth, hoping he could study with her. This
was three years after he first saw her perform. From the
moment Ted Shawn met Ruth St. Denis, two lives merged to
change American and world theatre and dance.

St. Denis wanted a male dance partner. Nijinsky was a
huge success in Paris, and the Castles were idolized as
ballroom performers. St. Denis knew that a male dancer in
her company would bring in larger audiences. When she
greeted the adoring young man in her new Riverside Drive
house, they hit it off immediately on all levels. They talked
far into the night. He danced for her and she was impressed
with his masculine dances of Greek, Slavic, and Aztec origin.
The next day, an astonished Ted Shawn was offered the
position of Ruth St. Denis's dance partner.

Ten days later they began a new tour; this time without
Mother St. Denis, whose importance slipped to second place.
Ruth and Ted were strongly attracted to each other, but Ruth
St. Denis hesitated before entering into marriage. She

remembered a childhood friend who had married young and aged fast. But puritanical morality won out, and the two were finally wed on August 13, 1914. The bride remained Ruth St. Denis, did not put on a wedding band, and did not promise to obey her husband.

She also never made him a full dance partner. He repeatedly asked for this status, knowing his contributions in their marriage and their career were vital, but St. Denis always replied that it was her reputation that attracted their audiences, and he would have to earn his own reputation. Ted Shawn, in Ruth's eyes, never managed to gain prestige equal to hers.

Although they lived together for fifteen years and were never divorced, Ruth St. Denis had been right in distrusting marriage for herself. "I was a very bad wife to a very good husband," she said. She felt that their wedding was the joining of four, not two, people (because of her theory of androgyny), and all four became confused. Although St. Denis deeply loved Shawn, she felt the tug of her own strong identity. Shawn had an equally strong ego, once calling himself "the Jesus Christ of the dance."

Still, they managed to make dance history. In 1917, they originated a kind of "musical visualization," creating dances to the symphonic works of masters like Beethoven and Schubert. In 1925, St. Denis performed her first dance without music, called *Tragica*. She believed that dance is an independent art and could be performed with or without the accompaniment of music.

But probably their most important contribution to dance was the formation of Denishawn, often called the first university of dance. Together, they managed Denishawn from 1914 to 1934. Here was where "modern dance" took root and flowered. The first location was Los Angeles. By 1918, students were coming from all over the country, and four years later, there were authorized Denishawn schools throughout the United States.

Classes were held out-of-doors on a platform with a canopy over it. This was to give the students a sense of

freedom and openness. Each morning, students placed one
dollar in a cigar box for lessons and lunch. Ted taught much
of the technique and did most of the administrating and
organizing work. "Miss Ruth" lectured and taught Oriental
technique, though she admitted that she was not too fond of
teaching and felt her real worth was as an inspiration to the
students.

Different forms of dance were taught. Shawn wrote, in
his autobiography, "The impact of [Ruth St. Denis's] broad
approach to the dance had strengthened my own
determination not ever to be trapped by one limited style of
dancing." He also defined the aims of the school: "The last
thing we wanted to produce was a facsimile row of pupils who
would be robot imitators of St. Denis and Shawn. Our role, as
we saw it, was to provide the stimulus, knowledge, and
experience essential to the development of dance artists, and
to give encouragement to the imaginative performer."

This made Denishawn vastly different from the ballet
schools to which parents sent their children to develop social
and physical grace. The pupils who came to Denishawn were
individuals who chose to be apprentices to the great masters.
The school had high standards; girls who studied there were
respected. Dancing was once again opened up to male
students who were interested in more than tap and ballroom.
And always, the behavior of the students was dictated and
supervised by St. Denis and Shawn.

Some of America's greatest dancers came out of
Denishawn. Doris Humphrey, teacher and choreographer,
credited Ruth St. Denis with providing her and the other
students, including Charles Weidman, Ernestine Day, and
Pauline Lawrence, with vision and vitality. Martha Graham
studied Oriental dance at Denishawn, varied it, and became
the most important dance personality of her time. Said Ms.
Graham: "Miss Ruth opened a door, and I saw into life."

From these Denishawn alumni came a third generation
of important dancers and choreographers—Agnes DeMille,
Jerome Robbins, Michael Kidd, and José Limon.

To subsidize Denishawn, a company of two stars and

approximately fifteen dancers went on tour for a part of every
year. At times, the company split in two, with some dancers
accompanying Ruth St. Denis on a classical concert-dance
tour and the rest going with Ted Shawn on the vaudeville
circuit. Other times, the entire troupe would put on a
program opening with dancers, barefoot and bare legged,
performing expressive dances followed by exotic ethnic
dances.

The authenticity of the ethnic dances greatly impressed
representatives of Japan and India. They asked St. Denis and
Shawn to visit their countries and help restore to the people a
sense of their traditional culture as well as to perform
American folk and American Indian dances. These were very
popular all over the United States. In performing them, each
dancer was given a challenging solo and an opportunity to
grow and learn.

The Denishawn company traveled to the Orient in 1925–
26. Their program was mostly Americana, although in India,
St. Denis danced *The Nautsch,* which delighted the people. On
that long trip, which included Japan, China, Indochina, Java,
and India, St. Denis and Shawn traveled to many remote
spots where they studied native dancing under the best
teachers. They ordered authentic costumes to be made and
watched the interminable epic dance dramas that were
popular throughout the Far East.

As Denishawn became successful, St. Denis and Shawn
strengthened their individual reputations. Ruth danced at the
William Randolph Hearst Greek Theater at the University of
California at Berkeley; Ted followed, performing with the
first all-male troupe since the ancient days of Greece.

They shared a dream of establishing a central Denishawn
House in New York. This would be a permanent home for
American dance as well as a personal home for them. The
house was dedicated in 1927. At the ceremonies, Ruth St.
Denis placed a hand on the building and quipped, "Every
brick a one-night stand!"

To finance the establishment of Denishawn House, St.

Denis and Shawn accepted an offer of thirty-five hundred
dollars a week to travel with the Ziegfield Follies. They left
Denishawn in the hands of Humphrey and Weidman and
began a grueling tour that lasted thirty-eight weeks; they
often did nine shows a week.

St. Denis was now fifty years old, and increasingly
dissatisfied. Her goal of combining her religion, art, and
physical love had not been achieved. She longed for inner
peace and independence, yet she was caught in a conventional
marriage and rigid schedules. She recognized the self-
centered nature of an artist's life, the need to place individual
work ahead of everything else. She felt she had to break away
from Ted Shawn. She credited him as being the finest male
dancer in the world, but instead of giving him equal billing,
she praised him for "twelve years of service."

The end of their marriage, and of the original
Denishawn, came after a series of performances at Carnegie
Hall. Ruth St. Denis was the first artist ever to perform four
straight shows there. Hundreds of people were turned away.
Dance critics from the *New York Times* and the *Herald-
Tribune* were assigned to cover her performances. At the close
of the series, St. Denis decided to make a speech. She was
touched by her reception and thanked her audience. She went
on to tell how she could now fulfill what she called her *own*
lifelong dream, Denishawn House. Not a word was said about
Ted Shawn. After that, Ruth and Ted separated and went
their own ways.

Although Ted Shawn continued his career and was
successful, establishing his famous summer dance festivals in
Jacob's Pillow, Massachusetts, Ruth St. Denis went into a
slump. Martha Graham, with her stark, evocative expressions
of the Great Depression, was more in tune with the times
than was Ruth St. Denis, who was dedicated to the expression
of beauty.

Ruth once wrote to Ted, "When you're fifty, you're
neither young nor old; you're just uninteresting. When you
are sixty, and still dancing, you become something of a

curiosity. And boy! if you hit seventy and can still get a foot
off the ground, you're phenomenal!" It was not until she once
again defined her aims that she snapped out of her decline.
She returned to the message of the old cigarette poster and its
temple of spiritual peace. St. Denis decided to design her own
temple of dance. There would be no obtrusive pillars; rather,
there would be adequate studio space, an altar-stage, and
room to display the graphic arts. She planned a Rhythmic
Choir, a Society of Spiritual Arts, and a Church of the Divine
Dance. Although this ambitious plan was never completed,
St. Denis went far in persuading churches of the important
part dance could hold in the service.

Ruth St. Denis slowly began to regain prominence as a
dance innovator. In 1937 she was invited to participate in
Dance International, performing with some of her well-known
former students, including Martha Graham and Doris
Humphrey. She was asked to form and to direct a Department
of Dance at the new Adelphi College on Long Island. And
later, St. Denis joined with ethnic dance expert Ms. Russell
Meriweather Hughes ("La Meri") to form the School of Natya.
La Meri performed authentic native dances from around the
world, and St. Denis interpreted the spirit of those dances and
of the people who originated them.

Although St. Denis became increasingly aware of the
limitations that age was placing upon her as a performer, she
continued to dance. She made less flamboyant turns and
fewer high leg extensions. Walter Terry said, "In a way, what
she did became miniature instead of expansive, but she never
lost perfection." Her ego continued to be enormous; she
always felt the need for attention and support. She once
stated: "I've climbed the ladder of success higher than any
American dancer except Isadora. And now I look back in
horror and realize that the rungs of that ladder were people."

Up to the time of her death in 1968, Ruth St. Denis was
active. She joined Ted Shawn occasionally to perform at his
Jacob's Pillow dance festivals and at Carnegie Hall,
Philharmonic Hall, and the New York Museum of Natural

History. She danced on television and planned movies, a television series, and her own Las Vegas act. She worked as a riveter during World War II. And she traveled and kept in contact with her many friends.

It was probably Ted Shawn, the person closest to Ruth St. Denis and most sensitive to her, who finally summarized her status as a dance revolutionary. "She is more than a great dancer. . . . She originated costume, scene, lighting, music, story, and movement, all blended with consummate art in the one unified whole."

Ruth St. Denis, at the end of her life, felt she had succeeded in combining her own three gods—her religion, physical love, art. And because she succeeded, she made dancing a true and lively art.

The Bettmann Archive

Margaret Sanger

According to Victor Hugo, "There is no force in the world so great as that of an idea whose hour has struck."

For Margaret Sanger, the hour began chiming in 1912 during a sweltering New York City summer. Working as a visiting nurse in the Lower East Side slums, she received a frantic call from a man named Jake Sachs. His wife, Sadie, was dying of blood poisoning, the result of an attempted self-abortion. After two weeks of intensive around-the-clock care, Sadie Sachs was out of danger. As Sanger was about to leave for a new job, Sadie broke down in tears. She didn't want any more children. She already had three, was old at twenty-eight, and was as frail in body as in spirit. The only suggestion the doctor made was that Jake sleep on the roof, and then he left.

Margaret Sanger soothed the woman and promised to help, but then she too, left. And she didn't return, being occupied with her other patients, her husband, three children, and a magazine column. Moreover, she had no birth-control information to give Ms. Sachs. A self-appointed guardian of purity, postal censor Anthony Comstock, had been largely responsible for the 1873 federal act which barred "obscene, lewd, lascivious, filthy, and indecent" materials from the mails, and in pre-World War I America, contraception information was considered to be most indecent.

In October, Jake Sachs called Margaret Sanger again. She arrived in time to see Sadie Sachs die from another desperate abortion try. This time when Sanger walked away, she carried with her the burden of Sadie Sachs and all "those poor, weak, wasted, frail women" like her, "pregnant year after year like so many automatic breeding machines."

The feeling of injustice never left her. As Emily Taft Douglas put it, Sanger's task now was "to liberate the masses of poor women from their age-old sexual servitude. She would no longer patch them up to repeat their pitiful ordeals and never again did she take a nursing assignment."

For Margaret Sanger, thirty-two years old, this was *the* social issue she and her generation had to tackle. She saw war, depressions, and colonialism as the inevitable results of overpopulation. However, in late Victorian America, there was still the problem of what one woman could do about birth control, and it took two years of resourceful preparation to even start moving.

Margaret Sanger was a beauty, scarcely five feet tall, slim, small-boned, and erect. Her eyes were wide and gray, and her hair was often described as a "bronze halo." Throughout her life, her delicate attractiveness contrasted with her aggressive social calling, just as the plain black dress she wore for speaking contrasted with her controversial statements.

Sanger was a romantic but worldly sophisticate. Her father bequeathed her an open mind. Sexologist Havelock Ellis added the idea that sex contained "peaceful and consoling and inspiring elements." With this combination, Margaret Sanger set out to prove to the world that sex for women was no longer merely for procreation. In her 1926 book *Married Happiness,* Sanger spelled out her beliefs that the double standard was destructive, for it promoted ignorance, and that having sex provided the radiant strength for all other feats. "To deny its expression cuts one off from the zest and beauty of life," she wrote. This was quite an inflammatory statement, even in the years of the "sexual revolution" and its propagandists Isadora Duncan, Dorothy Parker, and Edna St. Vincent Millay.

Sanger's choice of an activist existence was nourished back in her earliest Corning, New York, days when she first recognized that the rich had a "secret" for limiting the size of their families. She watched the executives in their large hilltop mansions raising one or two children, while the families of factory workers in the city below were crowded together in smoke-blanketed tenements, a new baby every year.

Sanger saw firsthand what too many children do to the poor. Her own mother was not even fifty when she died of consumption. She had raised eleven children. Her husband was a charming but irresponsible tombstone sculptor; her life was a morning-to-night struggle with chores, not only those normally demanded of a mother, but also those usually assumed by the father, such as disciplining the children and budgeting whatever funds were available. Margaret Sanger was convinced that her mother's frail health, surplus of babies, and all the responsibilities killed her. She was to see this situation repeated over and over again during her lifetime of dealing with women from New York to the Orient.

While Margaret Sanger empathized with her mother, it was Michael Higgins, her father, whom she adored. He was a philosopher without a trade. He collected fine books while his wife scraped together the makings of a meager stew; he arranged a speaking engagement for a famous free-thinker named Robert Ingersoll while he hadn't a job himself. In his thick Irish brogue, he told his children, "The one thing I've been able to give you is a free mind."

Higgins also withstood the torments of his more traditional fellow townsmen, ducking tomatoes when he challenged the local priest, and carrying his head high when

all doors to employment slammed shut in his face. His
daughter was to trod the same road of derision in her
adulthood, holding her head just as high while Teddy
Roosevelt called her cause "race suicide" and the clergy
labeled her a "lascivious monster."

Sanger recognized the bravery in her father and was
driven to measure the amount of courage within herself. As a
young child, she decided to cross a narrow railroad bridge
reaching from one side of the Corning River to the other. She
started across, knowing she'd be punished if she were
discovered. Then, when she had reached the middle, she
heard the roar of a coming train. Terrified, she dropped
between the ties and dangled there, watching the river swirl
far below. The train rushed over her, and when it had passed,
a fisherman who had watched the drama helped her to safety.
He urged her to go home, but Margaret was determined to
complete her self-imposed ordeal, so she again started across
the bridge. This time she made it. Margaret, at a very young
age, was convinced that she would always be able to
accomplish what she set out to do.

After that test, Margaret refused to be daunted. Once, at
the local school, she was criticized by a teacher for coming
late, so she stormed home, refusing to return. Her older
sisters, recognizing her capabilities, arranged to send her to
Claverack, a boarding school, and it was there that she
learned how to express herself by making speeches on all the
radical ideas she had picked up from her father, including
women's rights. She began Claverack a shy but determined
little girl and left with a budding flair for leadership.

After Claverack, Margaret Higgins accepted a teaching
job which she planned to hold until she was old enough for
medical school. But at this point, she was called home. Her
mother was dying, and in 1876, when she was not yet
seventeen, Margaret assumed the woman's role of
housekeeper.

After his wife's death, Michael Higgins collapsed with
grief; then he turned into a tyrant. One night, Margaret and

one of her younger sisters, Ethel, arrived home late from a
dance, so Michael locked them out. A few minutes later, he let
Ethel slip in but banned Margaret, claiming she was to
blame. Cold, humiliated, and furious, Margaret spent the
night with a friend, and soon after, she left home. She was not
to be reunited with her beloved father for many years.

This pride, however, helped rob Ms. Higgins of a medical
career. She had no money, so she lowered her sights to
nursing, despite a nagging illness (tuberculosis of the glands).
Her greatest interest was in maternity work, and Margaret
delivered many babies, relishing the joy of the new parents.
But at the same time, she had many poor patients who begged
her to tell them how to avoid another pregnancy. She did not
know how this could be done, and doctors, if they knew the
"secret," would not "corrupt" the young nurse by telling her.

Later, Margaret Higgins, her formal education over, was
assigned to Manhattan Eye and Ear Hospital, where, at a
dance, she met a wiry, dark architect. Ten years older than
Margaret, William Sanger knew many of the literati of New
York. He whisked her into a romantic whirlwind and, in
August 1902, demanded she marry him.

How Margaret reacted to this impetuous behavior is not
clear, for she wrote her sister: "I'm very sorry to have the
thing occur, but yet I am very very happy." As for Bill
Sanger, he confided later that he had felt threatened by
Margaret's many suitors and impelled to act as he did, for to
him, twenty-two-year-old Margaret was "a treasure and the
very embodiment of sunshine."

He found later that no mortal could hope to capture this
sunshine and hold it for long.

Margaret Sanger, though she lived to be almost eighty-
seven, was never a healthy person. As one physician put it,
she "seems to thrive on struggle." She suffered from
glandular disorders, gall bladder problems, appendicitis,
pleurisy, bursitis, insomnia, pneumonia, sacroiliac strain, and
coronary thrombosis. During her first pregnancy, six months
after the Sangers eloped, Margaret's tuberculosis flared up

again. She spent the period of her pregnancy in a sanitarium in the Adirondacks, returning to New York in the autumn to give birth. The child, a boy, was named Stuart. She returned to the sanitarium almost immediately, where she lapsed into depression until the doctors persuaded her to return home and fight for life.

At this point, Ms. Sanger made an effort to become a dedicated wife and mother, and no place seemed more appropriate for this role than the Sanger's suburban home. Bill had built a beautiful house in Hastings-On-Hudson, away from the city grime, but before they were completely settled in, the house burned down. Materialism was futile, Margaret decided after this disappointment. However, the house was rebuilt and the Sangers lived there for eight years, raising three children—Stuart, Grant, and Peggy. And then Margaret Sanger announced that she was certain she would suffocate if she had to spend the rest of her life outside the swing of society, tuberculosis or not, and the Sanger family moved back to New York City.

Ms. Sanger was determined to return to nursing. The Sangers moved into a large apartment, arranged to have the children cared for, and fell in with a circle of reformers that included Walter Lippman, Lincoln Steffans, Mabel Dodge, and Max Eastman. Margaret began writing a column for the socialist paper *The Call,* first, "What Every Mother Should Know" and then, "What Every Girl Should Know." No other publication would dare print the facts of anatomy, and when Ms. Sanger went so far as to discuss gonorrhea, Anthony Comstock stepped in to ban the publication.

This was a stormy era of aggressive socialist politicians like Eugene Debs and John Peter Altgeld, of trust-busting, of the IWW, and of brilliant John Reed and Bill Haywood. It was also a time of paradox for women—they were on a pedestal and in the streets battling for suffrage. Sanger, therefore, devised her own philosophy of socialistic feminism. "When women have raised the standard of sex ideals and purged the human mind of its unclean conception of sex, the fountain of

the race will have been cleaned," she declared. And "if the
unions [are] fighting for better wages and shorter hours, they
should be equally concerned with the size of the working-
man's family." She was now speaking before socialist
gatherings, her Claverack training developing into
magnetism. "To know Margaret Sanger," wrote an associate,
"is to realize that she is not merely a rebel, a crusader, an
indomitable fighter for a cause to which she has dedicated
herself, but that she is also a radiant rebel."

During this time, Sanger was working as a nurse and
was constantly appalled by the living conditions of the people
she visited. The Health Department reported that one-fifth of
all babies died; overcrowding was common. Bathtubs, toilets,
even sunlight were rare in the flats, and women used any
means to avoid the desperation which was inevitable with
each pregnancy. Since contraception was taboo, they resorted
to abortion by means of shoe hooks, knitting needles,
turpentine, or the local five-dollar abortionist. When all that
failed, more than one woman was driven to put her head in
the gas oven.

And then Sadie Sachs died, and Margaret Sanger
refocused her life. No longer would she just mouth the words,
"No woman can call herself free until she can choose
consciously whether she will or will not be a mother." To her,
abortion was an unnecessarily extreme alternative to
prevention. Sanger now would live her philosophy and work
to make contraception an acceptable choice in life.

Margaret Sanger found that doctors knew no more than
she did. She scoured the libraries, but except for books and
articles by Krafft-Ebing and Havelock Ellis, there was no
information on sex; Anthony Comstock had seen to that.
Slowly, Sanger found herself drifting apart from her socialist
friends, who were concentrating on economic reform. She
drew away from the feminists who were fighting for suffrage
and did not want to jeopardize their progress by attaching
themselves to such a controversial cause as birth control.

Most important of all, Sanger moved further and further away from her husband. She had long ago begun to question the romantic abandon that had attracted her to Bill. Like her father, he was irresponsible about money, spending it on opera tickets and Japanese robes rather than saving it, and though Margaret was at first flattered, she soon saw the similarity between the two men, and was fearful of it.

In October 1913, the Sangers decided to sail to France. Bill would study painting, and Margaret would try to discover how French women had succeeded in limiting their families since the time of the Napoleonic Code, which decreed that all children, not just the first son, would share equally in a man's estate. This had provided a strong incentive to overcome the inevitable result of what had been the poor man's only luxury —sex. Margaret and Bill also hoped to find some reason to reconcile.

While her husband painted, Margaret Sanger found out that the French "secret" was tampons, suppositories, and douches, and that this information was passed down from mother to daughter. She scribbled copious notes and purchased samples of contraceptives and then was anxious to get back to the United States and share what she had learned. Without articulating her feelings, she sensed she and Bill no longer had a basis for a common life, although they shared affection. Margaret urged Bill to remain in Paris to paint, and on New Year's Eve, she and the children sailed back to New York. Bill realized that, while he deeply loved his "sunshine," her devotion was to her cause.

On her return to New York, Ms. Sanger's first step was to publish a brash, down-to-earth newsletter called *The Woman Rebel;* its purpose was to "stimulate working women to think for themselves and to build up a conscious, fighting character." In the first issue, she introduced a brand-new phrase, *birth control.* In 1914, she organized the National Birth Control League, and Margaret Sanger's dream was in action.

Eight issues of *The Woman Rebel* were published before the Comstock Laws stopped its publication, but Sanger had already hit upon the evils of child labor, the exploitation of women in industry, health problems, social hygiene, and the rapidly growing population. "Woman must be mistress of her own body," she cried out in print.

Michael Higgins, back in Corning, shared his other children's embarrassment over Margaret's activities. He traveled to New York, hoping to convince her to settle down to a more conventional life, but while he was sermonizing, there came a knock on the apartment door. Two federal officers served Sanger with an indictment on nine counts of violating federal statutes. Margaret Sanger could be imprisoned for up to forty-five years.

Sanger invited the officers in. She began to explain the tragedy of Sadie Sachs, the hundred thousand known abortions every year, the despair of having too many children. The agents, and Michael Higgins, listened and were touched. The judge apparently was touched too, for when Sanger was arraigned, the trial was postponed for six weeks.

When Archduke Ferdinand's assassination ignited a war in Europe, Margaret Sanger was frantically organizing her contraception information and writing a pamphlet which she called *Family Limitation*. She trudged from printer to printer, but no one would publish it. Finally she succeeded in finding someone who would print a hundred thousand copies, although eventually a hundred times that number would be distributed. The pamphlets were put aside, however, when Sanger went to court.

This time the judge was not so sympathetic. He gave her eighteen hours to get herself a lawyer and a plea, and to prepare her case. Bill Sanger had returned home and joined her lawyer and friends in urging her to plead guilty. This Margaret Sanger would not do; it would be putting birth control on the same level with obscenity. Bill argued that she could do little for her cause if she were in jail. Finally, weary but decisive, Margaret packed a bag, wrote the judge and district attorney of her plans, and before the next morning, was headed for England. She had no money, no companions, no passport.

At sea, Sanger sent telegrams back home authorizing the release of *Family Limitation*. Next, she met a British government official who would help her enter England without a passport. In London, Sanger began the process of educating herself. She met the Drysdales from the Neo-Malthusian League, and she learned of Malthus, who had recognized in the late eighteenth century the danger to the economy of excessive population growth; she learned also of the Americans who had tried to educate the people on contraception only to be thrown into jail before any "harm" was done, and of Annie Besent, who fought the British courts after publishing writings of one of these Americans and who finally won an appeal from the higher courts.

Day after day, Sanger haunted the British Museum, studying the writers and philosophers who had tackled the overpopulation problem. And then she met the current prophet of sex research—Havelock Ellis.

From the beginning, there was a mutual romantic attraction. Ellis, tall, brooding, with white flowing hair and beard, was much older than Sanger, yet the two had such an emotional and intellectual affinity that they considered themselves "twins." Though Ellis was married, Sanger was to be his close friend until his death, bringing him gifts and representing his interests in America. But even Ellis could not hold Sanger, and eventually she left for Holland to continue her study of birth control.

Holland was far ahead of the world in this area, with the lowest maternity death rate in the world (the United States had the highest), the lowest infant mortality rate, the lowest venereal disease rate, and few prostitutes and illegitimate births. Two Dutch physicians had developed the diaphragm, which eventually spread throughout the world.

Sanger saw immediately that the Dutch did not consider birth control to be obscene; they believed it was necessary for

a progressive society. She wanted to bring this attitude to
America. Sanger learned also that medical skill was needed
to determine the best kind of contraception for each woman,
to keep medical records (which Holland neglected to do), and
to place birth control in the category of medicine. For her, the
time of pamphlet writing was over.

Although Sanger never espoused a formal religion, she
was a spiritual person with a sense of destiny. At different
times she embraced astrology and Rosicrucianism, and finally
she discovered that her own inner strength could see her
through any crisis.

She returned to London, and then a sense of foreboding
caused her to travel home to the United States. Just before
she sailed, the notice came that her husband was in jail for
selling a copy of *Family Limitation* to a man who claimed to
be a worried father, but who in reality had been sent as a
decoy by Comstock.

Faced with a fine or thirty days in jail, Bill Sanger
retorted, "I would rather be in jail with my self-respect than
in your place without it."

Margaret knew her sentence would be much harsher
than Bill's, but she sailed home immediately. The strange
premonition of doom still nagged at her, even when she
touched shore and found that public opinion was on her side.
Liberals everywhere were critical of Bill Sanger's trial, the
term *birth control* was in fairly wide use, and Anthony
Comstock was dead.

The first hint of disaster came when the new president of
the National Birth Control League denounced Sanger's tactics
as lawless and refused to support her at her trial. The
Academy of Medicine also backed away, after leaving a token
ten dollars for her cause. Margaret Sanger was without funds.
As a final, tragic blow, her daughter Peggy came down with
pneumonia, and, within a week, she was dead. Ms. Sanger
was shattered. This was later described as the greatest blow
of her life. Peggy's death numbed her.

Now Margaret Sanger began drawing upon her inner
strength. She refused a postponement of her trial, not

wanting to put off her work because of personal suffering. She would continue this way of living the rest of her life, ignoring even intense physical pain until her specific responsibility was taken care of. However, her sorrow touched the country, money began pouring in, and at her trial in December 1915, Margaret Sanger was no longer standing alone.

She was offered her freedom if she would make a simple promise to not break the law anymore. Sanger refused; she had done nothing obscene (and therefore illegal) and would not "admit" that she had. Threat of jail did not intimidate her. When her lawyer disagreed with her stand, she decided to plead her own case.

The tide of public opinion was with her now. Half the jury was made up of women. From England came a petition signed by such illuminaries as Marie Stopes and H. G. Wells; and then there was her image of heroine and grieving mother, standing against the world. It was too much for the government. The trial was postponed and finally declared *nolle prosequi*. Sanger, though relieved because she would not have to go to jail, was disappointed because the basic issue was not settled. She felt it was a good time to bring her message to the people of the country.

When she went on tour, Margaret Sanger saw that fame does not mean acceptance. Many women's clubs denounced her. She ran into Catholic opposition as her father had in Corning; and in St. Louis, the theatre she was to speak in was locked because of a Catholic threat of boycott. In total, however, the tour was a plus, and after three and a half months, Sanger was exhausted. Still, she was touched by stories told by desperate mothers throughout the country. One woman confided: "I wonder even if my body does survive this next birth, if my reason will." Sanger was convinced that speeches were not sufficient, and so, on October 16, 1916, she and her sister, Ethel Byrne, set up the first birth-control clinic. It was in Brownsville, Brooklyn.

The first day, she had one hundred forty patients; women stood in line from dawn to closing. Nine days later, a policewoman, posing as a neighborhood woman, came in and

picked up "What Every Girl Should Know." Very soon
thereafter, the clinic was raided.

Sanger was furious that a woman had conducted the raid,
and she refused to be carried off to jail; instead, she marched
ahead of the Black Maria. Once in the station house she
refused to be fingerprinted because she would not have her
cause connected with criminal activities. She was put
overnight in a cell infested with cockroaches, bedbugs, and
rats.

Ethel Byrne's trial came first, on January 8, 1917. She
was sentenced to thirty days at hard labor, and to protest the
harsh sentence, Byrne announced she would go on a hunger
strike. Sanger watched her sister deteriorate from starvation
and finally, breaking a promise not to interfere, she vowed to
the courts that Byrne would not break the law again. Ethel
Byrne was out of the battle, but she had become the first
American woman to employ physical defiance of injustice.

At her trial, Sanger wanted to test the constitutionality
of Penal Code Section 1142, which banned the dispensing of
contraceptive advice. Again, Sanger was offered leniency if
she would obey the law from then on. "I cannot promise to
obey a law I do not respect," she replied, and was rather
surprised that she got only thirty days in jail. Again, she
refused to be examined or fingerprinted, but did not plan a
hunger strike, which she felt would only be anticlimactic
after Byrne's ordeal. Anyway, the impending war was
grabbing all the headlines.

Sanger's confinement was rather easy. She spent her
time lecturing to the inmates on birth control, teaching them
to read and to write, and corresponding with her friends,
among them Eugene Debs, who wrote her, "You have in you
the stuff that stands; you are bound to win." Finally, the
month was up, and when she left the jail, Sanger was greeted
by a crowd singing "La Marseillaise." She later wrote, "All
the beauty and tragedy and hope of life's struggle seemed
crammed in that moment of my life."

Sanger garnered bits of wisdom from every experience.

Now she was convinced that it was up to the wealthy and intelligent women to influence the poor, because poverty mothers were too immersed in staying alive to fight for much more. She formed the Committee of One Hundred with the help of her socialite friend Juliet Rublee, who would stand by her side for many years, coordinating fund-raising activities for birth-control publications and, later, for clinics.

The years just prior to women's receiving the vote were taxing for Margaret Sanger. She was constantly blocked by hostility and by financial problems. She made a low-budget motion picture called *The Hand That Rocks the Cradle,* which could not be shown because it contained the words *birth control*. Her appeal for a reversal of that court decision was denied. But strangely, the purpose Sanger originally aimed for was achieved, for the same decision said that physicians may prescribe contraceptives to prevent or cure a disease, with disease meaning any change of state to the body that might bring on pain or illness. This broadening of the term was a big step forward for birth control.

Sanger continued lecturing and then, with her friends' backing, she founded a new publication called *Birth Control Review,* which was to be her platform for twenty-three years. She poured every cent she earned into the *Review,* denying herself all comforts. She lived in a shabby flat in Chelsea, her friends often loaning her clothes for her speaking engagements. As Armistice Day drew close, Margaret Sanger was running out of energy. She was told she must rest.

She was having a difficult time raising her children too. The boys lived at a boarding school, and Ms. Sanger was torn between spending time with them and working for birth control. She was very hurt when she was attacked for being a part-time mother. She took advantage of every opportunity to spend time with the boys. Once she was offered an advance by a publishing company for a book on labor relations. She accepted, and took her son Grant with her to California to spend time with her while she wrote the book. The book was called *Woman and the New Race.* It linked labor problems,

and all other social problems, to woman's "biological slavery."
She stressed the need for woman to define her own freedom.
The book came out in 1920, and a quarter of a million copies
were sold. Basking in this success, Sanger returned to
England.

England, in 1920, shone with such intellectual lights as
H. G. Wells, Harold Child, and Hugh de Selincourt, all of
whom eventually enjoyed romantic interludes with Sanger.
The atmosphere was one of love and of sharing love; the
enjoyment of sex was uppermost since they all believed
jealousy made woman a property of man.

Margaret Sanger was adored here, romantically and
intellectually. Wells once said of her, "Both [Alexander the
Great] and Napoleon were forced into fame by circumstances
outside of themselves and by currents of the time, but
Margaret Sanger made currents and circumstances. When the
history of our civilization is written, it will be a biological
history and Margaret Sanger will be its heroine."

Nevertheless, Sanger, unlike others such as Isadora
Duncan, reaped only the benefits of this free-love attitude,
and emerged unscathed. Her passion, of course, was always
birth control. "All the world of human beings is a passing
show," she wrote. "They come and go . . . but the idea of
human freedom grows ever closer around one's heart and
comforts and consoles and delights."

She visited war-devastated Germany at this time,
investigating rumors of a contraceptive jelly being developed
there. Her search took her from city to city; she finally found
a small factory which made the jelly, but it was too costly for
mass distribution. Nevertheless, she secured samples with the
idea of manufacturing a cheaper version.

With Sanger gone, Americans returned to an apathetic
attitude about contraception. She returned home in December
1920, eager to persuade people that birth control was
necessary for world peace. She had seen the misery of postwar
Germany; she believed that the overpopulated Far East,
particularly Japan, posed the next threat.

First, Sanger had to get the medical profession on her side. Juliet Rublee tried to help by inviting doctors to her apartment for dinner and then embroiling them in an argument about birth control. At the right moment, Rublee phoned Sanger, who appeared shortly thereafter, demurely clad, to answer all questions.

Slowly, support returned to her cause. University professors and the New York State Federation of Women's Clubs finally gave contraception their nod; books and pamphlets could now be passed out without interference by the law.

Sanger was in the process of organizing the first national birth control conference in this country when she was stricken again with tuberculosis of the glands. Urged to rest, she sailed back to England, where not only was she entertained and feted by her admirers, but she had her tonsils removed and immediately felt better. England, to her, was a tonic. When she returned home this time, she was ready for work, and she had a new beau in tow, J. Noah Slee, president of the 3-in-1 Oil Company. Like Havelock Ellis and H. G. Wells, he was much older than Sanger, but unlike the others, Slee eventually won Sanger, and to a limited degree, held her.

Sanger set up the American Birth Control League to help with the conference, set for November 11. The grand climax was to be a rally at Town Hall, paid for three weeks in advance and scheduled for seven in the evening. But the Catholic church stepped in, recognizing Margaret Sanger as a serious foe, and when she and her conference reached Town Hall, they found police blocking the door.

Sanger fought her way inside, climbed on the stage, and insisted she be arrested so she could take the case to court. Her audience crowded in after her, and the police moved to push them out. Anyone who approached the microphone was arrested; the people rioted. At the back of the auditorium stood Monsignor Dineen, secretary to Archbishop Patrick J. Hayes, quietly nodding his directions to the police. Finally, he ordered them to arrest Margaret Sanger. Again Sanger

marched to the station house, refusing to ride in the police
wagon. The people around her sang "My Country 'Tis of Thee"
and hissed at the police.

The next day the farce continued. Sanger appeared before
the judge, but the arresting police captain did not show up.
The assistant district attorney had to admit there was no
evidence, and the case was dismissed.

Sanger realized that Archbishop Hayes' church was a
powerful force in New York and that it had placed itself
squarely against all her goals. Although even the most
conservative press pictured Margaret as a defender of
constitutional freedoms rather than a radical extremist, she
knew religious opposition was not over.

The following year, Margaret Sanger was invited to visit
Japan, the only woman in a group that included Bertrand
Russell, Albert Einstein, and H. G. Wells. With her went her
thirteen-year-old son Grant and Noah Slee. The trip was
filled with confusion. While Japanese progressives, including
Baroness Shidzue Ishimoto, were on her side, the growing
military clique was not. First, she was denied a visa and her
ship reservations were cancelled. She finally headed for
China, hoping to get from there to Japan, but rumors
preceded her: she was a secret agent sent to deplete the
population so America could invade; she was a person bearing
"dangerous thoughts." Yet, when Sanger finally arrived and
began her tour, she met her most appreciative audiences. In
fact, it was said that "since the time of Commodore Perry, no
American has created a greater sensation in the land of the
Mikado than Margaret Sanger." Because of this tour, she
became less of a compassionate viewer of women's emotional
problems and more of a scientific evaluator of the political
implications of population growth. Despite the fact that
women in Japan were no more than exploited servants of the
male sex, Sanger found that decency rather than prejudice
met her everywhere. But the trip was hectic, and Sanger
came down with pneumonia.

After resting, the three moved westward through the

Orient. Sanger was sickened by the unfortunate condition of
the common people: coolies who barely eked out an existence;
the custom of drowning female babies; the uncontrolled
breeding. In Cairo, Grant came down with a serious case of
dysentery, and Sanger, again sensing a tragedy, was terrified
that she would lose him. But the boy recovered, and Noah
insisted on taking him to Switzerland. Later, Grant asked to
go home to his own life and friends. Sanger agreed and
continued to London, where she was to attend the Fifth
International Malthusian and Birth Control Conference.
Noah Slee met her there.

In England, Sanger's emotions were divided between her
work with the conference and her personal life. Noah Slee
wanted to marry her, but her old friends also vied for her
attention. She realized that while these great men worshiped
her, they also demanded her worship of them. Noah Slee, on
the other hand, was willing to adopt birth control as his
project. He also had the know-how and the capital to help the
cause.

It's not certain when the two wed. Though they
announced their marriage in 1924, it was evident that they
had married earlier, perhaps during this stay in London.
They made an agreement to always respect each other's
individuality, maintaining separate apartments in the same
house and taking nothing for granted, not even dining
together. They were not to interfere with the pattern of each
other's lives. As long as both kept to this agreement, the
marriage was successful.

Before leaving London, Sanger arranged to hold an
international conference in America in 1925. But, on reaching
New York, she found that birth control had again screeched
to a halt during her absence. Sanger set to work on a new
clinic, which she called the Clinical Research Bureau. Dr.
Dorothy Bocker was hired to run it, mainly as a research and
record center, testing contraceptive methods for other clinics
to eventually use. There were patients, of course, and
Sanger's heart went out particularly to the young Catholic

women who came to her knowing the vehement position their church took against birth control.

The Bureau was a contraception study center for scientists, doctors, and sociologists. In October 1923, Sanger presented the first-year report of the Bureau's activities at the Midwestern States Birth Control Conference. The next year, Sanger had to make the difficult administrative decision to replace Dr. Blocker with Dr. Hannah Stone, who was more experienced in gynecology. When Stone accepted the post, she made quite a sacrifice, for she was asked to resign her position at New York's Lying-In Hospital and was refused membership in the New York County Medical Society for many years. She worked for Sanger without salary and became, with her husband, Dr. Abraham Stone, a leader in the movement until her death. With her help, the Bureau was a great success and soon had to move to larger quarters. By the end of the twenties, evening sessions had been added, assistants had been hired, appointments had to be made two weeks in advance, and fifty-five new clinics had been set up throughout the country. The policy of the Bureau was to respect the decision from Margaret Sanger's court trial: contraceptives were to be given only when pregnancy would alter the condition of the patient's body.

Meanwhile, Dr. Stone and the newest Bureau physician, James F. Cooper, were developing a new version of the German contraceptive jelly to use with diaphragms, which Noah Slee was smuggling into his New Jersey factory from Europe. (American factories would not produce the particular type of rubber that was needed.) He was also packaging the contraceptive jelly as it was developed and loaned fifteen thousand dollars to a company for the production of an American-made diaphragm. Neither he nor Sanger involved themselves in profit making from any of these ventures, though they could have made millions.

The late 1920s were both good and bad for Margaret. She enjoyed great acclaim, and her movement gained respect. Arthur Schlesinger, Sr., called her the "outstanding social

warrior of the century." After years of poverty, she now had
financial ease, thanks to Slee, who built her a beautiful
English manor called Willow Lake above New York City.
Here she entertained her friends and family, establishing for
her parties a tradition of good food, entertainment, and
costumes, usually with an ethnic flair. In her forties,
Margaret Sanger was still very beautiful; Slee's daughter
once likened her to a ladies' magazine model with "delicate,
oval face, sloping shoulders."

Because of Dr. Cooper, Margaret Sanger also experienced
some success with the medical community. He traveled
widely; in one year he visited almost every state, telling
individual doctors about the advantages of recommending the
diaphragm and jelly. Thanks to him, many of the Bureau's
cases were written up in the *Medical Journal and Record,* and
medical people came to her Sixth International Conference. In
fact, it was here that Dr. William Allen Pusey, president of
the American Medical Association, gave the movement
official sanction.

But the Catholic church had not given up its fight
against Margaret, and after the Town Hall debacle, it was
open warfare. Catholic mayors of New York and Boston would
wait until she had reserved and paid for a hall and then
refuse to grant her permission to speak. In Cincinnati, the
Knights of Columbus warned it would cancel its own
conventions there if she were permitted to speak in the city,
and in 1925 and 1926, when Sanger was busy trying to force
birth-control bills through the legislatures of New York,
Connecticut, and New Jersey, the attacks on her moral life
were vicious. Other religious groups were coming around,
however; Sanger's first backing came from the Unitarian
Church of Cleveland in 1916, and ten years later, many
Jewish and Protestant groups had joined her effort.

Sanger's international conference opened in New York on
March 25, 1925, after months of frantic preparation and
tenuous financing (so tenuous, in fact, that even though she
had managed to bring her guest speakers to the United

States, she wasn't certain how she would get them back to their own countries). She was exhilarated with the success of the conference, however, and as soon as it ended, Sanger began formulating an even larger conference to be held two years hence in Geneva, home of the League of Nations.

While Sanger was working on this, her sister Mary and her father died. She had not visited Michael Higgins often these last years, although he lived nearby on Cape Cod in a cottage she had bought for him. Perhaps because she remembered him as the first positive influence on her life, she could not bear to see him old and incapacitated, and later, paralyzed.

The new Geneva conference tapped every bit of Margaret's energy and much of Noah's fortune. Her goal was to get an authoritative report on the threat of overpopulation to world peace. She saw Germany and Italy repopulating and taking new land. She heard that the Japanese military had conscripted ten million citizens for an army to conquer Manchuria.

And then, once again, her plans were halted by Catholic barriers; Italy, Spain, Belgium, and Catholic Germany demanded that her name be removed from the Geneva conference rolls to rid the conference of any controversial flavor. They insisted that no mention be made of birth control and all related books on display be removed.

Julian Huxley pleaded for retaining Sanger's name, but Sanger finally agreed to strike her name to save the conference. As it turned out, the delegates gave her a great ovation and an official statement was made saying no nation has the right to use expansion or war as a remedy for an overpopulation problem.

Sanger next planned a lecture tour through India, but collapsed before the plans materialized. While resting a few days in St. Moritz, she received word from New York that the Birth Control League was being reorganized by a days in St. Moritz, she received word from New York that the Birth Control League was being reorganized by a conservative block which sought to avoid any more controversy by taking respectable small steps over a long

period of time. Her newspaper was also being threatened, and
to avoid an internal split which could cripple the movement
for years, Margart Sanger agreed to let go, insisting only on
control of the Bureau, since this, she felt, was the core of the
movement. After sixteen years, this was all she had. Yet,
Sanger insisted, this was only the end of an era and another
would follow. In February 1929, she wrote, "I am a new, vital
being again, ready and free to forge ahead and fight as never
before."

Despite her spirited words, Sanger was depressed that
winter. Her son Stuart was suffering from a serious mastoid
condition and while she was taking him to the hospital on
April 15, she was called to the Bureau. When she got there,
she found the clinic ravaged, her files scattered, her staff
arrested. The Brownsville raid of eleven years earlier had
been repeated. Sanger learned that a policewoman, Anna K.
McNamara, had masqueraded as a patient a month before
and had set up the raid. Now, as before, Margaret Sanger was
taken to the police station, where she resisted fingerprinting
and saw herself booked on the same statute as she had been
previously.

This time the raid was denounced by the press, the
medical world, and social figures such as the Vanderbilts and
the Reids. When the trial opened on April 19, so many
spectators came that there was hardly standing room.
Sanger's attorney wanted to do more than merely defend the
1918 decision; he wanted to establish once and for all the
public's right to a birth control clinic. He also wanted on
record the fact that a mother's health was connected with the
spacing of her children.

Although it was never proven, the raid was most likely
instigated by the Roman Catholic hierarchy of the city. Mary
Sullivan, chief of the Policewoman's Bureau, who conducted
the raid, refused to reveal any connection with the church.
But Sanger later made a private investigation and reported
that because so many poor Catholics had benefited from her
Bureau, Catholic social workers had complained to Catholic

policewomen. Mary Sullivan was directed to raid the Clinical Research Bureau. The order was reported to have come from Archbishop Hayes.

But this was the last attack on Margaret Sanger. The trial magistrate decided that a doctor could recommend that a married woman have contraceptives and he could instruct her on their use. Because of this law and concurrent medical backing, the number of clinics in the following eight-year period expanded to 374. Sanger's own Bureau was now bursting with eighteen hundred patients a month, so Noah Slee bought a new clinic building on West Sixteenth Street. Another ironic twist—several months after the trial, Anne McNamara, the decoy patient, came back to ask for help in controlling the size of her own family.

As the 1920s drew to a close, Margaret Sanger and a group of her wealthy women friends worked to get a Doctor's Bill through Congress. This bill was drawn up with the help of medical experts and aimed to open the mails to birth control information and material sent from doctor to patient. It almost made it. To get the bill through, Sanger organized the National Committee for Federal Legislation for Birth Control, with branches across the country. This committee was eventually supported by the press, prestigious clubs, religious organizations, and twenty million women. But it was not supported by the Catholic church. Influential Father Coughlin, for one, denounced the bill as "a surrender to the ideals of paganism," especially at this time when the church was urging its people to populate the world.

Margaret Sanger trudged from congressman to congressman, tirelessly persuading them, even changing her accent to charm a Southerner. When the hearings came up in February 1931, she stood before the committee in her simple black dress, looking as conservative as her message was radical. In her slight voice, she bombarded the congressmen with statistics of maternal and infant mortality; she told them how, at her Bureau, each patient had undergone an average of 1 abortion for every 2.5 pregnancies and that seven hundred thousand abortions were being performed a year.

To the Roman Catholic spokesmen, backed by the Purity League, the Clean Books League, and the Society for the Suppression of Vice, Sanger pointed out that Catholics had a perfect right to depend upon self-control if they wished, but the rest of the American people should be able to enjoy the pursuit of happiness, health, and peace as they saw fit. Still, she lost. The bill did not pass.

Sanger's aim was to reintroduce the Doctor's Bill at the next session. The bill came close to getting through in 1934, when it was passed by a voice vote. But then, Pat McCarran asked that the bill be recalled and it went back to committee, where it died.

Nevertheless, the bill's objectives were gained with a court decision in *United States* v. *One Package*. This "package" was a bundle of contraceptives sent to Dr. Hannah Stone. The court decreed: "We cannot assume that Congress intended to interfere with doctors prescribing for the health of the people." The government appealed and lost. Birth control advocates were jubilant, although Sanger had been burned too often and knew that the government still had until 1937 to appeal again. But the attorney general announced he would abide by the earlier decisions, and this triumph, known as the "one-package victory" was the high point of the movement.

Meanwhile, Margaret Sanger was traveling extensively. She went to Germany to set up a birth-control clinic; then she went to Russia to inspect their birth-control program. There she found abortions were more prevalent than contraception, since the government wanted to boost the population and did not allow birth-control information to get to women. She came away disheartened.

In 1935, Sanger was invited to the All-India Women's Conference. It was during this trip that she spent two days with Mahatma Gandhi. She was in awe of his discipline and inner strength, but, practically speaking, they were at odds; Gandhi believed total abstinence was the only acceptable

method of birth control. In India, Sanger got her greatest
support from Mme. Pandit, future ambassador to the United
Nations. (She found encouragement there also, years later,
from Nehru.) This tour of ten thousand miles took her to
Rangoon, Malaya, and Hong Kong, where she had a gall
bladder attack and was hospitalized for two weeks. It wasn't
until 1937, after the "one-package victory," that she allowed
herself the surgery to take care of it. Margaret Sanger never
had time for her health.

She was very concerned about her sons' health, however.
Grant was attending Cornell Medical School. Stuart was
chronically ill with mastoiditis, and when he was preparing to
undergo his tenth operation, Sanger decided to move with
him to Tucson. There the Slees settled, and Stuart began
recuperating almost immediately. In time, he was sufficiently
recovered to enter medical school too.

As the war approached, Sanger was asked by Mme.
Chiang Kai-shek to visit China. On board ship Ms. Sanger
fell and broke her arm. Though the arm was set by the ship's
doctor, it had to be reset in Japan. Sanger was in great pain,
so an associate took her place in Shanghai. Then Sanger
learned that Shanghai had been bombed, and her friend had
just avoided being killed. At about the same time, Japan
closed all its birth-control clinics, placed Baroness Ishimoto,
the founder of birth control in Japan, under surveillance, and
forced Sanger to return home.

Reaction against birth control was occurring all over the
world. Birth control was damned in Germany, France, and
Italy. In America, Connecticut held to its ban against
contraceptives, and Boston said birth control was unpatriotic.
Doors were slamming in Sanger's face.

To add to her problems, Sanger's closest friends were
dying. Havelock Ellis died in 1939; Margaret wrote, "A
world's work done. What more can one ask of life? Finis." Dr.
Hannah Stone died suddenly in 1941. Noah Slee was well into
his seventies, and now Margaret Sanger stayed close to home
and her husband. Stuart and his wife gave Margaret her first

grandchild, a namesake, who became very close to her
grandmother, in a way replacing Margaret's own lost Peggy.

Slee's health deteriorated rapidly during these years, and
he was increasingly more depressed with his weakness and
incapacity. Ironically, it was during the months before his
death in 1943 that Noah Slee finally had his wife to himself,
and he relished that.

After the war, Margaret Sanger, now in her sixties, was
in poor health but indefatigable. She traveled to Sweden and
England, hoping to reactivate concern for birth control, now
at a low ebb. She instigated an international conference,
hoping to have Japan again exposed to her views, but General
Douglas MacArthur would now allow her in that country. The
reason printed in a Japanese newspaper was: "In view of the
pressure from Catholic church groups, it was believed
impossible for General MacArthur to allow her to lecture to
Japanese audiences without appearing to subscribe to her
views." The Catholics were influential, certainly, although
they numbered only one hundred thirty thousand against the
total population of eighty million.

MacArthur's stand was condemned by Eleanor Roosevelt
in her column, but even after MacArthur was removed from
Japan, Sanger was unable to get there. She suffered a
coronary thrombosis, which resulted in severe angina pains
until her death.

During these years, Margaret Sanger seemed to live only
to get the movement in motion again. She faced pain with
stoicism, ignoring it until the job at hand was over. When she
finally got to Japan, it was 1952, and her expectations of
welcome were multiplied beyond her dreams. A repeat trip to
India drew the same acclaim, although she realized that she
would not reach the poor people who needed her most. It was
at this time that the International Planned Parenthood
Federation was organized, and now Margaret knew her work
would be carried on.

Still, she would not relax. She was to prod to a finish the
project she had begun back in the 1930s. After the "one-

package victory," she felt the time had come when all women in America, even the poorest black and migrant worker, should have birth control information and material. For them, jellies and diaphragms were too complex and too expensive. Sanger's last great project, therefore, was getting support for a chemical contraceptive, preferably an injection, but perhaps in pill form. With her encouragement and the financial backing of a friend, Kate Dexter McCormick, work on an oral contraceptive was done by Drs. M. C. Chang, Gregory Pincus, and John Rock. For fear of Catholic reaction, neither the government nor philanthropic organizations would have anything to do with developing "the pill." It was years before "the pill" was ready for distribution in the 1960s. Then, however, women were eager for the new device, even though Margaret Sanger and many doctors knew it had to be improved and a "morning-after pill" might be more desirable.

Constant traveling sapped Sanger of her strength, but she never let up. She made three more trips to Japan, and to her joy, saw the birthrate there cut in half in ten years, thanks to her influence with the government. In 1959, seventy-five-year-old Sanger visited India once again. She met Nehru, less awesome than Gandhi but more satisfying to Margaret Sanger. Nehru agreed with Sanger's theories on population. It was during this trip that a nostalgic book called *Our Margaret Sanger* was presented to her, consisting of reminiscences by admirers from all over the world.

Returning to the United States, Margaret Sanger still battered Catholic barriers. Though President Dwight Eisenhower agreed to her plea that we help other nations curb their population growth, Catholic opposition forced him to back away. Sanger, furious, vowed to "straighten him out," but public opinion turned against her. In fact, a proposed television show with Sanger and Mike Wallace was canceled because of opposition from two priests.

Because Catholicism was her constant adversary, Sanger opposed John F. Kennedy in the presidential election the next year. She announced that if he won, she would leave the country. To her surprise, JFK declared that he would support giving contraceptive aid to other countries, and she was pacified. Later, Eisenhower, too, said, "the facts changed my mind," and with Truman, he headed the Sponsors Council for the Planned Parenthood World Federation.

Margaret Sanger was active until her death on September 14, 1966, just before her eighty-seventh birthday. She had moved to a Tucson nursing home because of her ailing heart, where, despite many visitors, she was often depressed. Yet, she had known the unique experience of giving birth to a movement, raising it, nurturing it, educating it, advancing it, and watching it develop into more than merely a respectable viewpoint.

She saw the Clinical Research Bureau renamed the Margaret Sanger Bureau, and its scope broadened to embrace not only birth control but infertility, male sexual problems, and physical, psychological, and emotional barriers to happy family life. The day before her death, almost fifty years after Margaret Sanger went to jail for her Brownsville Clinic, the U.S. Department of Health, Education and Welfare announced it would help in developing community birth-control programs. The time of the rich woman's "secret" was now in the past; birth control was for all women of all means.

Perhaps the greatest thrill came to Sanger the year before she died. The slight Irish girl who had battled the church of her ancestors lived to see Catholic lawyers band together and overcome the archaic Connecticut law against contraceptive use. In a way, she had won over the enormous Catholic institution. Margaret Sanger could rest. As Pearl S. Buck once said, "She started the fire of a great freedom."

Eleanor Roosevelt

As a woman, a human being, and a legend, Anna Eleanor Roosevelt has been deified and vilified. To Arthur M. Schlesinger, Jr., she was "a great and gallant—and, above all, a profoundly good—lady," while Francis Cardinal Spellman denounced her as an "unworthy American mother."

The press often viciously caricatured her in jokes and cartoons, but as Jean Monnet of the European Common Market saw it, "I think her greatest contribution was her persistence in carrying into practice her deep belief in liberty and equality. She would not accept that anyone should suffer —because they were women, or children, or foreign, or poor, or stateless refugees. To her, the world was truly one world, and all its inhabitants members of one family."

Columnist Westbrook Pegler covered these extremes in his comments about Ms. Roosevelt during his career. In 1938, he lauded her: "I think we can take the wraps off and call her the greatest American woman, because there is no other who works as hard or knows the low-down truth about the people and the troubles in their hearts as well as she does."

Fifteen years later he excoriated her: "The time has come

to snatch this wily old conspirator before Joe McCarthy's committee and chew her out. . . . She deserves far less respect than any conventional woman."

It was when Eleanor Roosevelt was viewed as a human being that she won approval and even honor, but when she was rated as a woman against the traditional standards of womanhood, Eleanor Roosevelt became an "unworthy American mother," commanding "less respect than any conventional woman."

Eleanor Roosevelt was unquestionably a compassionate person, but she was not a saint. She grasped lofty ideals, but her strong stubborn streak led her to indulge in murky backroom politics. She had a humble demeanor, but a forceful enough ego to plunge into a new active life at an age when others retire. Eleanor Roosevelt's mind was questioning and quick, but she was not an intellectual, and although she admired the arts and artists, she never profoundly appreciated other than the most traditional. To Harry Truman, Ms. Roosevelt was "the First Lady of the world," yet she courted ridicule by advertising mattresses, cold cream, and Selby shoes, and she edited a puerile publication called *Babies, Just Babies* while her husband was in the White House.

Ms. Roosevelt's strength lay in her acceptance of her own frailties. Through understanding her own weaknesses, she understood the weaknesses of others. Henry Kissinger once said, "She brought warmth rather than abstract principles" to her fellow human beings. This is what made her great. This, combined with the lasting changes she made in the image of conventional womanhood, also caused her to be hated.

If women like Margaret Sanger and Isadora Duncan opened new avenues of freedom in the female life style, Eleanor Roosevelt made these avenues respectable. She plunged into multitudinous activities that no First Lady before or after has undertaken. She entered politics timidly and ended up participating as vigorously as any Tammany boss. She remembered those who crossed her or crossed those she loved, and she used her position to lambaste them. Because she felt Carmine DeSapio caused her son's defeat in the race for New York attorney general in 1954, she dedicated herself to ousting DeSapio from party control, even though it took seven years of relentless campaigning against him. She even gave speeches in Italian, knowing DeSapio was unable to speak his forebear's language.

Eleanor Roosevelt interjected the female image into the male area of politics, yet no man called her "masculine," for she played the female role artfully. All the politicians could do was relent, because for every DeSapio or Father Coughlin she had as an enemy, Eleanor Roosevelt knew an Adlai Stevenson to ardently defend her. She always ranked high in popularity polls, often topping Harry Truman, George C. Marshall, Thomas Dewey, Herbert Hoover, and Douglas MacArthur—all contemporary national figures.

Grace Tully, one of Franklin D. Roosevelt's secretaries, remarked on the threat Ms. Roosevelt may have presented to some men: "If the term 'weaker sex' is to be transferred from the female to the male of our society, much of the psychological groundwork must be credited to Mrs. Eleanor Roosevelt."

Her achievements came late and were based on two strong characteristics. She had an inexhaustible drive which grew out of her upper-class Victorian sense of duty and charity toward the lower classes. She also had a consuming need to be accepted, which stemmed from her own feeling in childhood of not being accepted. Her favorite quotation was said to be "Back of tranquillity lies always conquered unhappiness."

Eleanor Roosevelt's life began unhappily. Just as she would later feel out of place as a wife and mother, young Eleanor felt unwanted as a daughter. She was born on October 11, 1884, the first child of dashing Elliott Roosevelt and Anna Hall Roosevelt, "one of the most beautiful and popular women in New York society." Her mother, the personification of feminine perfection, frankly considered the child "quaint," rather than lovable. Anna Roosevelt was not cruel, only unable to empathize with this solemn youngster who somehow was her daughter. Eleanor remembered how, as a child, she would stand in a doorway, thumb in mouth, and watch her mother cuddle her two younger brothers. Eleanor felt "a curious barrier between myself and these three."

When Eleanor was eight, her mother and one brother died within months of each other. Her father plunged into fatal alcoholism. Eleanor and her baby brother, Hall, were placed with her maternal grandmother, Mary Ludlow Hall. They lived in her two spacious homes—a mansion at Tivoli on the Hudson, and a brownstone on Thirty-Seventh Street in New York City.

To an observer, it would have appeared that Eleanor had just moved from one world of wealth and graciousness to another. Like Eleanor's old home, Grandmother Hall's city house was well-staffed with servants (who lived in poorly furnished, cramped quarters). The tall windows faced placid streets, the serene silence broken only by the clip-clop of horses drawing the carriages of the rich. (A few blocks away, tired horses pulled streetcars carrying those poor who had the few cents to spend on this convenience.) As a child, Eleanor was hardly aware of the financially less fortunate. She was involved with her own emotional survival.

Grandmother Hall was a widow who had been left with five lively children to raise, children who became so uncontrollable that she was at a total loss as to how to restrain them. She devoted all her time to the children and they were never allowed to work out their difficulties independently. (Eleanor later vowed that she would never let herself become so totally absorbed with her own children.)

When Grandmother Hall received Eleanor and Hall as her wards, she was determined to control them with a tighter rein than she had her own offspring, who were still living with her. Eleanor, therefore, entered a confined, emotionally restrained atmosphere. She had no friends and became increasingly insecure. She attached herself to her father, spiritually rather than physically, for he was seldom around. They corresponded lavishly, Elliot making grand promises to his little girl which he would never keep. She hung on these promises, as well as on his advice and admonitions.

It was chiefly from Elliot that Eleanor received the Victorian ideal of charity, an ideal that her father never practiced but one by which she would live. He died when she was not yet ten. Because she was unable to accept his death, she kept in touch with him by rereading his old letters.

Upon her father's death, Eleanor accepted the role of substitute parent to her young brother. She once said, "I want him to feel he belongs to somebody." Eleanor remained in this role until 1941, when Hall died of the effects of alcoholism.

A fortunate influence entered Eleanor Roosevelt's life when she was fifteen, an intensely shy and uncertain adolescent. She felt unattractive in the short, if sensible, clothes her grandmother made her wear, and uncomfortable in the steel back brace she was forced to put on for her posture. She was not particularly intellectual; her main occupations were reading, daydreaming, and observing the outlandish behavior of her aunts and uncles.

This was the child presented to Mlle. Souvestre, headmistress of an English finishing school called Allenswood. Here, Eleanor was "shocked into thinking." Mlle. Souvestre stimulated in her an active interest in current events, art, literature, philosophy, and languages. The teacher took a strong interest in the girl and even arranged to spend her own vacations traveling in Europe with Eleanor. Mlle. Souvestre encouraged Eleanor to make travel arrangements, to communicate in foreign languages, and even to venture into the streets of Florence alone. After three years with Mlle. Souvestre, Eleanor Roosevelt, if still quite immature in many ways, was a relatively poised, self-confident, and bright young lady. Then she was called back to New York to make her debut.

Eleanor was not at all interested in debuts, cotillions, and tea dances. Yet, she wanted her grandmother to be proud of her, or at least satisfied, so she accepted the role she had to play. Eleanor was far from being a popular debutante, despite the fact that her Uncle Theodore was president of the United States, and her Cousin Alice was the belle of the country. Although Eleanor had grown into a tall, willowy young woman, with soft wavy hair and intensely expressive blue eyes, she considered herself homely. While she could converse pleasantly, Eleanor felt embarrassed and altogether miserable. Her one outlet, acceptable both to herself and to her social peers, became charity.

She joined the Junior League, as many postdebutantes her age did; but unlike the others, Eleanor volunteered for active settlement work. She had already gained some experience working with troubled people; it was evident at Tivoli that Eleanor was the only member of the family able to cope with the wild sprees and emotional upsets of her aunts and uncles. At the Rivington Street Settlement House, she taught dancing and calisthenics to children. Eleanor Roosevelt was then nineteen years old, and she never forgot the misery she saw in her settlement work that year: "I had painfully high ideals and a tremendous sense of duty at that time, entirely unrelieved by any sense of humor or any appreciation of the weaknesses of human nature. Things were either right or wrong to me with very few shades, and I had had too little experience to know as yet how very fallible human judgements are."

In her autobiography, Ms. Roosevelt admitted that it took years for her stern standards to soften, and her sense of humor and levity never did develop to the degree her husband would have liked.

To some, Eleanor Roosevelt's betrothal to charming Franklin Delano Roosevelt was a blessing for her. To others, it was Franklin who was fortunate since her family branch of the Roosevelt tree was loftier. It was Eleanor who, during their courtship, introduced Franklin to the squalor of poverty and who later became an invaluable political partner to him.

Eleanor's future mother-in-law, Sara Delano Roosevelt,

was aghast. Her son was "too young" to get married, and too dashing and attractive for this ungainly girl, no matter how notable her family was. For months, Sara tried to break up the couple, but Franklin had made his choice.

Eleanor Roosevelt apparently had misgivings about marriage in general. Her parents' relationship had been stormy; they were ill suited to each other. She saw her Grandmother Hall's life distorted by her marriage and family. Still, for all young ladies, social acceptability meant marriage, and later, Eleanor wrote about marriage being the "lot of woman": "I had a great curiosity about life and a desire to participate in every experience that might be the lot of woman. . . . I felt the urge to be part of the stream of life, and so in the autumn of 1903, when Franklin Roosevelt, my fifth cousin once removed, asked me to marry him, though I was only nineteen, it seemed an entirely natural thing. . . . I know now that it was years later before I understood what being in love was or what loving really meant."

From the wedding day forward, Eleanor moved under someone else's yoke—first Sara's, then Franklin's—hoping for acceptance. Her marriage took place on March 17, 1905, and her Uncle Theodore, the president, gave the bride away. He also stole the limelight. One of his sons, Quentin, remarked, "Father always wants to be the bride at every wedding and the corpse at every funeral." Eleanor and Franklin were only two more in the audience as Uncle Ted entertained the guests with stories and jokes.

After the usual honeymoon in Europe, Eleanor Roosevelt moved directly into her mother-in-law's domain. Sara had obtained a house for "the children" near her own, and had furnished and staffed it. She brought Eleanor and Franklin to Campobello for the summers and to the Hyde Park family estate for holidays. In both places, Sara reigned and Eleanor Roosevelt was a guest.

Eventually, Sara Roosevelt built two handsome houses, side by side, on East Sixty-Fifth Street in New York City; one was for her and the other for Eleanor and Franklin, with connecting doors to serve as an umbilical link between them. Again, she furnished them both and hired the necessary servants. At first, her daughter-in-law could not run a household at all, later admitting she did not have the gumption to get up and learn. Eleanor Roosevelt remembered herself as "a completely colorless echo."

Only a few times in her life did she lose her quiet control before others; once when she realized that her home was not her own in any way and again when she cracked under the terrible strain of battling Sara Roosevelt for FDR's future after his attack of polio in 1921. Usually she did not rebel but just retreated into what she called a "Griselda mood" of sullenness.

Eleanor Roosevelt's first twelve years of married life were spent bearing children: Anna was born in 1906; James in 1907; Franklin, Jr., in 1908 (he died within one year); Elliott in 1910; Franklin, Jr., in 1914; and John in 1916. The children were handed over to nurses and governesses. Just as she did not feel confident enough to run a household, Ms. Roosevelt did not feel secure enough to handle her children, and the nurses usually ordered her around as much as they did the children. Eleanor even gave up her charity work upon Sara Roosevelt's warning that she might contaminate her own children by being in close contact with the poor.

She did, however, set the moral tone for the household, and because she was trying to avoid being like Grandmother Hall, who was lax with her offspring, Eleanor Roosevelt exerted too much discipline with her children. She was most rigid with Anna and most lenient toward Elliott, who seemed insecure and so like her father and brother.

Franklin made her job more difficult by not taking on enough of the disciplinary responsibilities. He felt that if the children were allowed to make mistakes, they would learn from them. He felt his own mother had been too domineering. (With her grandchildren, Sara Roosevelt was overindulgent; she loved to lavish expensive presents on them, especially when their parents denied them.)

As FDR's political career reached its height, life for his children became increasingly difficult. The two youngest boys were still teenagers, and their father was usually too preoccupied with the presidency to hear their problems. Ms. Roosevelt realized another problem; if her children accepted the inevitable special privileges offered them, they were criticized; on the other hand, they were considered ungracious if they refused.

Because of the turmoil of her own maternal experiences, Ms. Roosevelt later opened herself to all young people (occasionally becoming overinvolved, as with the Communist-led American Youth Congress, which she defended to the end). She declared that it was best for parents to serve as loving examples to their children, to not stifle them, and to let them grow up as independent people.

Eleanor and Franklin had different personalities. He loved sports, gaiety, and parties. Eleanor Roosevelt smiled and laughed easily, and loved to entertain, but she was basically too serious to be coy and flirtatious. She tried at first to share Franklin's enjoyment of games; she even overcame her fear of water and learned to swim. But, except for being skilled at horseback riding, Ms. Roosevelt was not athletic, so she stayed on the sidelines and became a gracious hostess. Gradually, she adopted the role of capable manager. Ms. Roosevelt performed all the necessary chores and duties which her husband required of her, becoming an able administrator and filling her "lot of woman" role exceedingly well.

Eleanor Roosevelt always had tremendous energy, much like her Uncle Theodore. As she developed, she learned to apply this energy effectively. FDR entered politics in 1911 as a New York state senator. While he was busy with his work, she did what was necessary to further his political career: welcoming politicians to her home, meeting congressmen and constituents, and greeting the press. She took it upon herself to visit the wives of the newspapermen because she heard they were lonely. Eleanor Roosevelt was always drawn to the lonely.

Besides entertaining, her main activity during these years was transporting the family and servants from New York City to Hyde Park to Albany to Campobello and back again. Still, it was invigorating; it was her first break with the old style of living—and with Sara Roosevelt. Even if Eleanor could not match her husband's sociability, she was intrigued with the political whirlwind he created around him. Living in Albany, and later in Washington, was an educational experience for her.

They moved to the nation's capital in 1913, when FDR was appointed undersecretary of the navy. Here, Ms. Roosevelt was given a definite social role, which mostly consisted of observing protocol and paying regular visits to the right people. She admitted that she was shocked by women who refused to be slaves to this custom. Such a woman was her cousin Alice Longworth, who was more interested in the men's world of political intrigue than in the women's world of calling cards. Eleanor felt, "My only chance of doing my duty as the wife of a public official was to do exactly as the majority of women were doing." She realized now that she was needed and accepted by her husband. This was all that she demanded of life.

FDR was popular and well liked by most, although there were those, like Henry Cabot Lodge, who considered him "a well-meaning, nice young man—but light." He served the Navy Department with tremendous energy. "I get my fingers into everything—there's no law against it," he once exclaimed.

When World War I came, Eleanor Roosevelt was finally called upon to fully release her great energy. She joined a Red Cross canteen and did everything—wrote postcards for the servicemen, sewed pajamas, poured tea, managed the finances, solicited funds, knitted, gave reports, ironed, scrubbed floors, and for the first time recognized the diverse

numbers of things she could do well. She was considered "the
dynamo" of the canteen.

Along with her energy, Eleanor Roosevelt also exerted
strong self-discipline, perhaps as a reaction to the lack of
discipline her father and brother displayed. After Hall died,
Eleanor lamented that his self-indulgence had laid waste to
his "generosity, warmth of heart . . . brilliance."

Ms. Roosevelt's self-discipline was both physical (she
exercised daily) and mental (she strove constantly to improve
her mind). During her child-bearing years she experienced
three months of illness before each delivery, but since she had
accepted "her lot" as household manager, she refused to let
this illness stop her from doing what was necessary. Neither
would she let her husband be beaten down by illness. In the
last years of Franklin's life, Eleanor took on many of his
social burdens, but she also urged him to continue on and not
accept invalidism. She believed that if he gave up his work,
he would collapse as did Woodrow Wilson.

While this stoicism worked *for* her, it also worked *against*
her. Eleanor Roosevelt admitted that often she could not
really savor life, even the years when her children were
small. She rarely enjoyed the sensual delights that her
husband relished—good food, gregarious people—and she
envied his ability to relax completely, even when burdened
with tremendous responsibilities. She could not provide the
camaraderie he needed, especially during the difficult World
War II years. During those years, Ms. Roosevelt traveled a
great deal, so FDR called in his daughter, Anna Roosevelt
Boettinger, to act as hostess in her mother's place. Ms.
Roosevelt later admitted that she resented her daughter's
intrusion, but could understand why FDR needed Anna. She
learned also to accept FDR's secretary, Marguerite (Missy)
LeHand's closeness with "the boss."

What Eleanor Roosevelt never forgave was her husband's
involvement with her own secretary, Lucy Mercer Rutherford
—first their love affair in 1918 and later his asking Ms.
Rutherford to visit him in the White House while his wife was

traveling. Eleanor Roosevelt was angry with Anna for not telling her about these visits or that Lucy Rutherford was in Warm Springs, Georgia, with the president when he died of a cerebral hemorrhage in 1945. She drew upon her inner strength and discipline and immersed herself in duty and work simply for self-preservation.

After she discovered FDR's unfaithfulness to her in 1918, she resolved that she could not continue living through her husband's accomplishments: "Somewhere along the line of development we discover what we really are, and then we make our real decision for which we are responsible. Make the decision primarily for yourself because you can never really live anyone else's life, not even your child's. The influence you exert is through your own life and what you become yourself."

In 1920, it looked as if the Roosevelts were aiming for the top. This was the first year women were voting. (Only later did Ms. Roosevelt appreciate the importance of suffrage: "I had learned that if you wanted to institute any kind of reform you could get far more attention if you had a vote than if you lacked one.") FDR was the Democratic party vice-presidential candidate, and although he lost the election, the campaign was instructive to both Franklin and Eleanor. He had faced the "forgotten man" and learned the average American's concerns. Eleanor absorbed the meet-the-public side of politics, and while she insisted that she was of no use on the trips, her letters back to the family were enthusiastic.

An important outcome of the campaign travels was Ms. Roosevelt's involvement with her husband's aide, Louis Howe. It was Howe who first recognized Eleanor Roosevelt's capabilities as an effective, energetic organizer. It was Howe who later convinced her to develop and use these gifts when her husband was paralyzed in 1921 with polio, and his future seemed empty.

In one way, the illness further damaged Franklin and Eleanor's relationship. From now on, Franklin would spend many weeks away from Eleanor, resting and exercising in

Warm Springs, Georgia. However, FDR's paralysis also bound
him to his wife. When necessary, she was his nurse; later she
battled his mother over his political career. Sara Roosevelt
wanted her son to retire to Hyde Park and spend his days
reading, writing, and collecting stamps. When Eleanor won
the "war," she became a major influence in her husband's life.
She also became an individual. She decided to go into politics
herself to keep her husband's name alive and to prepare the
way for his return to work.

With the help, encouragement, and advice of Louis Howe
and FDR, Eleanor Roosevelt began changing the traditional
image of the upper- and middle-class woman. From standing
behind her man, Eleanor moved beside him as an equal and
an indispensible partner. Her days as a "colorless echo" were
over. She could even tolerate, with amusement, her mother-
in-law!

Ms. Roosevelt volunteered to work with the Women's
Trade Union League and the Women's Division of the
Democratic State Committee. She delved into the problems of
women in labor—the forty-eight-hour work week, minimum
wages, and the right to unionize and strike. She urged an end
to child labor. Along with militant Rose Schneiderman and
political activists Marian Dickerman, Nancy Cook, and later,
Molly Dewson, Ms. Roosevelt said to women: "Get into
politics!" The male response to the idea was "Stay out!"
(Later, at a convention, Ms. Roosevelt learned firsthand just
how impotent women were: "They stood outside the door of all
important meetings and waited!")

She joined the League of Women Voters and the Women's
City Club. Eleanor Roosevelt became a popular speaker after
overcoming her high-pitched voice and nervous giggle. She
grew into leadership and took over the Women's Finance
Committee. She stumped for candidates, met party bosses,
organized local women, and wrote articles.

Remembering the hardships of World War I, she worked
for peace, helping to organize a contest for the best plan
telling how America might achieve and preserve world peace.
She urged U.S. participation in a world court. She briefed her

husband on what she was doing, teaching him about the trade union movement and solidifying his belief in the need for a new international organization. FDR was later to plant the seeds for such a group, and his widow was to be a vital force behind the United Nations during its first years.

Through the pain of his illness and recuperation, Franklin Roosevelt matured. He learned to be infinitely patient and persistent, assets he would use to get his programs through Congress in the next decade. He also learned to empathize with other unfortunate people, just as his wife had learned to do many years earlier.

At the 1924 convention, FDR came back with his legendary Happy Warrior speech to nominate Al Smith for president. At the same time, Eleanor Roosevelt was chairwoman of a special welfare committee proposing a progressive social welfare platform. Both Smith and the platform lost, but when FDR resumed his recuperation, Ms. Roosevelt went on to the New York state convention where she seconded Al Smith's nomination for governor. Here, she led a more satisfactory platform fight, winning inclusion of minimum wage, forty-eight-hour work week, and child-labor planks.

She continued to campaign vigorously for Smith, who was running against her cousin Theodore Roosevelt, Jr. She exploited the recent Republican administration's Teapot Dome scandal by following Theodore around the state in a car bearing a huge teapot on its roof. Though the Democrats lost the presidency, Al Smith won the governorship.

Four years later, Smith was to try for the presidency once more, and he wanted FDR, whom he thought he could control, to run for governor of New York. Franklin did not want to take that step yet; he felt he needed more time to strengthen himself. Eleanor went to the state convention alone. In the end, FDR agreed to become the candidate and he won.

Eleanor Roosevelt, who had been an introverted child, was now known for her warmth and graciousness. From being a young girl involved with her own needs, Eleanor Roosevelt had evolved into a mature individual concerned with others'

needs. She began her marriage unable to manage a
household, and now she was managing an area of politics and
even a new business. She had joined with two friends, Cook
and Dickerman, in establishing a furniture-making, pewter,
and weaving business on the Roosevelts' Hyde Park property.
Here, beside the Val-Kill brook, she built a cottage. It was to
this house that she would retreat when she wanted to be
alone; she'd never had a house that was truly her own before.
Sara Delano Roosevelt's mansion was not home to Eleanor.

Val-Kill Industries, though successful, did not quite fill
up Ms. Roosevelt's time. Nor did it do enough to improve her
mind, since she was involved more with the executive than
the creative aspects. So she joined Ms. Dickerson in buying
the Todhunter School (later the Dalton School) in New York
City. She taught drama, American history, and literature
there for several years with great dedication, even commuting
from Albany to teach two and a half days a week after FDR
became governor. The school was progressive and personal,
and Ms. Roosevelt escorted its wealthy and sheltered young
pupils on field trips to the city courts, business districts, and
slums.

Experience had broadened her intellect and ingenuity,
and trauma had developed her self-confidence. But, Eleanor
Roosevelt had not yet achieved self-fulfillment. She still had
the White House years to get through.

Her training ground for Washington was the governor's
mansion at Albany, from 1928 to 1932. Ostensibly she gave
up all personal political activities while her husband served
as an elected public official, but she was always busy. FDR
called upon his wife to make unannounced inspection tours to
state institutions, and she was astute and lucid in the reports
she gave him. She was also his intermediary. She received
huge volumes of letters containing appeals and confidences
from constituents, and not one letter went unanswered.

Eleanor Roosevelt was one of the few people near
Franklin Roosevelt who would not consistently say yes to
him. She was critical whenever she felt she had to be, and

often FDR was frustrated at not getting the supportive
answer he wanted from his wife.

If she was critical, she was always loyal. When Franklin
Roosevelt was reelected to the governorship by a landslide, it
was clear that the White House would be the next goal.
Eleanor Roosevelt had reached the point of admitting her
usefulness, but she was still a product of her upbringing and
environment, and she insisted that her activities and
speeches be for her husband's career betterment. FDR urged
his staff to consider the two of them "a team," and she
sincerely wanted to be his equal, but deep down she
considered herself a junior partner. Though her greatest
personal moments were to come after the White House years,
the twelve years in the nation's capital were nevertheless
historic, and they made Eleanor Roosevelt an historic figure.

Ms. Roosevelt moved into the White House with hesitant
steps. She recognized the possibilities there to help
individuals and the country through the depression crisis. She
also realized that there would be no privacy for her in that
goldfish bowl—no solitude, no escaping her mistakes. She was
concerned about her superficial knowledge of events and
facts: "More and more, as I grew older, I used the quickness of
my mind to pick the minds of other people and use their
knowledge as my own. A dinner companion, a casual
acquaintance, provided me with information which I could
use in conversation and few people were aware how little I
actually knew on a variety of subjects that I talked on with
apparent ease."

She constantly denied her influence in the White House,
and in one way she was right. As First Lady, she did have the
ear of the president; he paid attention to her ideas and
considered her beliefs, but when he disagreed, her power
ended. Franklin was the president.

For Eleanor Roosevelt, the White House was an
opportunity to aid the progress of women. She remembered
the activist women who helped and influenced her in the
early 1920s. When she began earning her own money by

doing radio work and writing columns, Ms. Roosevelt
established two places where unemployed working women
could rest and eat. One was in the Women's Trade Union
League clubhouse (for which she also helped pay off the
mortgage); the other was the Girls' Service League
headquarters in New York City.

The First Lady freely reminded the president whenever
she felt he was neglecting women in his appointments. She
would follow up her reminders with lists of qualified women.
She also fought any efforts to oust former President Hoover's
capable female appointees, such as Grace Abbott of the
Children's Bureau.

Although Eleanor Roosevelt had numerous official
functions to perform, she instituted her own personal projects
as well, such as teas and garden parties for those women her
husband had placed in executive positions but who were
routinely left off White House invitation lists. She organized
the "Gridiron Widows" get-together on the night of the
newspapermen's press party for the president. To this she
invited newspaperwomen and the wives of cabinet members
and newspapermen.

Ms. Roosevelt realized that Washington's female
reporters were in danger of losing their jobs since they were
not allowed to cover presidential press conferences and could
not make the contacts and receive the privileged information
that the male reporters could. Eleanor Roosevelt therefore
initiated First Lady press conferences and invited only
women reporters.

Press conferences were not the only new look in the
White House. Eleanor sloughed off most formality—she
greeted guests at the door rather than descending the grand
staircase after they had assembled, she refused to be waited
on or escorted, and she insisted upon running the White
House elevator for herself.

Eleanor Roosevelt was everywhere in those twelve years,
involved primarily in working for her husband's objectives

rather than for FDR himself. She traveled for the president, investigating slums, schools, bread lines, migrant camps, coal mines, hospitals, battlefields, and foreign lands, and she reported how the country and the people were responding to his programs. She worked as a staff member and diplomat without portfolio, as a New Dealer, and as a wife and mother.

Eleanor Roosevelt may have been politically naive, for she never ceased to reach for the highest goal, utopia. Two of her most publicized failures were Arthurdale and the overlong defense of the American Youth Congress (AYC). Arthurdale, a New Deal town of cheap prefabricated houses, turned out to be too costly. The idealistic young intellectuals of the AYC intrigued her and she stoutly defended them even after it was obvious that the leaders were Marxists.

Even though she had vowed to work only as her husband's backup, Ms. Roosevelt quickly became controversial. She had grown in her concern for humanity. During Wilson's administration she referred to her black servants as "darkies," and now she supported the rights of blacks, was a close friend of activist Mary Bethune, and resigned from the Daughters of the American Revolution when that group refused to allow contralto Marian Anderson to sing in Constitution Hall. Once she had distrusted Jews, but now among her closest friends were the Morganthaus. Later, she was to strongly support the Jewish state of Israel. Ms. Roosevelt sympathized with the Spanish Civil War, divorce, and sex education, all of which brought opposition from the Catholic hierarchy. She was criticized as commercializing her position as First Lady, but the greatest part of her earnings was turned over to the American Friends Society to be used for charity.

The country was almost as divided about the First Lady as it was about the president. Texas Governor W. Lee O'Daniel said of Eleanor Roosevelt, "Any good things [FDR] may have done during his political career are due to her, and any mistakes he may have made are due to his not taking up the matter with his wife." And Raymond Clapper remarked, "Half the trouble could be got rid of if the president would haul her out of the place."

Her revolutionary First Lady image was tested in the 1936 campaign. The Republican party contrasted the active Ms. Roosevelt with Alf Landon's wife, a "homebody" who would stay put in the White House. The country chose the Roosevelts by a landslide vote that November.

That same year, Eleanor Roosevelt was gratified to see women for the first time sharing equal power with men on the platform committee. When Secretary of Labor Frances Perkins eulogized her as "gallant and courageous and intelligent and wise," the audience gave her a standing ovation.

Just as Ms. Roosevelt was persistent in airing her feelings to her husband, she was equally determined to have him listen to the views of others. She arranged dinners where the president was forced to sit next to a radical with a plan for improved medical care, a pacifist, or a "do-gooder." On her own, she warned FDR during his last term about the reorganization of the State Department, indicating that he should not expect the full truth from the replacements, only appeasement. She urged him to pressure Winston Churchill when England vetoed Count Carlo Sforza, an anti-Fascist, as new Italian Foreign Minister. She expressed reservations about FDR's Yalta agreement with Stalin.

Despite all she had fought for and achieved during those years, Eleanor Roosevelt said, "I was lost somewhere deep inside myself." When the president died, she was sixty-four years old. Although she felt lonely, his death was not as devastating to her as the death in 1953 of her long-time secretary, Malvina Thompson. At that time, Ms. Roosevelt said, "I learned for the first time what being alone was like."

With FDR gone, she had to find new goals. "In my early married years the pattern of my life had been largely my mother-in-law's pattern. Later it was the children and Franklin who made the pattern. When the last child went to boarding school, I began to want to do things on my own, to use my own mind and abilities for my own aims. When I went to Washington, I felt sure that I would be able to use opportunities which came to me to help Franklin gain the objectives he cared about—but the work would be his work and the pattern his pattern. . . ." Touchingly, she ended, "I was one of those who served his purposes."

Now she was free to express ideas and wishes which reflected herself, something she could not do while Franklin Roosevelt was alive. She was alone, but her work was not ended. There was much to do—lecturing, traveling, and writing magazine articles, a newspaper column, and fifteen books. There were also the United Nations, political campaigning, a television talk show, and teaching at Brandeis University. She evolved from an amateur with a wide span of interests to a professional, astute in national and international politics. And when President Harry Truman asked her to accept the position of United States delegate to the U.N. General Assembly, she accepted.

As she began this job, she commented, "For the first time in my life I can say just what I want." She soon learned, however, that freedom to speak in the U.N. was just as limited as it had been when she was First Lady; she was still representing America's, not Eleanor Roosevelt's, beliefs—and sometimes they were in conflict.

She also recognized quickly that discrimination against women was just as rampant in the U.N. as it was in Washington. She had been put on the Social, Humanitarian, and Cultural Committee of the General Assembly, which suited her until she understood why she had been assigned there; it was to keep her away from the political committees. She knew she was one of the few women at the U.N.: "If I failed to be a useful member, it would not be considered merely that I as an individual had failed but that all women had failed, and there would be little chance for others to serve in the near future."

She studied hard and listened intently, trying to learn as

much as she could. She was considered the only delegate
familiar with all the background material of the committees
on which she served. And although she understood her
weaknesses and tried to overcome them, she never
underestimated her influence. "I think [the delegation] won't
like to propose anything they think I would not approve of!"
she wrote to a friend.

Ms. Roosevelt was asked to help set up the Commission
on Human Rights and was selected to be its first chairperson.
The primary concern of the commission was drafting a
Declaration of Human Rights for the U.N. charter. As
progress with this was made, she felt her feminist
consciousness rising. Indian delegate Ms. Hansa Mehta
complained that the opening sentence, "All men are created
equal," was sexist. Ms. Roosevelt first argued that in America
"all men" was taken to mean "all people." She recognized,
however, that what was often considered trivial made up a
vast network of propaganda that weakened female power.
Eventually, the sentence was changed to "All human beings
are born free and equal." She complained that the male
members of her own delegation moved too slowly and
indecisively. She also felt that more women should have the
chance to help formulate U.N. policies.

Because she was interested in getting to know the other
U.N. female delegates, she began inviting them to her
apartment for tea. She soon realized that the women
discussed their problems more easily in this casual
environment. She then began to invite male delegates, too, for
the purpose of untangling knotty political problems in a
congenial atmosphere. "So, against odds," she once wrote to
John Foster Dulles, "the women inch forward, but I'm rather
old to be carrying on this fight."

While equality for women was often a result of her
efforts, Eleanor Roosevelt was actually involved in other
problems. She sincerely believed that world peace depended
upon a strong United Nations, and therefore she was not in
favor of the Truman Doctrine, which had the United States
sharing Great Britain's responsibility toward Greece and

Turkey, ignoring the U.N. Eleanor Roosevelt was also among the first to notice the growing rift between the United States and the U.S.S.R. She learned firsthand the difficulties of dealing with Russian diplomats and was often frustrated by them.

Ms. Roosevelt continued as U.N. delegate until 1952, when she handed in the customary resignation to the incoming president, Dwight Eisenhower. Mr. Eisenhower accepted her resignation, and she joined the American Association for the United Nations as a volunteer worker.

In her last speech before the U.N., Eleanor Roosevelt talked about the inferior status of women in politics, stressing that the important decisions were still made by men and that even though there were women in parliaments of Communist countries, they were not active in the policy-making realm. She traveled to many countries in her later years, visiting and interviewing Nikita Krushchev in Yalta, enjoying the surge of progress in Israel, studying the shifting status of Japanese, Indian, and Pakistani women, and conferring with political leaders.

Ms. Roosevelt also kept in close touch with American leaders. In 1948, she was asked to participate in a Truman-Roosevelt presidential ticket, but she refused, stating that if the ticket were defeated, it would be interpreted as a defeat in the battle for political equality for women. In the next two presidential elections Ms. Roosevelt campaigned for Adlai Stevenson. In 1960, she tried to get him nominated with John F. Kennedy as his vice-president. (It was not until she met and spoke to John Kennedy personally in 1960 that she could support his candidacy. That was when she experienced his ability to inspire hope.) When JFK became president, Ms. Roosevelt worked on his Tractors for Freedom committee, served on the Peace Corps Advisory Council, and gave him a long list of qualified women for federal appointments (out of his first two hundred forty appointments, only nine were female).

She also began lecturing on behalf of an equal rights amendment. Remembering her work in the 1920s with the

Women's Trade Union League, she said, "Many of us opposed
the amendment because we felt it would do away with
protection in the labor field." She felt that with unionization
protection was available, but equality was still not a fact.
President Kennedy appointed her chairperson of his
Commission on the Status of Women, a position she held until
her last debilitating illness, aplastic anemia.

Eleanor Roosevelt never ceased to be controversial.
Although cartoonists became kinder when her protruding
"Roosevelt teeth" were replaced after an automobile accident
in 1945, her work incited other attacks. In her column she
opposed state aid to parochial schools and was strongly
attacked for this view by Cardinal Spellman. He accused her
of waging an Anti-Catholic campaign, and the country drew
sides. An uneasy peace was made when Cardinal Spellman
wrote a clarifying letter to Ms. Roosevelt and paid a visit to
her home. He agreed that direct federal aid to parochial
education was unconstitutional. He advocated instead
auxiliary aid for all children.

Though she was rather puritanical and a teetotaler, in
1948 she was cited in a divorce suit by the wife of former FDR
bodyguard Earl Miller. Ms. Roosevelt denied any involvement
with Miller beyond friendship. She had known him since the
1930s, when he was a state trooper in Albany. He became her
chauffeur and was a frequent guest at her Val-Kill cottage.
Her sons were angry and upset at the idea of a public divorce
trial, and during this time Eleanor Roosevelt became severely
depressed. The case was finally cleared up privately by Mr.
Miller and his wife.

Eleanor Roosevelt, born into a sheltered world in the
1880s, died at the start of the 1960 upheavals. She never
stopped being a force, and her presence was felt even as her
life was fading. She kept in contact with blacks and the poor
in her seventh decade just as she had supported their
predecessors in the 1930s. She urged the young to live
"bravely, excitingly, imaginatively," and she advised the
United States to stay out of Vietnam and take the question to

the United Nations. She had gone through it all before—wars, discrimination, and a personal existence as a "colorless echo."

She had learned that the "capacity for understanding grows with the effort to understand" not "abstract principles" but individuals: "It was the sight of a child dying of hunger that made the tragedy of hunger become of such overriding importance to me. Out of my response to an individual develops an awareness of a problem to the community, then to the country, and finally to the world. In each case my feeling of obligation to do something has stemmed from one individual and then widened and become applied to a broader area."

Eleanor Roosevelt was the personification of the changes that took place in the traditional role of womanhood from the nineteenth century to the twentieth. She exemplified the human ability to learn, to develop, and to change. She possessed many attributes long considered masculine—strength, courage, determination, stoicism, discipline, energy. (It could be said that she was a female counterpart of her uncle, Theodore Roosevelt, who was a most "masculine" president.) At the same time, Ms. Roosevelt retained all the traditional "feminine" qualities—compassion, emotionalism, flexibility, graciousness, honesty. And since she was human, she displayed some of these qualities to a disadvantage. Honesty, for example, sometimes surpassed candor and became tactlessness.

Ms. Roosevelt died a few weeks after her eightieth birthday. She fought her increasing invalidism to the end, just as she had urged her husband to do. She had done her duty; she had known universal acceptance. Adlai Stevenson delivered her eulogy and said, simply: "We are lonelier. Someone has gone from one's own life who was like the certainty of refuge, and someone has gone from the world who was like a certainty of honor."

America has not replaced Eleanor Roosevelt.

World Wide Photos

Rachel Carson

On April 14, 1964, a woman died. She was a gentle, shy, private, serious yet witty lady. Her name was Rachel Carson and her funeral was held in the Washington National Cathedral. Pallbearers included Stewart Udall and Abraham Ribicoff, and an enormous funeral wreath was sent by Prince Philip of England.

Rachel Carson was dead, but she left a legacy. After centuries of human domination and destruction of the earth, a new respect had been born for the interrelationship of all living things, and this concern was now a leading national priority. Ms. Carson lived just long enough to see her "revolution" snowball into one of the most determined movements of the time. Said Ribicoff: "This gentle lady ... aroused people everywhere to be concerned with one of the most significant problems of mid-twentieth century life— man's contamination of his environment."

Rachel Carson was not happy muckraking; she preferred to investigate the coexistence of people and nature. Yet, as it turned out, she is remembered more for her indictment in *Silent Spring*, than for the poetic and prize-winning *The Sea Around Us* and *Edge of the Sea*. This would have surprised her, for she did not put great weight upon the sociopolitical power of her words and knowledge. "It would be unrealistic to believe one book could bring a complete change," she once said. Few utterances have been so mistaken, for the *New York Times* called Carson "one of the most influential women of her time."

During the almost five years Rachel Carson spent writing *Silent Spring,* the United States underwent tremendous change. She began the book in the late 1950s, during a period which has been called "the McCarthy era of the conservation movement." The Department of Agriculture (later called by Ralph Nader "the Department of Agribusiness") was servant to one group, the farm bloc. It was dedicated to eradicating insects, although out of the three million known species, only one percent could be classed as "pests." In 1957, the Department of Agriculture would not consider any evidence that pesticides were harmful to the environment, no matter how expert the source.

The Department of Interior, traditionally more sympathetic to environmentalists, was then under the direction of Douglas McKay, who freely leased public lands, fired many wildlife specialists, and called conservationists "punks." Ecologists were suspected by some of being somehow subversive, a danger to American industrial growth.

Then in the sixties changes began to take place. Traditional principles were challenged, established religious groups lost a great deal of their influence, and the nation was injecting itself into a bitter, unpopular war at the other side of the world. In this environment, the new priority of conservation of the earth's resources, perhaps the most important problem ever to confront the human race, mushroomed into the public consciousness. Although Carson did not coin the word *ecology,* it was she, more than anyone else, who pushed the conservation problem and the facts before her fellow humans and demanded not only recognition of them, but also rectification from both the technological community and the public.

One government official claimed, "There is no question that *Silent Spring* prompted the federal government to take action against water and air pollution—as well as against persistent pesticides—several years before it otherwise would have moved."

Virginia Apgar, M.D., stated, "There are a great number of questions yet unanswered about the environment we all live in, and there will be more as new drugs, new chemicals such as pesticides and fungicides, increasing pollution and changing social mores continue to alter our environment. The four P's—pills, pesticides, psychedelics, and pollution—pose questions of environmentally-caused birth defects we have only begun to suspect should be asked."

Carson had a message and was driven to write it down, despite debilitating personal setbacks, a long, losing battle with cancer, and volumes of facts, data, experiments, and leads to be followed and assembled. Why Rachel Carson? She had won many public and professional honors for her previous books on the sea. She had introduced to the public the fascination and complexity of the oceans. Carson now had financial security, after decades of worry and scrimping. Although she never married, she had an adopted son and an aging mother to care for. And Carson certainly had other interests, other books to write, as well as a desire for some private perusal of the natural world around her.

She took on her crusade for many reasons—the welfare of future generations; her love of the environment; her reputation; her unique experience, acquaintances, and personal knowledge from her government work; and her anger about the lack of concern for life she saw in other people about her.

These feelings were not new to her. Carson had been sensitive to the delicate balance of nature all her life. Several months after World War II ended, while still working for the Fish and Wildlife Service of the Department of the Interior, she wrote to *Reader's Digest,* asking if the magazine would be interested in an article on the DDT war being waged against insects and the effects of the chemical on fish, birds, and the whole scheme of nature's checks and balances. *Reader's Digest* was not interested.

Neither was anyone else, and Carson gave up the article idea to concentrate on her second book and her government work. But concern gnawed at her.

Isolated warnings were being voiced by other scientists who were worried about what they considered to be a sophisticated and systematic destruction of the earth. It was 1957 when Carson finally took on the project of *Silent Spring*. Olga Huckins, a friend who lived near Cape Cod, wrote a letter to a local newspaper condemning the heavy spraying against mosquitoes in the area, which caused the deaths of songbirds and of bees, grasshoppers, and other necessary insects, while the mosquitoes remained as numerous as ever. A copy of the letter went to Carson, beseeching whatever help she could provide. Huckins ended her letter: "Air spraying where it is not needed or wanted is inhuman, undemocratic, and probably unconstitutional. For those of us who stand helplessly on the tortured earth, it is intolerable." When *Silent Spring* was published five years later, Rachel Carson acknowledged that Olga Huckins' letter had propelled her to start that book.

Rachel Louise Carson was born on May 27, 1907, in Springdale, Pennsylvania. It was a genteel era, an age of innocence in the Allegheny valley, or so it would seem to later generations. It's curious that Rachel Carson was to gain her greatest satisfaction from the sea, for she was raised far from any ocean. It is curious also that while she was enthralled by the sea, Carson was indifferent to water sports, seafood, and water-living pets. Her closest nonhuman companions were cats, and when one died, she grieved deeply. Slender and pretty, she dressed in simple, tailored clothes, and spoke in a quiet, low voice. She loved reading, especially books on the sea.

One admirer, former Secretary of the Interior Stewart Udall, likened her to Emily Dickinson, who was also reserved and sensitive. Ms. Carson found it a great strain to speak in public, a responsibility after her books became so successful.

Yet, when Rachel Carson discussed her interests—nature, the sea, the Maine coast, and her cats, close friends, and family—she became animated and charming. She had a fine sense of humor which her coworkers claimed saved their often tedious and bureaucratic chores from being totally boring. Carson also had great inner toughness. One reviewer saw this strength as "unassuming competence [which] suggests that should she meet a shark on her next research dive, she might even be able to interest him in a friendly armistice."

Rachel Carson's love of nature derived from a solitary childhood. Her mother, Maria McLean Carson, was her main companion. It was the elder Ms. Carson who gave to Rachel a love of music, books, and the wild woods which surrounded their modest farm. Maria Carson had been a schoolteacher before she married Robert Warden Carson and bore three children. Rachel was the youngest, born when Ms. Carson was thirty-seven, and because the child was sickly, Maria Carson spent a lot of time with her. Together they would take long walks, discovering the mysteries of the outdoors. Rachel learned to observe the countryside as an ecologist might, viewing the living organisms within their particular environments. Her sensitivity was acute. She felt a spiritual kinship to the creatures which she later wrote about—worms, snails, insects, and birds. Often she would study an infinitesimal organism under her binocular microscope and then place it carefully back in its home. It's no surprise to learn of her abhorrence for the "glorification of cruelty" demonstrated in hunting for sport.

She was not concerned with the great impersonal forces of nature. She mentioned believing in the existence of God, but apparently did not concern herself with theological specifics. Once, when her mother told her that God created the world, Rachel replied, "Yes, and General Motors created my Oldsmobile. But *how* is the question."

Rachel was bright and creative and went through

childhood and adolescence determined to be a writer. When she attended school, she was more readily accepted by her teachers than by her peers, for she was intellectual and introverted. She did not follow the fads of the 1920s, and she had a sense of her own potential. When she entered Pennsylvania College for Women on a scholarship, Rachel planned to major in literature.

Rachel Carson became a lyric writer, but only after arduous, disciplined, and meticulous work. Although she always found the research stimulating, the writing was grueling. She would leave her office and write long into the night, relaxing before sleep with a volume of Thoreau or Melville.

She took writing so seriously and so respected the manuscripts she later submitted to her publishers that she refused to allow editors free rein to rework her books. She carefully followed their progress and was aware of how each stage of production was faring. Writing was a private part of Carson's life, the area no one touched.

In her second year of college, Ms. Carson took a required course in biology and the direction of her life changed. A new world opened up and she wanted to explore it. Carson switched her major to zoology. She graduated magna cum laude in 1928 and attended Johns Hopkins University for her master's degree. Then she taught, first at Hopkins, then at the University of Maryland.

In 1935, Carson's father died and Rachel took on the responsibility for her mother; two nieces were also left in her care when her older sister died. It was the Great Depression and Carson needed more income, so she took a civil service examination with the hope of getting a government job. She got the highest score; she was the only woman who took it. In 1936, Rachel Carson joined the Fish and Wildlife Service of the Department of the Interior, and at the same time returned to free-lance writing, mainly newspaper features.

She was a responsible head of the family and a dutiful daughter. Her mother took care of the housework and later helped with her daughter's correspondence. Rachel, apparently, set the tone for the small feminine household. She was trusted and loved. (Ms. Carson was later to reinforce this trust when another niece died, leaving an eight-year-old son, Roger, whom Rachel Carson adopted when she was almost fifty.)

Carson was a private person, but not antisocial. During the war years she accepted invitations to many Washington parties, and whenever possible, she joined friends for field trips to Hawk Mountain Bird Sanctuary in Pennsylvania or to other nature spots.

In September 1937, Carson sold her first story to a major magazine, *Atlantic*. It was called "Undersea" and formed the basis for her first book, *Under the Sea Wind*, published by Simon and Schuster.

Writing this book revealed to Rachel Carson the difficulties of trying to become absorbed in her subject while having to devote most of her time and energy to her family, friends, and job. Her book was published in 1941, one month before Pearl Harbor. Fewer than sixteen hundred copies were sold in its first six years. (Later, Carson bought the rights to *Under the Sea Wind* and Oxford Press published it along with *The Sea Around Us*, which put Rachel Carson in the unique position of having two books on the *New York Times* best-seller list at one time.)

Meanwhile, Carson continued with her government duties. She progressed from junior aquatic biologist to biologist and chief editor of conservation booklets. These pamphlets included hints on stretching wartime food supplies by substituting lesser known seafoods for the more popular varieties. Carson struggled along on a modest salary, supplemented by the payments she received for occasional magazine articles. She even tried, unsuccessfully, to change jobs, applying to *Reader's Digest*, the New York Zoological Society, and *National Audubon*. Since her first book sold so few copies, Carson could not yet live on her writing income alone.

It was during these war years that Carson realized that

vast amounts of information were being gathered about chemicals, poisonous gases, and the general environment—gathered to help the military effort. Discoveries which might have taken scientists decades to make in peacetime would have to be evaluated when the war ended. Rachel Carson used much of the information concerning the sea, as well as chemicals, in her books.

After the war, Carson began carting home volumes of scientific data to study at night. She was researching her next book, *The Sea Around Us*. During this time, she also produced a series of twelve government booklets called *Conservation in Action*. These contained some of the government's first ecological statements. In the booklets, Rachel Carson denounced the needless waste of American natural resources: "Entire species of animals have been exterminated, or reduced to so small a remnant that their survival is doubtful. Forests have been despoiled by uncontrolled and excessive cutting of lumber; grasslands have been destroyed by overgrazing. . . . We have much to accomplish before we can feel assured of passing on to future generations a land as richly endowed in natural wealth as the one we live in."

These booklets were precursors not only of *Silent Spring,* but also of the ecological movement, for they indicted short-term profits reaped from long-term hazards brought about by techno-agricultural irresponsibility.

The Sea Around Us was published in 1952 by Oxford University Press. During the writing, Carson gained the friendship of literary agent Marie Rodell, who was a great help, not only in the business aspects of publishing, but also because she gave encouragement and support as the deadline trauma engulfed Carson.

The book was an immediate success, both with critics and the public. The diversity of the sea was presented in a fluent manner, easy to read and to appreciate. For many, this was an introduction to the sea and the sea islands which Carson claimed should be preserved as natural museums. Like all her writing, *The Sea Around Us* was well researched, and included information from the top-level government conferences she attended and from the specialists she knew. It was, in the words of the *New York Times,* "a classic."

The book brought her material and professional honors from the start. She received the George Washington Science Award for an advance chapter publication. The *New Yorker* ran a "Profile on the Sea" and became a Rachel Carson supporter. (*New Yorker* had offered her a large sum to postpone book publication one year, but Carson refused, feeling Oxford Press deserved first consideration. The *New Yorker* readjusted its own schedule and ran the "Profile" just before the book came out.)

The Sea Around Us appeared on the *New York Times* best-seller list for eighty-six weeks. Rachel Carson received fellowships, money, rave notices, and the National Book Award. She was given several honorary doctorate degrees and became a sought-after speaker. The book was then produced as a film and earned an Academy Award for best documentary.

Most important to Rachel Carson, she was now able to quit her job and devote all her time to studying and writing. She bought a strip of land on the Maine seacoast, which became a laboratory and second home. (After her death, this land was expanded to almost four thousand acres by the Interior Department, and became the Rachel Carson National Wildlife Refuge for migratory birds, water fowl, small animals, and marine life.)

One time, Carson and her niece went down to the beach at midnight. The spring tide was up, and she knew there would be great surf activity. They turned off their flashlights and watched the "diamonds and emeralds" thrown about on the sand, the phosphorescent foam sparkling along the entire shore.

Suddenly they saw a firefly. It apparently was confused, mistaking the flashes in the water for other fireflies. The firefly dipped low, got caught in the water, and was tossed onto the wet sand.

The two rescued the firefly and put it in a pail, hoping it would be safe there. Carson considered writing a children's story about the experience, but *Silent Spring,* and then death, precluded that.

Meanwhile, Carson was preparing her next book which she envisioned as a counterpart of *The Sea Around Us.* The main character of that book had been the ocean and its physical nature. The new book featured the tough, adaptable life found in the narrow region where water and land meet, *The Edge of the Sea.* It came out in 1955, earning further accolades for the author. Rachel Carson enjoyed the enthusiastic acceptance of the books, but found she had to limit the time she could give to their promotion. Not only did travel and speeches cut into her writing schedule, but her family demanded more attention as well. In the mid-fifties, Rachel's ailing niece came to live with her, bringing along her son Roger.

Rachel Carson loved Roger. He was the inspiration for an article which was posthumously expanded into a book called, *A Sense of Wonder.* As her own mother had done, Carson took the boy on long walks through the countryside, introducing him to the world of nature and instilling in him a self-perpetuating involvement with the earth, sky, and water.

"A child's world is fresh and new and beautiful, full of wonder and excitement. It is our misfortune that for all of us that clear-eyed vision, that true instinct for what is beautiful and awe-inspiring, is dimmed and even lost before we reach adulthood. If I had influence with the good fairy who is supposed to preside over the christening of all children I should ask that her gift to each child in the world be a sense of wonder so indestructible that it would last throughout life, as an unfailing antidote against the boredom and disenchantments of later years, the sterile preoccupation with things that are artificial, the alienation from the sources of our strength."

When Carson's niece died, Roger made new demands on Carson's life, and also brought new vivacity. She built a large house in Silver Springs and enjoyed the youthful spirit that now invaded it. She once claimed that now she relished Christmas more than ever because she shared the exuberance of a young boy opening his packages of "space-age toys."

When Rachel Carson began her next book, *Silent Spring,* her days as a gentle, informative naturalist were over. Her crusading era had begun, and it was to last until her death.

Writing *Silent Spring* was the most exhausting work she had ever undertaken. She had to provide an unshakable foundation for her thesis that industrial civilization was destroying the earth. Fifty-five pages of sources at the end of the book indicate that she elicited evidence from authorities all over the world.

Said Frank Graham, Jr., in his book on the aftermath of *Silent Spring,* "She came to believe that the full horror of the story lay for the most part unguessed at, even by herself."

She hoped that her book would "not degenerate into vaguely mystical ideas, or smack of the emotional arguments of the fringe groups. . . . Science must be the foundation for [the] work, as it always had been in the past, but it must be given another dimension by the sympathy and compassion without which the finest scientists in the world are dehumanized."

Carson followed the various court cases protesting pesticide spraying around the country, for example, the gypsy moth trial in Long Island. Cities, fields, gardens, marshes, farms, fish ponds, houses, and vehicles were all being liberally sprayed, although the gypsy moth thrived only in the woods. Because of mass spraying, countless animals and plants were killed, but the gypsy moth continued to thrive. In 1973, over fifteen years later, citizen groups were still protesting the continuous spraying for an insect that had proven to be highly resistant.

While writing *Silent Spring,* Carson attended the 1959 Washington hearings on the "cranberry scandal." This resulted in a ban against cranberries sprayed with aminotriazol. The next year she served on the National Resources Committee of the Democratic Advisory Council and attended meetings of the Women's Committee for the New Frontier. She also updated *The Sea Around Us,* explaining that the ocean had already been greatly changed, and she correctly predicted widespread pollution of the sea within ten years due to waste material and to radioactivity.

Her work was often hampered by illness. Even before she learned she had breast cancer in 1960, Carson was already ill with sinus infections and an ulcer. Later she underwent radiation treatment; her eyesight failed; an infection in her legs kept her in bed for weeks. Only intense dedication propelled her to keep at the book.

But finishing *Silent Spring* did not end her work; she was now faced with defending it. The accusations she had leveled were too far-reaching and too overwhelming to be ignored by industry and the general public.

Carson wrote: "The crusade to create a chemically sterile, insect-free world seems to have engendered a fanatic zeal on the part of many specialists and most of the so-called control agencies. On every hand there is evidence that those engaged in spraying operations exercise a ruthless power.

"It is not my contention that chemical insecticides must never be used. I do contend that we have put poisonous and biologically potent chemicals indiscriminately into the hands of persons largely or wholly ignorant of their potentials for harm."

She went on to state why, where, and how these chemicals have brought harm or extinction to animals, plants, necessary insects, and possibly humans. The last point was especially timely, because 1962 was also the year of the Thalidomyde scare. Several thousand babies were born deformed because pregnant women had taken a tranquilizer, Thalidomyde, put on the market without adequate testing.

"Although chemical manufacturers are required by law to test their materials for toxicity, they are not required to make the tests that would reliably demonstrate genetic effect, and they do not do so," wrote Carson. Although Thalidomyde was not a pesticide, the testing situation was similar. In fact, one of the reviewers of *Silent Spring* pointed out that medical controls, though inadequate, were actually better than those for agricultural chemical products. Carson found a polarization of scientists: there were those willing to deduce certain possibilities from proven facts; and there were others who denied the possibility of any evidence without definite proof, thus virtually using the public as guinea pigs.

"What the public is asked to accept as 'safe' today," wrote Rachel Carson, "may turn out to be extremely dangerous."

Arsenic was one example of a long-used pesticide which has been proven to be a carcinogen. Ms. Carson rated several other pesticides as direct carcinogens and even more which indirectly contributed to cancer. Although the latter were implicated by circumstantial evidence, the evidence was impressive and resulted in at least temporary withdrawal of the products from widespread use.

Carson described the dangerous chemicals which were available on supermarket shelves, often in glass bottles which a child might knock over and splatter. Much of her information and her accusations are still pertinent a decade later. Over two hundred basic chemicals were being used in the 1970 pest control programs. They are used in over sixty thousand separate compounds, each reacting differently in various organisms and in different surroundings.

Chlordane, Dieldrin, Aldrin, and Endrin, all more toxic than DDT, have been dusted liberally over farms and suburbs. Parathion is so toxic that one chemist who swallowed .00424 ounce of it became paralyzed and died before he could reach the antidote he had prepared. This chemical, now illegal in New York City without a special permit, was sold door to door in Miami, and has killed in recent years over a hundred people and poisoned many more.

Also in the early 1970s, public places were freely and abundantly sprayed against insects; restaurants used Lindane in their vaporizing units, although this chemical had been banned from home use; airplane interiors were sprayed to a point which could have been dangerous to the crew as

well as the passengers; rugs and clothing were routinely
sprayed against beetles before they were sold; and garden
sprays were hailed as indispensable to any home gardener
who wanted to avoid crab grass and thus criticism by
neighbors.

DDT was the most widely used pesticide when Carson
wrote her book. Gradually it has been banned for mass aerial
spraying in many countries (including the United States since
early 1973). DDT, however, is persistent and cumulative. It
remains in the soil and is passed from organism to organism,
turning up in far-off lands and waters and in all kinds of
products, including milk, tobacco, and leafy vegetables. As it
moves up the food pyramid, it accumulates. In 1969, *Chemical
Week* admitted that "DDT's marketing problems began in
earnest with the publication of the late Rachel Carson's *Silent
Spring.*"

Ms. Carson also denounced the destruction of natural
beauty through the indiscriminate use of herbicides. Native
plants, important indicators of soil conditions, were being
eradicated in many areas, labeled "pest" by those "who make
a business of selling and applying chemicals." Carson allowed
that there were benefits in carefully regulated spot spraying.
But for most pests—insect or plant—she advocated
alternatives to mass spraying.

Some alternatives were basic, for example, planting
marigolds among the roses to lure away aphids. "The best and
cheapest controls for vegetation are not chemicals but other
plants," Ms. Carson claimed. She advocated releasing
predator insects to feed on pest species; this was proven
workable when a wasp native to Korea and China was
imported to combat the Japanese beetle in the United States.
Also basic is getting away from one-crop farming by rotating
and by mingling sympathetic crops (for example, when dill is
planted with tomatoes, the dill lures tomato worms away
from the tomato plants). Systems of checks and balances were
fairly common in the past, when farms were smaller.

Other alternatives are more sophisticated: genetic

manipulation of certain insects which would eventually weaken and eradicate the whole species; sterilization of male insects to mate unproductively with females; sexual attractants to lure insects into traps; ultrasonic and electronic methods of pest control; hormonal interference in plant growth—for example, stimulating early growth of weeds which would be killed by heavy spring frosts. Carson acknowledged that these methods are often slower than mass chemical spraying, but they are safer, cheaper, and more effective in the long run. She also urged resisting the impulse to try new methods before they are well tested.

Silent Spring was received with every reaction but apathy. Carson was called the "nun of nature" by some and the "quack of nature" by others. Big Business derided the book as "baloney" while politicians wrote Carson asking her for effective ecology statements to use in their campaigns. More than a hundred thousand copies of the book were sold in the first three months after its publication.

One chemical company threatened her publisher with a suit if the book came out, but then withdrew the threat upon publication. Another company intimated that Carson was misled by "sinister forces working to undermine the capitalist system."

Because Carson's facts were irrefutable, one way her challenge was met was with ridicule. Some who felt they had been attacked countered in a viciously personal way, charging her with oversensitivity to carcinogens because she herself was suffering from cancer. One congressman wondered why she was so concerned with genetic damage when she wasn't even married. Others charged that her case was one-sided; here Rachel Carson agreed, saying that up to the time of *Silent Spring,* all statements on pesticides were praises of their effectiveness.

Despite the uproar from agricultural chemicals businesses, positive reactions were also immediate. By the end of 1962, over forty bills were pending in various state legislatures to regulate use of pesticides. A loophole in the

Department of Agriculture's federal insecticide, fungicide, and rodenticide act was closed. (This loophole allowed manufacturers accused of producing a hazardous pesticide to continue selling their product while the decision was appealed. Now the manufacturer had to prove a product's safety or withdraw the product.)

The Agriculture Department began supervising the registration and labeling of all pesticides, although it still proved neglectful in prosecuting violators. In 1967 there were almost twelve hundred violations out of five thousand samples.

In 1963, President John F. Kennedy urged his Science Advisory Committee to carefully study the pesticide problem. When the committee report came out, it claimed pesticidal pollution could be greatly reduced without lessening efficiency in pest control if more attention were paid to bioenvironmental controls (Rachel Carson's "alternative methods"). Dr. Jerome Wiesner of the committee said indiscriminate use of poisonous chemicals was "potentially a much greater hazard than radioactive fallout."

In the spring of 1963, Senator Abraham Ribicoff was named acting chairman of a subcommittee to study environmental hazards. The report of his subcommittee blamed industry and government for not recognizing ecological problems and for not getting at the facts and the solutions.

Rachel Carson was pleased by the "environmental revolution" her book inspired. She felt great satisfaction that her own sense of responsibility had pricked the public conscience. She regretted not having written *Silent Spring* ten years earlier, for she still had so many projects she wanted to delve into. Carson gathered more awards, including the Schweitzer Medal, and she was named Conservationist of the Year, received various board memberships, and was accepted into the American Association of Arts and Letters.

Although in pain, she remained optimistic. She died in April 1964 at the age of fifty-six.

The prospect of a silent spring remains before the human race and the planet which supports it. Still, the rain of pesticides has lessened and legal action has begun to abate, if not halt, the destruction. Most important is the public awareness ignited by Rachel Carson. And there are the memorials she began, inspired, or aided to preserve natural areas against "civilizing" intrusion—the Rachel Carson Seacoast Fund, the Sierra Club, the Nature Conservancy, and the Rachel Carson Fund for the Living Environment.

It took a generation beyond her own to grasp fully the meaning of Carson's work. Peace, love, and reverence for all life has become a motto for many of the young in the last third of the twentieth century.

"Miss Carson," said Senator Ribicoff, "you are the lady who started all this."

12

The Bettmann Archive

Margaret Mead

Anthropologist, folk heroine, ultimate liberated woman, and, perhaps most of all, national oracle—in all these capacities, each with its element of truth, Dr. Margaret Mead is as much a natural outgrowth of her childhood environment as she is a product of her chosen career.

"For me, being brought up to become a woman who could live responsibly in the contemporary world and learning to become an anthropologist, conscious of the culture in which I lived, were almost the same thing."

In her lifetime, Dr. Mead has lived among three generations and has been a spokesperson for each. She is probably the best-known anthropologist of all time. Bringing to the public a respect for as well as a knowledge of primitive cultures, she has linked the primitive with the sophisticated. She has utilized her information about South Pacific peoples to formulate and to present her own ideas about the American culture. That all this was to be her life's work was determined years ago by the family she was born into on December 16, 1901, near Philadelphia, and within which she developed as a person and as a woman.

In her autobiography, *Blackberry Winter,* Mead wrote:
"The content of my conscience came from my mother's
concern for other people and the state of the world, and from
my father's insistence that the only thing worth doing is to
add to the store of exactly known facts. But the strength of
my conscience came from Grandma, who meant what she
said."

Margaret Mead today is concerned with the world and its
people. She is curious about the new and the future as well as
the present and the past. And she is always strong and
authoritative, to the consternation of some of her colleagues,
who have called her a busybody and a Pollyanna.

Emily Fogg Mead, Margaret's mother, was a small,
pretty woman, a feminist who could never fully apply
feminist principles to her own life. She was a college graduate
and a former Hull House worker. She raised four children (a
fifth died in infancy) and ran a physically and intellectually
mobile household. She edited her husband's manuscripts
which, combined with her homemaking responsibilities, left
too little time for independent interests. Yet her "concern for
other people and the state of the world" impressed her eldest
daughter. This concern manifested itself in Emily Mead's
sociological studies, eventually leading to a Ph.D. She was
particularly interested in the adaptation of Italian
immigrants to American society; the Mead family spent many
springs, summers, and autumns in Hammonton, New Jersey,
where Ms. Mead worked on her field of interest. But it was
finally Margaret who would live out the goals that her
mother had set for herself. Emily Fogg Mead relished her
daughter's success and helped Margaret with her book
indexes in later years.

Margaret's father, Edward Sherwood Mead, taught
economics at the Wharton School, wrote several books, and
edited a railroad magazine. He was involved with the
formulation, more than the application, of ideas. He was
intrigued, for example, with theories of making money, but
did not apply his knowledge. Margaret Mead later said she

most respected her father's abilities to concentrate and to criticize, but his acuity did not extend to understanding other people.

Margaret Mead knew his lack of sensitivity well. When she was nearing college age, her father decided he could not afford the expense. Too proud to admit that he was short of funds, he made excuses, such as, she would only get married anyway and waste the education. He brought a physician friend to the house to state that tiny Margaret was too "weak" for college, suggesting that she study nursing instead. This proposal Margaret found contradictory, since she had taken on most of the household chores in addition to her school program the previous year, which indicated her physical and mental strength.

However, the center of the Mead household was neither mother nor father, but Margaret's paternal grandmother, Martha Ramsey Mead, a Montessori teacher, school principal, wife, and mother, who had tread an individualistic path all her life. She brought the past into the Mead home, to simmer with and flavor the present. She was a tremendous influence on Margaret, who eventually brought old family traditions to her own family.

In her later years, Margaret Mead recognized and deplored the trend of isolating the old in retirement cities. "We're putting people away in these institutions much too early and leaving them all alone with nobody but other people who are dying, which is a horrible way to live. A society that does it has done something terrible to itself and has robbed its children of their right to know about the past from the grandparents' generation."

It was also Martha Mead who provided the children with the necessary discipline and with their unique education. Margaret Mead never doubted either the infallibility of her grandmother's threats or her school theories. She later wrote that her schooling before college consisted of two years in kindergarten, one year (half days only) in the fourth grade, and six years in high school. Martha Mead felt the traditional

school system was outdated and confined; children needed
freedom to learn. As a result, while other grade-school
children were spelling three-letter words, Margaret, Richard,
Elizabeth, and Priscilla, were studying botany and algebra.

To supplement this erratic education dictated by her
mother-in-law, Emily Mead hunted for experts in various
fields to teach her children different crafts—drawing, basket
weaving, music, and leather work. Not only did Margaret
Mead later utilize this idea with her own child, but for
decades she was a leading spokesperson for interdisciplinary
research. She encouraged talented personnel trained in
different disciplines to invest in one common study,
merging their specialized information to form a whole,
definitive work.

From these two women—her mother and her
grandmother—Margaret Mead learned her pattern of
womanhood, which combined a tradition of nurturing with
individualism. Because Emily Fogg Mead always dressed
neatly after rising, Margaret Mead dressed carefully in the
morning. Because her grandmother had combined career and
family, so did Margaret continue working after her only
daughter, Mary Catherine Bateson, was born. She made sure
Cathy was provided with warmly personal surroundings and
devoted maternal care, just as Dr. Mead had known in
childhood.

Margaret Mead said of her grandmother, "She was
unquestionably feminine—small and dainty and pretty and
wholly without masculine protest or feminist aggrievement."
Dr. Mead's own daughter once told a reporter, "My mother
thinks being female is marvelous. She wouldn't be a man for
anything." All three generations refused to reject femininity,
nor did they restrict it within its outdated boundaries.

Mead's childhood experiences in femininity permeated
her career. In anthropology, she focused much of her attention
on women and children, gathering information male
anthropologists had neglected. In America, Margaret Mead
became a symbol of zest and accomplishment for older women.

"Menopause relieves anxiety, releases creativity. The reproductive years are a rival to creation. With their end comes a kind of exhilaration," she once wrote, talking as much about her vital mother and grandmother as about her own experience.

Yet, this concentration on "woman's work" has brought criticism, particularly from the New Feminists. In *The Feminine Mystique,* Betty Friedan wrote: "From [her] anthropological observations, she might have passed on to the popular culture a truly revolutionary vision of women finally free to realize their full capabilities in a society which replaced arbitrary sexual definitions with a recognition of genuine individual gifts as they occur in either sex. . . ." Margaret Mead, says Friedan, often "seems to be arguing in functional terms, that while woman's potential is as great and various as the unlimited human potential, it is better to preserve the sexual biological limitations established by a culture."

Nevertheless, Dr. Mead became a standard bearer for emancipated women during a century seriously lacking in female inspiration. (Even Friedan admits that Mead's "influence has been felt in almost every leader of American thought.") From her position as a leader, Margaret Mead, while supporting the twentieth century revolt of American women, stated that the basic fault of the movement has been its superficial aims. What Mead envisions for women is a revolution which cuts deeper than the worker's revolution or the suffrage movement did, and goes beyond yearnings for new opportunities, changes, and freedoms. Self-determination for women must go beyond their biological capabilities of bearing, nursing, and raising children; but rather than discarding the traditional functions, women must utilize them for the betterment of all people. Men and women both need to adopt the formerly feminine virtues of patience, endurance, and steadfastness.

"I believe we are faced with the necessity for a revolution that will be as fully as important for women—and so for all

human beings—as the development of civilization was for
men and only incidentally for women." Civilization freed men
from their daily search for food, but women's lives remain
centered on the needs of children. "The crucial question today,
I believe, is how we shall begin to reorder our lives so that
having a small number of children can enrich the lives of both
children and adults. . . . If we look to the future, the current
moves for women's right to determine and control their own
activities—all related to the development of an industrial
society and growing egalitarianism—are no more than pale
reflections of what will be accomplished once we realize the
immensity of the break with the past."

Obviously, the Mead family was unique. A childhood
friend once told Dr. Mead: "In my family I was a child. In
your family's house I was a person!" Margaret grew up with a
strong sense of her own worth and potential. When she was
young, her father called her "The Original Punk" and her
brother, "Boy-Punk," which indicated to Margaret that she
was the norm and Richard the variation.

Almost seventy years later, Margaret Mead, a small,
round, serene lady—gray haired and gray eyed, with a fringe
of gray bangs across her forehead—is strong minded and
positive in her convictions. One colleague remarked that
when Dr. Mead believes a fellow scholar is wrong, "she is
truly like one of those terrible Indian goddesses, standing on
her victims with her tongue sticking out."

Mead's parents made her feel important. When the two
youngest daughters, Elizabeth and Priscilla, were born,
Emily Mead gave Margaret a notebook so that she could
record the babies' progress and achievements. Margaret Mead
kept up this notebook practice all her life, in field studies as
well as with her own daughter. Always Mead looked for traits
that linked family members, and recently, she found that her
granddaughter has the same alert, sparkling, dark eyes as did
her grandmother, Martha Ramsey Mead.

With notebook and pencil, Margaret, the budding
anthropologist, soon recorded differences between Elizabeth

and Priscilla; this led to pondering why one sister would behave differently from the other in certain situations. Young Margaret reasoned that the order of birth was important in a child's development. She also suspected back then what she later verified in *Sex and Temperament* and *Male and Female,* that gender was not the determining factor in a person's behavior.

She called herself a family stage manager, arranging the atmosphere in which her brother and sisters could perform. Richard would sing; Elizabeth would dance; Priscilla would look beautiful. She continued with her sisterly interest even as the children grew older. When Priscilla was ready for college, Margaret did not want her to become just another society matron, beautiful but skilled only in parlor conversation. She encouraged her, therefore, to attend a socially-oriented university. There Priscilla soon got her fill of superficialities, and on her own, switched to a more academic environment (and won a Phi Beta Kappa key).

Young Margaret Mead's "home" was not a physical structure, it was this family. They moved often. In winter, when her father taught at the Wharton school, the Meads lived in Philadelphia so he would not have to commute. The rest of the year the family lived in other places, first in Hammonton where Emily Mead pursued her studies and, later, on a farm in Bucks County. (An interest in people rather than places continued into Margaret Mead's adult life. She preferred to share apartments and houses instead of secluding herself and her family. Her basic "home" was an attic office of the American Museum of Natural History in New York City, where she began working in 1926. She shared apartments with each of her three husbands, and then she shared a commune house in Greenwich Village with another family. Her latest apartment is shared with anthropologist Rhoda Metraux.)

When Edward Mead finally agreed to finance his daughter's education, Margaret entered his alma mater, DePauw University, in 1919. During her one unhappy year at

DePauw, Mead learned the heartbreak of sorority-fraternity social rule. Because she would not adopt the rigid conventions of dress and behavior, Margaret Mead was not pledged to a sorority, and consequently, she was out of the college social whirl completely. Yet, she had, by now, a proud independence, so she did not retreat into sulky isolation or haughty disapproval. Instead, she drew upon her old stage-manager ability and helped set up college shows.

She also continued studying people and their behavior. She could understand the agony that results when an arbitrarily rejected person continues to crave acceptance into an exclusive society. She came to believe that no person or group should be favored at the expense of others.

Mead's one year at DePauw was made a bit more bearable by her engagement to a young Pennsylvania seminarian, Luther Cressman. She was excited more about her future as a minister's wife, working with the parish people and raising a large family of children, than she was about Luther Cressman himself. She had joined the Episcopal church at age eleven, when she decided that this religion gave the opportunity to express spiritual feelings in the manner most amenable to her. There was no distinct religious upbringing in the Mead home, and again, Margaret Mead was allowed to choose her own way at an early age, even in an area usually well defined by parents.

When Margaret Mead left DePauw, she had decided that coeducation was limiting for bright girls; they were not praised for doing well academically even though, Mead noted, bright girls did far better in school than bright boys. In 1920, she entered Barnard College and a stimulating period of her life.

During the Barnard years, Margaret Mead changed her career plans and met her lifelong friends. Her father had impressed upon her that "the most important thing any person could do was to add to the world's store of knowledge." Mead had considered writing, painting, and politics, but finally decided that in social science any individual could find a satisfying way to work for the world's betterment. In her senior year, when she took a course under Franz Boas and Ruth Benedict, Mead narrowed this down to anthropology.

Mead moved into an apartment with a group of women students of different ages, all intellectual and talented. They called themselves the "Ash Can Girls," and they considered themselves the "free generation," loving openly with no demands and postponing marriage and children for careers. More important, Mead learned the high degree of loyalty and trust that is possible among women.

Although Ruth Benedict was not an "Ash Can Girl" and was already established in the field of anthropology, she and Margaret Mead became close friends. Mead later said that Benedict was the only person who read everything Mead wrote and vice versa. Their friendship was firmly cemented when a tragedy occurred one weekend during Mead's senior year. Mead was caught in a situation of having to decide which of two desperate school friends needed her more. One friend was depressed after a hospital stay; the other was temporarily blinded by hysteria. Mead chose to remain with the blinded girl, whose need seemed more immediate. When the weekend was over, Mead checked on the other girl and found her depressed friend had committed suicide. Mead was desolate. She felt terribly guilty.

It was Ruth Benedict who most consoled Mead, explaining that she was not to blame and that contrary to our society's beliefs, there are times when suicide is the most noble choice.

Margaret Mead graduated from Barnard in 1923, planning to earn her master's degree in psychology by the end of that summer and to begin graduate work in anthropology in the fall. She planned to study immigrant groups and American Indians.

That fall she married Luther Cressman, but she kept her own name, as Emily Fogg Mead encouraged all her daughters to do. Years later, Mead's own daughter followed the same example. Cressman and Mead settled into marriage easily, advising other couples on how to solve problems, and apparently having none themselves. "I had what I thought I wanted . . . a marriage in which there seemed no obstacles to being myself," said Mead.

But marital contentment and academic advancement did not satisfy her ambition and drive for long. In the summer of 1924, Mead attended a meeting of the British Association for the Advancement of Science in Toronto. She was stirred by the presentations of real accomplishments. She heard active field anthropologists discuss "their people."

"I learned the delight of intellectual arguments among peers. I, too, wanted to have a 'people' on whom I could base my own intellectual life." Margaret Mead decided to do field work; this was the first break in the smooth plans she had made for her life with Luther Cressman.

Margaret Mead's Ph.D. dissertation was almost completed. Cressman was interested in studying in Europe, and Mead received a fellowship to work in Polynesia during 1925-26. She had chosen Polynesia, a dangerous area, because her fluency in French and German could help her there. She immediately set out to read the many accounts written by missionaries and early explorers of their experiences in the area. Her Columbia adviser, Franz Boas, urged her to study Polynesian adolescents and try to determine if the difficulties so common in the same age group in Western cultures were biologically or culturally induced. He emphasized that the Polynesian culture was disappearing, and Mead was anxious as she prepared for the long trip to Samoa (chosen because a steamship made regular stops there).

In 1925, Margaret Mead was academically well prepared, but lacked knowledge of the practical aspects of anthropological field work. She was not prepared for the daily trial of mere existence. She did not realize the discipline needed to work regularly without supervision. She had not foreseen the loneliness, or the "frustrated gentleness," rather than frustrated sex, that was so difficult to bear in the field, or the problems in dealing with officials. Later in her life,

Margaret Mead would be generous with her written notes and with advice to young field workers, telling them how to work cameras, tape-recorders, and generators, and how to protect their belongings against the humidity.

Fortunately, Dr. Mead met friendly people. Stopping in California, she learned that she must add a good lamp to her supplies, which until then included only a flashlight, camera, some clothes, a typewriter, a strongbox, and notebooks. In Hawaii she was given squares of muslin for wiping the children's noses, and a blue silk pillow, so she could sleep anywhere. She received letters, one of which introduced her to the staff of the medical department in Samoa. One of the nurses there taught her the Samoan language.

Margaret Mead, small and young with bobbed brown hair and a slender figure, became quick friends with the Samoan children, who called her Makelita. She learned to sleep on a pebble floor, to sit cross-legged for hours, and to eat raw fish. She learned to wash in the village shower and change clothes in front of anyone who happened by. She learned also that a field worker "must live all day in a maze of relationships without being caught in the maze"—he must chronicle, but not become involved.

"The anthropologist," she wrote, "is trained to see form where other people see concrete details, to think in terms which will bring together a wedding in a cathedral and a ceremony on a small South Sea island, in which two middle-aged people with three children sit down and solemnly eat one white chicken egg. Seen in terms of the social history, both are marriages: both are socially sanctioned ways of recognizing that two people, a man and a woman, now publicly assume complete responsibility for their children, although in one society the children are born before the ceremony while in the other, the ceremony must come first."

Dr. Mead completed her study of Samoan adolescent girls in nine months. She noted that biological human nature was altered by the customs of society, and her resulting book, *Coming of Age in Samoa,* was an immediate best seller.

Critics called it "a remarkable contribution to our knowledge of humanity."

Beginning with this book, and continuing throughout her life, Margaret Mead wrote up her field notes as quickly as possible. She had seen the notes of other anthropologists wasted because they were not written up immediately. When a scientist died, often no one was able to decipher his notations.

Margaret and Luther's marriage was ending. Their plan had been based upon his working in the ministry and her with American Indian groups. Now Margaret was doing field work abroad and Luther had left the ministry. Furthermore, Mead had learned that she could probably never bear children, so her belief that Luther Cressman would be a good father for her children was irrelevant to their marriage. Their original life outline was no longer valid.

Sailing home from Samoa, Dr. Mead met a brilliant young New Zealand psychologist named Reo Fortune, who was later to become her second husband. They parted in Europe, and Mead continued on to New York. There, while writing *Coming of Age in Samoa,* she began her new job as Assistant Curator of Ethnology at the American Museum of Natural History. In 1928, her book was at the printer's and Mead took a leave of absence to study on a fellowship in New Guinea with Reo Fortune.

Theirs was a marriage in which each could work as an individual contributing to the whole. With Fortune, Mead felt she was able to move into areas more inaccessible and more savage than she could have attempted alone. For the next eleven years, she worked with six different tribes. Five of those years were spent with Reo Fortune.

The first tribe they studied together was the Manus, and from this study came her second book, *Growing Up in New Guinea.* After the Second World War, Dr. Mead returned alone many times to visit the Manus, to stay in the house they built for her, and to chronicle the changes which had occurred since that first trip: "I have seen what few people have ever seen, people who have moved from the Stone Age into the present in thirty years—kids who say, 'My father was a cannibal, but I am going to be a doctor!'"

While touching base in New York in 1930, Mead and Fortune accepted an offer to study the Omaha Indians for the museum's Anthropology Department. Reo was to investigate the "visions" often reported by the Indians; Margaret was to study the women. It turned out to be a disappointing venture —beginning with the stifling Nebraska weather and their battered old car, and ending with their finding an uninspiring culture which seemed to offer nothing from the old and nothing that was new. Mead said she would have rather studied the Navaho Indians, who still retained their strong traditions, but they "belonged" to another anthropologist, and colleagues did not tread on each other's "people."

On her next field trip to New Guinea in 1931, Mead found the material for one of her most quoted books, *Sex and Temperament*. Reo and Margaret studied three contrasting tribes: the placid Arapesh, the violent Mundugumor, and the Tschambuli with their reversed sex roles. From these tribes they wanted to determine: Are there innate differences between people which are applicable to both males and females? Can human beings be categorized into tempera-mental types, and can there exist male and female versions of these types? What happens to a nonconformist individual in a society which emphasizes one type of temperament?

Fortune and Mead joined Gregory Bateson, another anthropologist, in New Guinea. The three drew upon various "peoples" to devise four culturally defined temperamental types. (The fourth "people"—the Bali—would be studied and included later.)

The Arapesh tribe expected its members to be peaceful and involved with growing food and children. They did not tolerate aggressiveness, punishing a member who even aroused anger in another. (Mead found this tribe a bit dull, for they had no art, no ritual, and little variation.)

The Mundugumor were a cannibalistic tribe, fierce and possessive. Unwanted babies were routinely tossed into the river, a habit which tortured Margaret Mead, who deeply wanted a child herself. She admitted abhorring the tribe.

The third people studied by Mead and Fortune had sex roles that were opposite those of Western cultures. The Tschambuli women, brisk and hearty, were the business people. Their daughters were bright and competent. The men and boys were petty, had temper tantrums, and liked to learn new dance steps and gossip.

While pondering the differences in the customs of the tribes, the three anthropologists began studying themselves and their own native cultures. They discovered that American-born, tiny Margaret Mead and aristocratic, British, towering Gregory Bateson were basically the same temperamental types—nurturing and parental, yet Bateson would not be considered "feminine" anymore than would the Arapesh men be called "maternal."

Reo Fortune, in contrast, was more aggressive, the product of a masculinist environment. His marriage with Dr. Mead had already begun showing signs of strain. Fortune found it difficult to adjust to marriage with a famed and vigorous woman. And, although she shared his energetic enthusiasm for their work, confident, independent Margaret Mead found it fatiguing to be constantly boosting his ego:

"I fully realized that it was essential to respect the sensibilities of men reared in other cultures, and that their sense of masculinity could be impaired by being asked to behave in ways they had been taught to regard as feminine. . . . But I thought then—as I do now—that if we are to have a world in which women work beside men, a world in which both men and women can contribute their best, women must learn to give up pandering to male sensitivities, something at which they succeeded so well as long as it was a woman's primary role, as a wife, to keep her family intact, or, as a mistress, to comfort her lover. Because of their age-long training in human relations—for that is what feminine

intuition really is—women have a special contribution to
make to any group enterprise, and I feel it is up to them to
contribute the kinds of awareness that relatively few men . . .
have incorporated through their education."

Mead and Fortune were divorced in 1935, and shortly
thereafter, she married Gregory Bateson. Meanwhile, she had
returned to the American Museum and begun work on *Sex
and Temperament.*

In this book, she emphasized the different ways in which
gender behavior was stylized in the Arapesh, Mundugumor,
and Tschambuli tribes. Fourteen years later, she continued
the comparison in *Male and Female,* pointing out the cultural
and temperamental differences displayed by men and women.
She also discussed characteristics which seemed related to
primary differences between the sexes. With both books,
Dr. Mead was attacked as being too feministic by the
antifeminists and too traditional by the feminists.

In March 1936, Margaret Mead and Gregory Bateson
arrived in Bali to begin a joint two-year study of the highly
civilized Polynesian people who lived there. It was in Bali
that they made breakthroughs in the techniques of recording
primitive life. They devised a way of taking massive numbers
of photographs, developing them fast, organizing them, and
accompanying them with recorded notes.

In 1939, Margaret Mead gave birth to a baby girl. Since
she had suffered several miscarriages, when she found out she
was pregnant, she took extreme precautions to prevent
another loss. She planned a prepared childbirth with no
anesthesia; she secured wet nurses so the hospital would not
have an excuse to give the baby a bottle if she could not nurse
immediately, and she demanded the baby be in her hospital
room as much as possible. Because Margaret Mead chose to
have and care for her child in that manner, many women
emulated her, starting a trend toward prepared childbirth
and breast-feeding on demand.

Mead hired a nurse for Mary Catherine Bateson, but she
undertook the feeding and much of the care-taking herself.

Immediately the family began to move from place to place, much as the Mead family had done years before. Because Gregory Bateson was working much of the time in England, Dr. Mead and the baby moved into her parents' home in Philadelphia. Next, they went to New York; while Dr. Mead taught at New York University and worked at the museum, an English nurse cared for Cathy. As the war years approached, the Mead-Bateson family shared an extended family relationship with psychiatrist Lawrence Frank and his family in Greenwich Village. Consequently, Cathy Bateson grew up with many people around her.

By this time, Margaret Mead was no longer working with just one other person but with many others. As the war ended, so did her marriage and her years as a wife-partner. For the next part of her life, Dr. Mead functioned as an individual among many associates.

Although Mead now had a child to care for and no longer did much extensive field study, she did not cut down on her work. When she became a grandmother thirty years later, Mead was still handling a full work schedule and making plans. Becoming a grandmother, she admitted, had given her a jolt because she realized that a series of events in which she had no active part had changed her status forever.

In 1942, Margaret Mead accepted the position of executive secretary of the Committee on Food Habits of the National Research Council. She studied American food preferences and how Americans coped with food shortages. She lectured in England and wrote *And Keep Your Powder Dry*, about America's strengths and weaknesses.

After the war, Mead joined her old friend Ruth Benedict in a series of studies of contemporary societies; she wrote three books on different cultures existing at that time. She also joined the first research study group of the National Institute for Mental Health and the World Federation for Mental Health. She served as president of the WFMH in 1956.

Always, Mead remained at the American Museum in her

crowded attic office. In 1970 she became curator emeritus of
ethnology, and in the next year, her dream of forty-five years,
the Hall of the Peoples of the Pacific, was completed. This hall
is an effective minirecord of Mead's life and work. She has
illustrated the unique twentieth-century story of New Guinea
primitives who had never seen a canoe, a bicycle, or a horse
and buggy, who stepped "straight from the Stone Age into an
airplane with virtually nothing in between."

Almost a half-century ago, Margaret Mead used simple
devices to record such tribes; today, just as her "people" use
modern tools, Mead uses sophisticated equipment to present
their culture to the rest of the world.

"This Hall," claims Mead, "has been made with television
in mind," made for the new generation which witnesses the
whole world daily in its home through that medium of
communication. Dr. Mead herself uses television extensively
to communicate and to teach. She also uses the college lecture
hall. She set up N.Y.U.'s department of anthropology and
Fordham University's Liberal Arts College, and has taught at
Columbia University and lectured at the Universities of
Cincinnati and Rhode Island.

Margaret Mead still views society as an anthropologist,
applying her observations and theories to the contemporary
world in books, magazine articles, and columns. She has a
strong statement on almost every aspect of society. Like
Eleanor Roosevelt, Dr. Mead has been called a "den mother"
of the world's people. She urges respect for world laws and a
strong world organization to speak for all the people. She
encourages social scientists to search for ways by which
primitive people can learn to be coworkers with the more
sophisticated. It is by studying the primitive peoples, she has
said, that we can learn about our potentials and our
limitations.

The responsibility of anthropologists, she believes, is to
the people they are working with. They have the obligation to
advise governments "as to how to modulate the shocks, or
how *not* to go in and insist on changing the methods of burial

that upset everyone unnecessarily." Governments must be counseled "on what sorts of education will bring people from the Stone Age most rapidly into the modern world; on what sorts of labor practices may upset the village life and upset relations between young and old, or upset marriage relationships."

Realizing her own worth—always the "Original Punk"—Mead is free with advice: "One of the jobs of the anthropologist is to get people to see that many of the things that we think of as universal were only invented yesterday and don't fit anymore today." She feels the "lifetime marriage" concept is out of date and doomed to disappear. The human lifespan is much longer now and the childbearing rate is much lower than it once was. Instead, she proposes two types of marriage. The first is a relationship between two people who do not want to have children. Here, the marriage could be dissolved easily with a minimum of emotional trauma. The other type of marriage she recommends is a parental one. This would be for couples who want children and who are willing to take the responsibility for them. Mead also advocates encouraging parents, children, relatives, and friends of all ages to mingle, helping each other in individual ways.

"The only legitimate cause for divorce is the death of a marriage, that is, when one partner feels the relationship has died."

Regarding sex, the former "Ash Can Girl" says: "I think sex should be related to something. If you break off every time you're disappointed I don't see where it leads—this demand for instant happiness."

To Margaret Mead, a whole new era began the day the atom bomb was dropped. (A manuscript she had nearly finished she tore into bits, for she felt that it was now out of date.) Dr. Mead has become one of the few older spokespeople for the young, a firm believer that every child born after the Second World War belongs to one era and all those born before belong to another. She sees this "generation gap" as a product of history, not of age. She also considers this gap to be temporary, for the pre–World War II generations will die and the younger people will gradually assume power over a world that has always known computers, instant worldwide communication, and the threats of instant annihilation, overpopulation, and pollution.

Therefore, while most of the pre–World War II generation looks on with horror at what some of the postwar generations reject, such as orthodox religion, competition, and cleanliness, Margaret Mead is often considered by the young as part of their world. To this she replies, "No, I belong to my own generation. Because we are now seeking many of the same things, this does not mean I belong to your generation. I cannot ever belong to your generation, as you cannot ever belong to mine. But I can try to explain."

She explains that learning itself is rewarding, and that young people must look to older people as consultants. "We must create new models for adults who can teach their children not what to learn, but how to learn, and not what they should be committed to, but the value of commitment."

Dr. Mead once said, "At this moment we have virtually the whole of man's life spread out before us—people who are living as they may have lived for the past thirty thousand years and astronauts who are beginning to live as we will live tomorrow. On my first field trips I worked with the comforting knowledge that everything I reported was unique, vanishing, and would be useful for anthropology. Today those people and I live in the same world, and my knowledge of their past has changed the world climate so that it is ready for them to assert their rights as human beings. . . . We're not going to go back."

Of all her activities, Margaret Mead's greatest goal seems to be implicit in that last sentence: to look backward, but not to move backward; to convince people that "we're not going to go back," yet remembering at the same time that "only if we accept our past, can we go ahead in the future."

Bibliography

The symbol (P) which follows some entries indicates that the material is available in a paperback edition, but not necessarily from the publisher cited.

CHAPTER 1: ANNE HUTCHINSON

Battis, Emery. *Saints and Sectaries: Anne Hutchinson and the Antinomian Controversy in the Massachusetts Bay Colony*. Institute of Early American History and Culture. Chapel Hill: University of North Carolina Press, 1962.

Boorstin, Daniel J. *The Americans: The Colonial Experience*. New York: Random House, 1958.

Cockshott, Winnifred. *The Pilgrim Fathers, Their Church and Colony*. London, England: Methuen and Co., 1909.

Douglas, Emily T. *Remember the Ladies*. New York: G. P. Putnam's Sons, 1966.

Dunn, Richard S. *Puritans and Yankees: The Winthrop Dynasty of New England, 1630–1717*. Princeton, N. J.: Princeton University Press, 1962.

Flexner, Eleanor. *Century of Struggle: The Woman's Rights Movement in the United States*. Cambridge, Mass.:

245

Harvard University Press, Belknap Press, 1959.

Morris, Richard B. *The New World*. Life History of the
United States. Vol. 1. New York: Time-Life Books, 1963.

Sinclair, Andrew. *The Emancipation of the American Woman*.
2d ed. (Original title: *Better Half*.) New York: Harper
and Row, 1970.

CHAPTER 2: MERCY OTIS WARREN

Anthony, Katherine. *First Lady of the Revolution*. New York:
Doubleday and Co., 1958. Reprint ed., Port Washington,
N. Y.: Kennikat Press, 1971.

Brown, Alice. *Mercy Warren*. 1896. Reprint ed., Spartanburg,
S. C.: Reprint Co., 1968.

Butterfield, L. H., ed. *The Adams Papers, Adams Family
Correspondence*. Cambridge, Mass.: Harvard University
Press, Belknap Press, 1963.

———. *Diary and Autobiography of John Adams*. Cambridge,
Mass.: Harvard University Press, Belknap Press, 1961.

Commager, Henry S., and Morris, Richard B., eds. *The Spirit
of Seventy-Six: The Story of the American Revolution as
Told by Participants*. New York: Harper and Row, 1967.

Ellet, Elizabeth. *Women of the American Revolution*. Vol. 1.
Philadelphia: George W. Jacobs and Co., 1900. Reprint
ed., New York: Haskell House, 1969.

Forbes, Esther. *Paul Revere and the World He Lived In*.
Boston: Houghton Mifflin Co., 1942.

Hutcheson, Maud M. "Mercy Warren, 1728–1814." *William
and Mary Quarterly*, July 1953, pp. 378–402.

James, Edward T.; James, Janet W.; and Boyer, Paul S., eds.
*Notable American Women 1607–1950: A Biographical
Dictionary*. 3 vols. Cambridge, Mass.: Harvard University
Press, Belknap Press, 1971.

Morison, Samuel E. *Harrison Gray Otis, Seventeen Sixty-Five
to Eighteen Forty-Eight: The Urbane Federalist*. Boston:
Houghton Mifflin Co., 1969.

Tudor, William. *The Life of James Otis of Massachusetts*.
1823. Reprint ed., New York: Da Capo Press, n.d.

Ward, Christopher. *The American Revolution.* New York:
Macmillan and Co., 1952.
Whitten, Mary O. *These Were the Women, U.S.A. 1776–1860.*
New York: Hastings House, 1954.

CHAPTER 3: EMMA HART WILLARD

Fairbanks, A. W., ed. *Emma Willard and Her Pupils, or Fifty
Years of the Troy Female Seminary, 1822–72.* 1898.
Flexner, Eleanor. *Century of Struggle: The Woman's Rights
Movement in the United States.* Cambridge, Mass.:
Harvard University Press, Belknap Press, 1959. (P)
Holbrook, Stewart H. *Dreamers of the American Dream.*
Mainstreams of America Series, edited by Lewis Gannett.
New York: Doubleday and Co., 1957.
James, Edward T.; James, Janet W.; and Boyer, Paul S., eds.
*Notable American Women 1607 to 1950: A Biographical
Dictionary.* 3 vols. Cambridge, Mass.: Harvard University
Press, Belknap Press, 1971.
Lutz, Alma. *Emma Willard: Pioneer Educator of American
Women.* Boston: Beacon Press, 1964.
Morison, Samuel E. *The Oxford History of the American
People.* New York: Oxford University Press, 1965.
Scott, Anne F., ed. *The American Woman: Who Was She?*
Englewood Cliffs, N. J.: Prentice-Hall, 1971.
Sinclair, Andrew. *The Emancipation of the American Woman.*
2d ed. (Original title: *Better Half.*) New York: Harper
and Row, 1970.
Willard, Emma. *Journal and Letters from France and Great
Britain.* 1833.

CHAPTER 4: MARGARET FULLER

Chipperfield, Faith. *In Quest of Love: The Life and Death of
Margaret Fuller.* New York: Coward, McCann and
Geoghegan, 1957.
Curtis, Edith R. *Season in Utopia: The Story of Brook Farm.*
New York: Russell and Russell, 1971.

Deiss, Joseph Jay. "Men, Women, and Margaret Fuller."
  American Heritage, August 1972, pp. 42–47.
————. *The Roman Years of Margaret Fuller*. New York:
  Thomas Y. Crowell Co., 1969.
Flexner, Eleanor. *Century of Struggle: The Woman's Rights
  Movement in the United States*. Cambridge, Mass.:
  Harvard University Press, Belknap Press, 1959. (P)
Holbrook, Stewart H. *Dreamers of the American Dream*.
  Mainstreams of America Series, edited by Lewis Gannett.
  New York: Doubleday and Co., 1957.
James, Edward T.; James, Janet W.; and Boyer, Paul S., eds.
  *Notable American Women 1607 to 1950: A Biographical
  Dictionary*. 3 vols. Cambridge, Mass.: Harvard University
  Press, Belknap Press, 1971.
Miller, Perry. "I Find No Intellect Comparable to My Own."
  American Heritage, February 1957, pp. 22–25.
————, ed. *Margaret Fuller—American Romantic: A
  Selection from Her Writings and Correspondence*. New
  York: Doubleday and Co., 1963. Reprint ed., Gloucester,
  Mass.: Peter Smith, n.d.
Morison, Samuel E. *The Oxford History of the American
  People*. New York: Oxford University Press, 1965.
Mumford, Lewis. "Have Courage!" *American Heritage*,
  February 1969, pp. 104–11.
Sinclair, Andrew. *The Emancipation of the American Woman*.
  2d ed. (Original title: *Better Half*.) New York: Harper
  and Row, 1970.
Twayne, Arthur. *Margaret Fuller*. New York: Twayne
  Publishers, 1964.
Whitton, Mary O. *These Were the Women, U.S.A. 1776–1860*.
  New York: Hastings House, 1954.

CHAPTER 5: SUSAN B. ANTHONY

Anthony, Katherine. *Susan B. Anthony: Her Personal
  History and Her Era*. New York: Doubleday and Co.,

1954. Reprint ed., New York: Russell and Russell, 1974.

Bird, Caroline. *Born Female*. New York: David McKay, 1968.
(P)

Brown, Dee. *The Year of the Century: 1876*. New York:
Charles Scribner's Sons, 1966.

Flexner, Eleanor. *Century of Struggle: The Woman's Rights
Movement in the United States*. Cambridge, Mass.:
Harvard University Press, Belknap Press, 1959. (P)

Friedan, Betty. *The Feminine Mystique*. New York: W. W.
Norton and Co., 1963. (P)

Gattey, Charles N. *The Bloomer Girls*. New York: Coward-
McCann, 1967.

Holbrook, Stewart H. *Dreamers of the American Dream*.
Mainstreams of America Series, edited by Lewis Gannett.
New York: Doubleday and Co., 1957.

James, Edward T.; James, Janet W.; and Boyer, Paul S., eds.
*Notable American Women 1607 to 1950: A Biographical
Dictionary*. 3 vols. Cambridge, Mass.: Harvard University
Press, Belknap Press, 1971.

Lyon, Peter. "The Herald Angels of Woman's Rights."
American Heritage, October 1959, pp. 18–21.

Massey, Mary E. *Bonnet Brigades*. New York: Alfred A.
Knopf, 1966.

Morison, Samuel E. *The Oxford History of the American
People*. New York: Oxford University Press, 1965.

O'Neill, William L. *Everyone Was Brave: The Rise and Fall of
Feminism in America*. Chicago: Quadrangle Books, 1969.

Rossi, Alice S., ed. *The Feminist Papers: From Adams to De
Beauvoir*. New York: Columbia University Press, 1973.
(P)

Scott, Anne F., ed. *The American Woman: Who Was She?*
Englewood Cliffs, N. J.: Prentice-Hall, 1971.

Sinclair, Andrew. *The Emancipation of the American Woman*.
2d ed. (Original title: *Better Half*.) New York: Harper
and Row, 1970.

Thomas, Henry, and Thomas, Dana L. *Fifty Great Americans*.

New York: Doubleday and Co., 1948.

Chapter 6: Dorothea Lynde Dix

Commission on Hospital Care. *Hospital Care in the United States*. Commonwealth Fund. New York, 1947.

Dix, Dorothea. *Memorial in behalf of the pauper insane and idiots in jails and poorhouses throughout the commonwealth: To the Legislature of Massachusetts*. 1843.

Flexner, Eleanor. *Century of Struggle: The Woman's Rights Movement in the United States*. Cambridge, Mass.: Harvard University Press, Belknap Press, 1959. (P)

Holbrook, Stewart H. *Dreamers of the American Dream*. Mainstreams of America Series, edited by Lewis Gannett. New York: Doubleday and Co., 1957.

James, Edward T.; James, Janet W.; and Boyer, Paul S., eds. *Notable American Women 1607 to 1950: A Biographical Dictionary*. 3 vols. Cambridge, Mass.: Harvard University Press, Belknap Press, 1971.

Marshall, Helen E. *Dorothea Dix: Forgotten Samaritan*. Chapel Hill: University of North Carolina Press, 1937. Reprint ed., New York: Russell and Russell, 1967.

Martin, John Bartlow. *The Pane of Glass*. New York: Harper and Brothers, 1959.

Morison, Samuel E. *The Oxford History of the American People*. New York: Oxford University Press, 1965.

Roberts, Mary H. *American Nursing: History and Interpretation*. New York: Macmillan and Co., 1954.

Scott, Anne F., ed. *The American Woman: Who Was She?* Englewood Cliffs, N. J.: Prentice-Hall, 1971.

Sinclair, Andrew. *The Emancipation of the American Woman*. 2d ed. (Original title: *Better Half.*) New York: Harper and Row, 1970.

Tiffany, Francis. *Life of Dorothea Dix*. 1918. Reprint ed., Detroit, Mich.: Gale Research Co., n.d.

CHAPTER 7: JANE ADDAMS

Addams, Jane. *Twenty Years at Hull-House*. New York:
    Macmillan Co., 1966. (P)
Conway, Jane. "Jane Addams: An American Heroine." In
    The Woman in America, edited by Robert J. Lifton.
    Boston: Houghton Mifflin Co., 1965.
Flexner, Eleanor. *Century of Struggle: The Woman's Rights
    Movement in the United States*. Cambridge, Mass.:
    Harvard University Press, Belknap Press, 1959. (P)
Holbrook, Stewart G. *Dreamers of the American Dream*.
    Mainstreams of America Series, edited by Lewis Gannett.
    New York: Doubleday and Co., 1957.
James, Edward T.; James, Janet W.; and Boyer, Paul S., eds.
    *Notable American Women 1607 to 1950: A Biographical
    Dictionary*. 3 vols. Cambridge, Mass.: Harvard University
    Press, Belknap Press, 1971.
Meigs, Cornelia. *Jane Addams: Pioneer for Social Justice*.
    Boston: Little, Brown and Co., 1970.
Morison, Samuel E. *The Oxford History of the American
    People*. New York: Oxford University Press, 1965.
Neumann, William L., ed. *Jane Addams: A Centennial
    Reader*. New York: Macmillan Co., 1960.
Oakley, Violet. *Cathedral of Compassion: Dramatic Outline
    of the Life of Jane Addams, 1860–1935*. The Women's
    International League for Peace and Freedom.
    Philadelphia: Press of Lyon and Armor, n.d.
O'Neill, William L. *Everyone Was Brave: The Rise and Fall of
    Feminism in America*. Chicago: Quadrangle Books, 1969.
Scott, Anne F. *The American Woman: Who Was She?*
    Englewood Cliffs, N. J.: Prentice-Hall, 1971.
————. "Saint Jane and the Ward Boss." *American Heritage*,
    December 1960, pp. 12–17.
Sinclair, Andrew. *The Emancipation of the American Woman*.
    2d ed. (Original title: *Better Half*.) New York: Harper
    and Row, 1970.

Thomas, Henry, and Thomas, Dana L. *Fifty Great Americans.*
    New York: Doubleday and Co., 1948.
Tims, Margaret. *Jane Addams of Hull-House, 1860–1935.*
    New York: Macmillan and Co., n.d.

CHAPTER 8: RUTH ST. DENIS

Cohen, Selma J., ed. *Doris Humphrey, an Artist First: An
    Autobiography.* Middletown, Conn.: Wesleyan University
    Press, 1972.
Conyn, Cornelius. *Three Centuries of Ballet.* Houston, New
    York: Elsevier Press, 1953.
DeMille, Agnes. *The Book of the Dance.* New York: Golden
    Press, 1963.
Kinney, Troy, and West, Margaret. *The Dance: Its Place in
    Art and Life.* New York: Tudor Publishing Co., 1936.
Maynard, Olga. *The American Ballet.* Philadelphia: Macrae
    Smith Co., 1959.
St. Denis, Ruth. *An Unfinished Life.* [1939.]
Seroff, Victor. *The Real Isadora.* New York: Dial Press, 1971.
Shawn, Ted. *Ruth St. Denis: Pioneer and Prophet.* 1920.
———, with Gray, Poole. *One Thousand and One Night
    Stands.* New York: Doubleday and Co., 1960.
Terry, Walter. *Miss Ruth: The More Living Life of Ruth St.
    Denis.* New York: Dodd, Mead and Co., 1969.
Walker, Katherine S. *Dance and Its Creators:
    Choreographers at Work.* New York: John Day Co., 1972.

CHAPTER 9: MARGARET SANGER

Ditzion, Sidney. *Marriage, Morals, and Sex in America: A
    History of Ideas.* New York: Octagon Books, 1970.
Douglas, Emily T. *Pioneer of the Future: Margaret Sanger.*
    New York: Holt, Rinehart and Winston, 1970.
"Every Child a Wanted Child." *Time*, 16 September 1966, p.
    96.

Friedan, Betty. *The Feminine Mystique*. New York: W. W.
  Norton and Co., 1963. (P)
Holbrook, Stewart H. *Dreamers of the American Dream*.
  Mainstreams of America Series, edited by Lewis Gannett.
  New York: Doubleday and Co., 1957.
Jenness, Linda. "Margaret Sanger's Pioneering Role: How
  Women Won the Right to Birth Control." *The Militant*,
  16 March 1973, p. 5.
Kennedy, David. "Birth Control in America." *Commonweal*,
  12 June 1960, p. 299.
Ketchum, Richard M. "Faces from the Past." *American
  Heritage*, June 1970, pp. 52–53.
Komisar, Lucy. *The New Feminism*. New York: Franklin
  Watts, 1971.
Lader, Lawrence. *The Margaret Sanger Story and the Fight
  for Birth Control*. New York: Doubleday and Co., 1955.
Leech, Margaret, and Broun, Heywood. *Anthony Comstock*.
  1927.
Margaret Sanger: Biography of the Birth Control Pioneer.
  Pulp Publishing Co., 1938.
Morison, Samuel E. *The Oxford History of the American
  People*. New York: Oxford University Press, 1965.
"Rebel With a Cause." *Newsweek*, 19 September 1966, p. 34.
Sanger, Margaret. *Margaret Sanger: An Autobiography*. New
  York: W. W. Norton and Co., 1938. (P)
————. *My Fight for Birth Control*. Pulp Publishing Co.,
  1938. Reprint ed., Elmsford, N. Y.: Pergamon Press, n.d.

CHAPTER 10: ELEANOR ROOSEVELT

Churchill, Allen. *The Roosevelts: American Aristocrats*. New
  York: Harper and Row, 1965.
Davis, Kenneth S. *The Politics of Honor: A Biography of
  Adlai Stevenson*. New York: G. P. Putnam's Sons, 1967.
Erikson, Joan M. "Nothing to Fear: Notes on the Life of
  Eleanor Roosevelt." In *The Woman in America*, edited by
  Robert J. Lifton. Boston: Houghton Mifflin Co., 1965.

Gannon, Robert I., S. J. *The Cardinal Spellman Story*. New
York: Doubleday and Co., 1962.

Gallagher, Robert S. "Before the Colors Fade: The Radio
Priest." *American Heritage*, October 1972, pp. 38–41.

Janeway, Elizabeth. "First Lady of the U.N." *New York
Times Magazine*, 22 October 1950, p. 12.

Kearney, James R. *Anna Eleanor Roosevelt: The Evolution of
a Reformer*. Boston: Houghton Mifflin Co., 1968.

Lash, Joseph P. *Eleanor and Franklin*. New York: New
American Library, 1973.

_____. *Eleanor: The Years Alone*. New York: W. W. Norton
and Co., 1972.

Morison, Samuel E. *The Oxford History of the American
People*. New York: Oxford University Press, 1965.

Muller, Herbert J. *Adlai Stevenson: A Study in Values*. New
York: Harper and Row, 1967.

Roosevelt, Eleanor. *Autobiography of Eleanor Roosevelt*. New
York: Harper and Row, 1961.

_____. *It's Up To the Women*. 1933.

Roosevelt, Elliot, and Brough, James. *An Untold Story: The
Roosevelts of Hyde Park*. New York: G. P. Putnam's Sons,
1973.

Chapter 11: Rachel Carson

Brooks, Paul. *The House of Life: Rachel Carson at Work*.
Boston: Houghton Mifflin Co., 1972.

Carson, Rachel. *The Edge of the Sea*. Boston, Houghton
Mifflin Co., 1955. (P)

_____. "Our Ever-Changing Shore." *Holiday*, July 1958, pp.
70–71.

_____. *The Sea Around Us*. New York: Oxford University
Press, 1961. (P)

_____. *The Sense of Wonder*. New York: Harper and Row,
1965. (P)

_____. *Silent Spring*. Boston: Houghton Mifflin Co., 1962. (P)

_____. *Under the Sea Wind: A Naturalist's Picture of Ocean*

Life. New York: Oxford University Press, 1952. (P)

Clark, Austin H. "From the Beginning of the World." *Saturday Review*, 7 July 1951, p. 13.

Graham, Frank, Jr. *Since Silent Spring*. Boston: Houghton Mifflin Co., 1970.

Harvey, M. K. "Using a Plague to Fight a Plague." *Saturday Review*, 29 September 1962, p. 18.

Rudd, Robert L. *Pesticides and the Living Landscape*. Madison: University of Wisconsin Press, 1964. (P)

Strother, Robert S. "Backfire in the War Against Insects." *Reader's Digest*, June 1959, pp. 64–69.

Udall, Stewart L. "The Legacy of Rachel Carson." *Saturday Review*, 16 May 1964, p. 23.

Woodwell, George M. "Toxic Substances and Ecological Cycles." *Scientific American*, March 1967, pp. 24–31.

Chapter 12: Margaret Mead

Barrett, Mary E. "Margaret Mead: First of the Libbies." *Cosmopolitan*, September 1972, pp. 160–65.

Bird, Caroline. *Born Female*. New York: David McKay Co., 1968. (P)

Current Biography. 1951. New York: H. W. Wilson Co.

Friedan, Betty. *The Feminine Mystique*. New York: W. W. Norton and Co., 1963. (P)

Komisar, Lucy. *The New Feminism*. New York: Franklin Watts, 1971. (P)

"Margaret Mead Today: Mother to the World." *Time*, 21 March 1969, p. 74.

Mead, Margaret. *And Keep Your Powder Dry*. New York: William Morrow and Co., 1942. (P)

————. *Blackberry Winter: A Memoir*. New York: William Morrow and Co., 1972.

————. *Coming of Age in Samoa*. New York: William Morrow and Co., 1928. (P)

————. *Cooperation and Competition Among Primitive Peoples*. Boston: Beacon Press, 1961.

———. *Male and Female*. New York: William Morrow and Co., 1949. (P)

———. "Return of the Cave Woman" ("Sex on the Campus: excerpt from Women in Mass Society."). *Saturday Evening Post*, 3 March 1962, p. 6.

———. *Sex and Temperament in Three Primitive Societies*. New York: William Morrow and Co., n.d. (P)

———. "Women: A Time for Change." *Redbook*, monthly column, March, April and May 1970.

———, and Bunzel, Ruth L., eds. *The Golden Age of American Anthropology*. New York: George Braziller, 1960.

Packard, Vance. *The Sexual Wilderness*. New York: David McKay Co., 1968. (P)

Sargeant, Winthrop. "Profile." *New Yorker*, 30 December 1961, pp. 31–34.

"Speaking Freely." Margaret Mead interviewed by Edwin Newman. Telecast from the American Museum of Natural History, New York City, September 1971.